Teaching Geography 11-1

Teaching Geography 11–18

A Conceptual Approach

David Lambert and John Morgan

Open University Press
First Edition

Open University Press
McGraw-Hill Education
McGraw-Hill House
Shoppenhangers Road
Maidenhead
Berkshire
England
SL6 2QL

email: enquiries@openup.co.uk
world wide web: www.openup.co.uk

and Two Penn Plaza, New York, NY 10121-2289, USA

First published 2010

A catalogue record of this book is available from the British Library

ISBN-13: 978-0-33-523448-6 (pb) 978-0-33-523447-9 (hb)
ISBN-10: 0-33-523448-8 (pb) 0-33-523447-X

Library of Congress Cataloging-in-Publication Data
CIP data applied for

Typeset by YHT Ltd, London

Printed and bound by CPI Group (UK) Ltd, Croydon, CR0 4YY

The McGraw·Hill Companies

Contents

Preface

The promise of geography in education

Describing, interpreting and imagining landscapes: the promise of geography

The promise of geography in education? This needs explaining.

When we make promises we often do so because we aspire to achieve something. Promises are often optimistic and ambitious, like a New Year resolution. Making promises however is sometimes hazardous as they are sometimes difficult to keep. We sometimes disappoint ourselves, and others, when we forget the promise or when it becomes obscured or lost in the 'noise', possibly supplanted by other priorities. Therefore, promises frequently need to be recast, reaffirmed or restated.

    As we worked to shape up this book, we realized increasingly that we were involved with what geography education promises. What this book attempts is an analysis of what geography education promises. The result of our analysis is, we hope, a significant contribution to how geography in schools, colleges and other educational settings can be theorized.

Take a look at the photograph. You can find a colour version of this on www. geography.org.uk/adifferentview. This is a picture of Royston Heath, taken from a field near the village of Litlington in south Cambridgeshire. It is in the afternoon on a beautiful late autumn day and we are looking towards the south east.

The boulder clay soil has been ploughed (it looks quite dry at the end of the summer) and prepared. In the foreground, and beyond the recently ploughed field, it looks like the winter wheat is already growing. On the skyline there is beech woodland – typical for a chalk escarpment in the south of England (look at its dry valley pointing to us). Some of this has been ploughed in the past. Some of the land in this photograph may have been ploughed almost continuously for a thousand years or more. Much of the Heath is common land and has been grazed by sheep for even longer. Indeed, in among the greens and bunkers of the golf course on the Heath (but just out of view) are iron-age burial mounds, further evidence of a long history of human occupation. Royston itself is at the crossroads of Ermine Street, a product of Roman occupation, and to this day the Coach and Horses public house stands at the town centre.

The ruined building evidences more recent history, part of the US airbase that was established during the latter part of the Second World War (the 355th Fighter Group which between 1943 and 1945 housed 2000 USAAF personnel). East Anglia is littered with such remains (and still has several active military bases to this day). Recently, the remains of a person were found in this building – a lonely wanderer who had been using it as a shelter. He wasn't discovered for days as people who live in the villages around here usually get from 'a' to 'b' in their cars. In some ways they are 'insulated' from the countryside – and much else besides.

The driver you can see is possibly returning from the nearby Tesco with the weekly shopping and lives a suburban lifestyle, albeit in a 'village'. Between us and the chalk escarpment, but concealed from view, is a dual carriageway road and an electrified rail line linking Cambridge and London in around 45 minutes. It is hard to tell from this serene photograph, but the full picture of the area is one of great development pressure. House prices are well above the national average. The trains are packed at peak times and are expensive. The Royston crossroads bottleneck has been relieved with a bypass (which is where the supermarket is located), and continues to expand rapidly with suburban estates.

A geographical approach

The above provides a pretty standard and familiar 'geographical' account. In essence, we employ the idea of landscape as a text – a palimpsest with stories to tell as we peel off each layer. In doing so we are applying a number of concepts that are used frequently by geographers; for example, the way we have written this text implicitly tries to capture a sense of the place. Consequently, we also draw from a number of physical and human observations and processes to provide a deep description of the place. Crucially, we also draw from knowledge and understanding that comes from elsewhere – that is, in addition to that supplied by the photograph – and we begin to interpret the picture, using the geographical concepts of place, space and spatial relations. We synthesize aspects of the physical environment (the rock and the soil) with human and social activity (farming and shopping) in order to make sense of this part of the world. This, then, is the promise of geography: it helps us to understand the world and the part we play in it.

But this application of a geographical lens is not straightforward. Geography cannot simply be seen as a 'window' on the world. Thus, we are cautious – and perhaps a little contentious – about the categories we use in our interpretation. For example, the scene is self-evidently 'rural' – or is it? Whether there is any rurality left in England depends on what we mean by rural, but in economic and cultural terms most of us are connected to the British urban system. Furthermore, through the food we eat, the films we watch, the energy we consume and the social networks we join, we are connected to global space. Commonplace terms like 'globalization' and 'interdependence' are used frequently in the media to capture this sense of the modern world, but in truth these are complex ideas that we need to work with carefully and critically.

An approach to geography in education

In this book we argue that geography is a valuable subject resource for the school curriculum. We hope to do this by showing how geography contributes to our understanding of the observed world (or parts of it). For example, a geographical perspective shows that a deep understanding of Royston and its surrounds is impossible without a scaled approach that enables us to grasp more fully a number of deceptively simple questions: who lives there, where have they come from, what do they for a living? These questions encourage a global perspective, showing how the place links to other places across the world.

Thus, Royston is a unique place, but it is not in totality a singular place. The uniqueness of the precise features that produce this place do not conceal that Royston shares many characteristics with other small market towns as it is subject to and experiences several economic, social and other processes that are commonplace and universal. Thus, for instance, the empty shops on Royston High Street, which many locals link to the presence of an expanding supermarket on the edge of town with free parking, is a widespread phenomenon. In other words, the place responds to general social, cultural, environmental and economic forces with fairly predictable results, but sometimes in a particular way. Royston is not exactly like anywhere else, to the extent that some people identify with it and would not want to live anywhere else.

This book provides a fresh approach to understanding the place of geography in education. Through a conceptual approach it shows the promise of geography in education and the key role that teachers play in fulfilling this promise with young people. We are in effect saying to geography teachers, 'use your geography': use it to help you engage and excite interest in young people to understand the world; use it to help you design and plan your teaching.

To do this is very challenging. It requires more than 'imparting knowledge'. It requires a form of intellectual engagement with the discipline so that its perspectives and insights can be applied in an educational setting. This is not to suggest that school teachers should be forced slavishly to follow the whims of the academic discipline, but it is to suggest that school geography is aware of contemporary thought in the discipline. This is the source of intellectual excitement that nourishes the relationship teachers create with young people. These days we appreciate more openly than ever before that young people themselves are agentive in their own learning, and part of the promise of geography in education is that it encourages discovery. This means young people asking good questions and being engaged in knowledge making about the world – encouraged as the Geographical Association would put it, to acquire a 'different view'.[1] Geography, partly through the ideas it has created and uses, provides frameworks to help achieve this. In this book we have tried to contribute to this process with a three-part analysis:

Part 1   Concepts, contexts and histories

This part offers the reader:

- an overview of geography in schools. This is akin to a squinting of the eyes and trying to make out, once we have blurred the detail, what we are left with. What is geography in schools really for? What is its overarching narrative?
- an argument for the continuance of a role for geography in schools based on an analysis of contemporary 'knowledge society' and how education has a crucial role to prepare young people to engage with this: what we call 'capability';
- advocacy over the role of teachers by reworking the relationship teachers have with the subject. We are clear that teaching is an intensely practical activity, but is underpinned by intellectual effort. Without the latter it lacks efficacy.

Part 2   Reconstructing concepts

In Part 2, the main part of the book, we offer you a series of essays on a selection of geography's big ideas. We need to provide some 'health warnings'.

We are aware that our approach to concepts is rather different to that taken by geography educators in the past, where there is a reliance on the psychology of learning. Instead, we see concepts as sites of contestation, and because of this are likely to possess multiple meanings that cannot be reduced to a single straightforward definition. This means that the discussions of the concepts found in these chapters do not represent anything like the 'final word'. Each is an exploration informed by our own experience as geography educators and our interpretation of contemporary debates in geography and education. They are intended to provoke thought and prompt readers to develop their own ideas. This is a deliberate ploy and we hope makes for an exciting read. Geography, like all dynamic areas of disciplinary thought, is in a constant 'state of becoming'. Indeed, it might be argued that geography is a discipline that involves creating concepts in response to changes in the nature of the world. In the chapters in this part, we attempt to portray how a selection of influential ideas has been thought through and developed in geography, and its implications for teaching geography.

Furthermore, our choice of concepts is not definitive! We could have chosen to follow the rubric of the 2008 National Curriculum with is seven 'key concepts'. We thought that this would be needlessly restricting. We also wanted deliberately to deter any unwitting assumption that these seven concepts define school geography. They do not – any more than an examination specification does. Some will be surprised that we seem to have ignored certain ideas, such as 'interaction', 'location' or 'change' that of course are important in geography. However, close reading of the chapters in this part will show that we have certainly addressed these ideas and many more besides. What we can claim to cover is a variety of challenging debates in the discipline that have informed its development. We have tried to focus on developments that have purchase not just in geography, but on geography in schools and what it can promise education.

Part 3   Curriculum challenges

This part has one major chapter (Chapter 11) that explores the media cultures in which young people are often immersed. In the course of writing this book, we became increasingly aware of the way that all the concepts that we were discussing are routinely accessed through the products of media culture. Many of the places, spaces, themes and issues that we teach about in geography are 'known' through films, television news and documentaries, newspapers and, more recently, websites and blogs. Although this may sound obvious and in many ways it is taken for granted, there has been very little discussion of the implication of the fact that so much geographical teaching is mediated. This chapter provides an introduction to some important debates about media education in relation to geography.

Chapter 12 is essentially a reflection on the book as a whole – taking us right back to the present discussion about the promise of geography in education. Here, we have opened up the idea of a conceptual approach to geography that, for example, takes us well away from geography as mimesis, as a way to present the world objectively to young people as facts to be learned. We have nothing against facts of course, so long as we use them carefully and perhaps cautiously (as in the photograph, which we are not entirely happy to describe as 'rural'). The final chapter, drawing strength from the conceptual discussions that make up the bulk of this book, takes this point further. What the final chapter does in effect is suggest what the characteristics of a moral geography education might be.

We hope that readers of this book will find as much to excite and engage them as we did in writing it. Above all, we hope you share our belief in the promise of geography.

Notes

1   A different view is the Geographical Association's 'manifesto' launched in 2009 (www.geography.org.uk/adifferentview).

PART 1
CONCEPTS, CONTEXTS AND HISTORIES

1   A modern school geography

This chapter sets the scene for the book as a whole. Its central claim is that school geography can be understood as an engagement with the 'project of modernity'. Modernity is seen as a description of major social and material changes, and the growing consciousness of the novelty of these changes. School geography teaches about major social and material changes such as economic shift, environmental transformations, and cultural development, and offers students frameworks for understanding and evaluating these. The chapter adopts a historical perspective, showing how geography teaching can be seen as responding to wider economic and social changes.

Introduction

Geography – as a school subject – provides a way of helping young people in schools to learn about, and reflect on, aspects of the world. This engagement with the world means that geography is constantly changing as society changes although, as we will see, this connection is not simple and straightforward. This is true of other school subjects such as history and English, too, though of course they look at the world through different perspectives and with different methods. This is another way of saying that the school curriculum is a reflection of the culture of society. It is a selection from that culture and, as such, there are always arguments and discussions about how that selection should be made, and who gets to decide (Williams 1961).

This chapter provides a short historical account that places post-Second World War geography teaching in its wider economic, social and cultural contexts. It attempts to illustrate how geography teaching is always engaged with questions of social change.

Modernity

We start by explaining how we use the idea of 'modernity' in this chapter. Berman (1983) began his influential book *All that is Solid Melts into Air* by defining modernity as 'a mode of vital experience – experience of space and time, of the self and others, of life's possibilities and perils'. In Berman's words, 'to be modern is to find ourselves in an environment that promises us adventure, power, joy, growth, transformation of ourselves and the world – and, at the same time, threatens to destroy everything we have, everything we know, everything we are' (p. 15). The emphasis in these quotations is on 'feeling' but this experience – the maelstrom of modern life – is the product of social processes that are driven by 'an ever expanding, drastically fluctuating capitalist world market' (p. 16).

Modernity is thus both an experience and a social project. Berman gives a powerful summary of the social processes that are at the heart of the modern project. These include: scientific discoveries, technological knowledge that has led to and created industrialization that in turn has generated new forms of corporate and social power, the rapid growth of urban environments, demographic upheavals resulting in increased geographical mobility, mass systems of communication, the development of powerful national states, and a vastly expanding, but volatile, capitalist market.

Modernity then is a structure of feeling that allows men and women to make sense of the social processes of modernization. As O' Shea (1996: 11) puts it, modernity is 'the practical negotiation of one's life and one's identity within a complex and fast-changing world'. To be modern is to somehow make oneself at home in the maelstrom, to relish the process of modernization 'even as it exploits and torments us, brings our energies and imaginations to life, drives us to grasp and confront the world that modernization makes, and to strive to make it our own' (Berman 1983: 348)

Though modernity is a temporal concept (to do with the passage of time), geographers have shown how it is impossible to understand modernity in an aspatial fashion (Gilbert et al. 2003; Ogborn 1998; Pred and Watts 1992). The social processes of modernization lead to the destruction of old spaces and the construction of new ones. Most obvious are the development of large cities, and within those, the clearing of land for roads, railways, new housing, places of work such as office blocks and factories, and new spaces of consumption and leisure. Similarly, processes of industrialization required raw materials that are dug from the ground (or beneath the sea), pipelines, roads and railways, the increased intensification of agricultural production and the clearing of forests. In all this space it not merely a 'container' in which modern life is played out. The way space is used is the product of political, economic, social and cultural processes, and in turn the organization of space offers opportunities and constraints for the further development of those processes. These spaces offer new opportunities to define what it means to be human. But this is far from straightforward.

Consider, for instance, the experience of migration. As capitalism developed, workers were required to work in the factories concentrated in large towns and cities. Men and women who had previously lived a settled life in rural areas were attracted by the 'bright lights' and prospects of higher wages. They left behind them families, lovers, and friends and their attachment to the places in which they grew up. Another example is the development of new types of work that have relied on the supply of women workers. For many women, this has allowed them to take on new and expanded identities, to leave behind the idea that a 'woman's place is in the home'. Of course, this development is uneven and contested. Once again, modernity is both a feeling and a project.

We want to suggest that a productive way of thinking about the work of geography teachers in schools is to see the subject as a way of helping young people understand and make sense of the modern adventure. This is because its content is concerned with the social processes that make up the modern project. At the same time, it is concerned with helping students to make sense of and evaluate the impacts of these processes. When thought about in these terms, school geography takes on a particularly important role. Once again, this is not straightforward, since there is no simple and authoritative response to the changes wrought by the experience of modernity. Instead, when carefully taught, geography offers a means of reflecting on the process and experience of historical-geographical change.

Education is clearly part of the project and experience of modernity. The building of schools is an obvious investment in the 'future'. But schools are also about preserving valued aspects of the past or reproducing existing patterns. The school curriculum becomes a site of conflict over what values to uphold. School geography sits in a pivotal position because it is both forward-looking and progressive, and at the same time seeks to conserve tradition. Having outlined how we are using the idea of modernity, the next section discusses the geographical imagination that informed school geography in the immediate post-war period, paying attention to the broad economic and social contexts in which geography was taught.

A world to win: geography education 1945–64

> War shook up the geography of England, unsettling people and their objects, transforming landscapes, moving things to where they weren't before.
>
> (Matless 1998: 173).

Historians often refer to the post-war period as one of general 'consensus' about economy, politics and culture, one in which it was recognized that there should be a sharing of the 'good things' in life, rather than these being restricted to the rich. Sinfield represents this 'settlement' in stark, materialist terms:

> Historically and currently, in most of the world, human societies have been and are generally controlled by force. If you don't do what powerful people tell you, they hit you, lock you up, throw you out of your house or burn it down, don't let you grow enough to eat or earn enough to subsist ... Since what people of my generation call 'the war', meaning 1939–45, a distinctive attempt has been made in Britain and other parts of Europe to arrange things differently.
>
> (Sinfield 1989: 1)

To win the war, Sinfield argues, people were encouraged to believe that there would not be a return to widespread injustice and poverty. Full employment and the welfare state created a sense that society was moving towards fairness, where remaining 'pockets of poverty' would soon be eliminated. The 'good things' in life – healthcare, education, housing, financial security – which previously had been the preserve of the upper classes, would be generally available.

In this period, most states in Europe were intent on the renewal and reconstruction of their public services. Education played an important part in this reconstruction. The expansion of the educational offer to all children required the building of new schools and the recruitment of teachers (Grosvenor and Burke 2008). Matless (1998) argues that debates about landscape during the inter-war period had veered between 'tradition' and 'modernity', but that after the war, the idea of the rational and ordered development of space and resources came to dominate.

Planning was concerned with the ordered and rational development of landscape. It was informed by a modernist aesthetic that valued smooth lines, orderliness and tidiness. It suggested that in order to preserve England's valued landscapes it was necessary to adopt practices of land-use management and planning. During and after the war this 'planner-preservation' discourse had real power since it was argued that 'when we build again', the mistakes and excesses of the past should be avoided. It was envisaged that after the war there would be a need for a reconstructed town and country. Reconstruction was based on the need for an ordered landscape, where everything was in its place. This was not simply about conservation (keeping things as they are) but planning and preservation (intervening to bring about appropriate change).

An example of this type of thinking is found in a publication published in 1943 on the occasion of the Royal Institute of British Architecture's Rebuilding Britain exhibition. The cover of the catalogue shows two soldiers imposed on an aerial view of London, with the city spread out at their feet. As Matless (1998) notes, these men could be representative citizens from anywhere in Britain. The catalogue calls for the rebuilding of a 'new' Britain: 'Now is the opportunity for making the new Britain that we all desire' (RIBA 1943: 3). The catalogue explains how the processes of industrialization and urbanization had led to cities becoming 'choked', 'grossly overburdened with the weight of humanity and transport' (p. 9). This uncontrolled growth is unworthy of the people of Britain: 'We have not merely put a blight on our landscape, we have put a blight on ourselves' (p. 9). The catalogue calls for a national plan and the removal of inefficient urban agglomerations. The answer to these issues is town planning. The text is illustrated with examples of 'good' and 'bad' planning. For example, there is a picture of Peacehaven on the South Coast, which 'must be the saddest monument to the Great Peace that was ever built' (p. 48), and two of the Pioneer Health Centre in Peckham, which is praised for its attempts to bring families together to 'play games, dance, swim, meet your friends, and have regular medical attention to keep you in good health' (p. 31).

Thus, Matless (1998) suggests, in the post-war period, this notion of planned, ordered and rational development dominated political thinking, and geographers aligned themselves with this movement, with influential figures such as Dudley Stamp chairing influential committees on land utilization. This way of thinking about the appropriate use of space is exemplified in Stamp's conclusion to the book he published towards the end of the war, based on his famous land-use survey of Britain:

> Under the town and country planning act of 1944 the whole of Britain is now under planning control ... But there is good planning and bad planning and there is still the need for a clear national policy which will equate the land needs of industry, housing, food production, forestry, sport and recreation.
>
> (Stamp 1946: 79–80)

There was a clear scheme of value here, and the geographer's role was to adjudicate on the appropriate use of land. This focus on order and planning permeated geography texts such as Stamp and Beaver's (1954) *The British Isles: A Geographic and Economic Survey*, which was a regional inventory of the resources of Britain and descriptions of the location of industry, and was reproduced in books for school students such as Preece and Wood's (1954) *Modern Geography. Book 2: The British Isles*, which celebrated the achievements of industrial production and agricultural improvement. The focus was on ideas of progress and economic development, and, in keeping with the overall tone of textbooks before and after the Second World War, stressed the industriousness of the nation and its abundance of natural resources, that allowed Britain to become much greater and more influential than her size would suggest. Industry served both as a description of economic activity and the characteristics of her people. Thus, Fairgrieve and Young's (1952) textbook on the British Isles, *Real Geography*, was organized as a series of 'sample studies' of how people make a living from the land, which means the emphasis is on primary and secondary activity. The reader is shown how we rely on water from Wales, a farm in the Cheviot Hills, the Black Dyke mills of Bradford, the Ashington collieries in the north-east, the iron and steel industry on Clydeside, the fishing villages of the east of England, the Kent hop-fields and finally to London. As a text, the idea of a journey has the effect of knitting together the different parts of the economy into a single whole, stressing how what goes on in one place is linked to life in other parts of the nation. In this way the diversity of economic life is used to tell a story of commonality. The text works to reinforce an imagined geography of the nation through stressing the way in which people are all similar, making their homes and going about their work:

> In this book we have seen that even in the comparatively small area of the British Isles there are many different ways of living and contributing to the well-being of other people – lonely farms on the hills, rich farms in the lowlands, villages, towns and cities by the sea or inland and in each of these are dwellings that people call home, where life is all the richer because of what other people are doing both in the homeland – and the world.
>
> (Fairgrieve and Young 1952: 172)

Despite this consensual view of Britain's geography, historians recognize the fact that there were important divides around class, gender and region (e.g. Rose 2003). Organized as it was around a 'man-land' paradigm, geography developed as a largely descriptive subject and did not explore political and social issues in any depth, and reflected the fact that school geography was dominated by educated, middle and upper-class men (as Walford's 2001 history of geography in British schools confirms). However, as the post-war period developed, this representation of Britain's geography was out of step with the realities of life in the new schools.

The historiography of the 1950s and 1960s is increasingly contested; however, most commentators seem to agree that this was a period of tumultuous economic, social and cultural change, and that there was a distinctive geography to these changes:

> Whether by day or by night, the United Kingdom's surface when viewed from the air changed markedly between 1951 and 1970. Superimposed on old patterns were the new field shapes and changed watercourses stemming from intensive farming. The new motorway system was taking shape; new towns and universities were springing up on greenfield sites; housing geography was in flux.
>
> (Harrison 2009: 123).

Production was increasing rapidly, and rising wage levels allowed for the development of consumer affluence. In this context, education spending increased to unprecedented levels. Politically, this was a period of consensus, underpinned by the assumption of full employment. The economy was changing. There was a series of occupational shifts as a greater percentage of the workforce worked in services, and the trend was towards semi-skilled and professional employment. In addition, women were entering the workforce in greater numbers, and Britain welcomed migrants from Ireland and the New Commonwealth and Pakistan.

It is important to note that these shifts were not evenly felt throughout Britain, and there existed persistent regional divides. Jones (2003) argues that 'The pace and unevenness of economic change raised problems for education' (p. 41). Occupational shifts led to greater demand for higher levels of education and certification, and led to the expansion of higher education in the 1960s. The uneven nature of this shift mixed with new patterns of settlement to create geographical polarization, with the growth of skilled, professional jobs in the new industries located in the suburbs and new towns. While the older inner-city areas did not lose the 'dead-end, low-paid and unskilled jobs', they lost the skilled jobs associated with the 'aristocracy of labour'. There emerged a division between the blighted urban areas and the suburban location of new industries, and this was reflected in terms of school quality and type. Throughout the 1950s there was an unyielding, urban-based concern about continuing social and cultural divides. As the Newsom Report put it in 1963, 'Some schools have everything, and some virtually nothing' (p. 250).

Added to these economic and social divides was the issue of immigration and generational difference. In *The Uses of Literacy* Hoggart (1957) noted the impact of popular culture – especially American popular culture – on what he depicted as settled working-class communities. Overall, the 1950s saw an 'emerging generational conflict over cultural and moral meanings, which had strong implications for schooling' (p. 43).

These changes were linked to the new economic status of young people. They had, for the first time, money in their pockets, and were targeted by a commercial consumer culture. This affected those still at school. Abrams (1959) spoke of the twin forces of 'proletarianization' (in which the manners and mores of the working classes gained more general acceptance) and 'Americanization', both of which implied a break from the paternalism of officially directed children's culture. As Jones comments:

> The sense of a cultural decline, in which childhood was implicated, and the focus on youth culture as a battleground of opposing forces, were commonplaces of the period, and formed a striking counterpoint to the optimistic discourses that attended educational expansion.
>
> (Jones 2003: 43)

The overall movement of the post-war educational settlement had been to expand the range of provision to more and more children. However, this settlement was challenged by forces of economic and cultural change that demanded creative educational responses. These included the rise of affluence as reflected in the consumption of goods such as cars, washing machines and televisions, and the growth of a more home-centred, geographically mobile society that challenged traditional forms of place-based community. These changes eventually led to calls for a radical renewal of the school curriculum. These are considered in the next section.

Box 1.1

GLOBAL MODERNITIES

While this chapter is predominantly concerned with exploring the geographies of British modernity within the framework of the nation state, it is important to recognize that school geography has also played an important part in narrating the story of global modernity. This box enquires as to how school geography constructed Britain's relationship with the rest of the world.

Any attempt to answer this question must recognize the importance of Britain's colonial past. Research on early school geography textbooks has highlighted the derogatory representations of 'other' people. Thus, one of the 'founding fathers' of geography, Halford Mackinder (1911: 83) urged that 'Let all our teaching be from the British standpoint', and wrote that, 'The gaining of so extensive a territory by Britain is one of the greatest miracles of history'. The trend at the end of the 1800s was to emphasize the differences between races. There was an acceptance of the achievements of other civilizations (though the 'negro' race was less likely to be complimented on its achievements). These representations accord with Edward Said's (1978) argument in his influential text *Orientalism* about how the 'East' has been represented by academics, novelist and others situated in the 'West'. These representations comprised a 'discourse' that he defines as a tradition whose material presence or weight, not the originality of a given author, is really responsible for the texts produced out of it. This suggests that there were particular ways of representing other people and other places that became common sense and unremarkable, and that geography textbooks reproduced these uncritically.

Though old prejudices lingered, it is important to recognize that in the post-war period there was a distinct move away from the racial imaginaries that had informed geographical thinking in the nineteenth century, in the form of environmental determinism. In the post-war period there was more focus on development and environment. All of this was framed within a regional geography approach in which 'numerous bulky, regional geographies of the non-western world were published' (Power 2003: 49). These were related to Britain's own histories in relation to these areas, and opportunities to travel. Each expedition allowed for the writing previously undocumented space. Power labels these as 'Colonial geographies of modernity'. (49)

A number of criticisms of these regional approaches were made in the 1960s as geography underwent a shift from a regional, descriptive approach to a systematic, 'scientific' subject. For instance, it was argued that there were no formal rules for recognizing, defining, delimiting or describing 'regions', and regional approaches were seen as focusing on the unique and failing to identify more general laws governing development in all regions. In the 1950s and 1960s geographers became increasingly interested in developing more general models of development that were underpinned by ideas of 'modernization'. In effect, these divided the world into 'modern' and 'traditional' societies and assumed that the path of development would be to increase modernization. Geographers were interested in the spatial patterns of development that could be measured through indicators of development. Examples of such modernization included the move towards large urban centres, agricultural modernization schemes and transport systems. Geographers' contribution to this was to map the modernization process and develop the spatial aspects of modernization theories. School textbooks were rewritten to accommodate the theories and models of Rostow, Myrdal and Friedman.

However, a familiar characteristic of school geography in the post-war period is its tendency to focus on spatial patterns rather than explore the social processes that help to shape them. The effect of prioritizing such 'geographical theories of development' was that they tend to ignore the economic, social and political circuits of which development is part. It was this that the development of 'World Studies' in schools challenged (see Hicks and Townley 1982). World Studies tended to operate with a much broader sense of what development means, infused by non-governmental organization (NGO) thinking and new 'value-based' pedagogical approaches. The explicit aim was to 'teach for a better world' (Fien and Gerber 1988). World Studies sought to promote an alternative conception of development, one that recognized the voices and experiences of people in the 'Third World'. It was part of an 'anti-development' critique that eventually led to the rise of global perspectives in the school curriculum, and which was reflected in the rise of critical geographies of development in the academic subject. For example, Taylor (1985) wrote of the 'error of developmentalism' that assumed the world is made up of around 150–200 nation states, all following their own path to development. Instead, he argued, nation states should be seen as interdependent, inextricably linked together as part of a 'World economy'. Though Taylor adopted the political sociologist Immanuel Wallerstein's World-systems theory, this was part of a more general trend for geographers to recognize the importance of understanding the global nature of society, as evidenced in influential titles such as *A World in Crisis?* (Johnston and Taylor 1986) and *Global Shift* (Dicken 1998).

These developments mean that geography has become increasingly concerned with the study of global issues in the past decade, and the global dimension is evident in schools. However, it is perhaps ironic that this has not been accompanied by an increased breadth of studies of places. Critics such as Standish (2009) argue that this is because teaching about global issues in geography has become more concerned with promulgating particular moralistic values rather than learning geographical knowledge. The 'anti-development' arguments of the 1980s have moved to centre stage in geography teaching as part of a wider loss of faith in the project of Western modernity. For Standish, the 'developmentalist' perspective whereby each nation state is pursuing its path to industrialization and modernity is rarely found in school geography, where the desirability of large-scale development is frequently questioned: 'Instead, Western anxiety over environmental limits and socio-political unrest, projected on to the developing world, has become the main prism through which development is viewed' (Standish 2009: 137).

Within geography as an academic subject, recent years have seen moves to deconstruct the ways in which geographical knowledge is based on a colonial geographical imagination (e.g. Gregory 2004). In this work, geographers have uncovered how processes of exploration, travel and techniques of observation and mapping all serve to reinforce the distinction between 'us' and 'them'. There are clear links with the argument about modernity that we are making in this chapter. Post-colonial culture is reflected in global media culture and is a result of the processes of mobility and hybridization (Sharp 2009).

1964-80 geography as a modern subject

In discussions of geography education, it is common to note the break between a regional approach that dominated until the 1960s and the modern 'new' systematic geography that transformed the subject in schools. It is less common to relate these changes in content and approach to the broader processes of modernization that were shaping educational debates in this period. The Labour government came to power in 1964 on a programme of economic modernization within the framework of a mixed economy. The driving force was Prime Minister Harold Wilson's 'white heat of technology'. The Labour government sought to use planning mechanisms to coordinate public and private sector activities, to subsidize and promote technological change, and use regional policy to diversify the economic base of old industrial regions. In this, education at both school and university levels would be a focus of investment and a site of reform. Ross (2000: 25–6) identifies three forces that led to pressures to reform the school curriculum:

1   The growth in the amount and organization of knowledge, particularly scientific and technological knowledge. This originated at the level of higher education, but filtered down to the 16–18 curriculum and subsequently the 11–16 curriculum.
2   The changing understanding of the processes and consequences of teaching and learning. This meant that different groups of students were considered to require different forms of knowledge and curriculum.
3   The development of a changing, plural society. This included increased affluence and consumerism, the recognition of social, cultural and linguistic diversity, and technological developments.

In line with its approach to planning and coordination, the Labour governments of the 1960s relied on the advice of a 'new educational establishment'. A changing economy and society required a modern curriculum, and the Schools Council was established in 1964 charged with the task of developing new relevant and appropriate approaches to the curriculum.

In secondary schools, the developments were driven and supported by examination reform. Most significantly, the introduction of CSE in 1965 allowed for curriculum innovation and experimentation. Its effects were contradictory. On one hand, it served to strengthen the academic/non-academic divide and led to an increase in 'streaming'. On the other, it stimulated school-based curriculum development, notably through the mechanism of Mode 3 examinations in which schools developed their own assessments, reflective of the needs of their students, which were then subject to approval from exam boards.

The renowned Schools Council geography projects were the result of this process of reform (see Rawling 2001: chapter 2). They were infused with large measures of technocratic positivist geography that have continued to shape the way in which the subject is taught in schools. In the debate that preceded the setting up of the Schools Council, there was widespread agreement for the need for teacher autonomy; the issue was how to support that autonomy. There was a general acceptance that the 'increasing pace of change', the 'knowledge expansion' and more extended schooling warranted new approaches to enable schools to respond more quickly and effectively to social changes. An important part of this was the planned change to raise the school leaving age. Few disputed that the traditional curriculum was unsuited to most of the pupils who left school at 15.

The 'new' geography was a problem-solving geography. An example is Brigg's (1977) series 'Introducing the new geography'. It 'uses a concept-based, problem-solving approach to geography, which is appropriate to modern thinking in geography'. One of the exercises is for students to calculate the 'Shape Index' of Southport. Graves (2001: 126) comments that 'I would argue that a visual inspection of the map of a town is a sufficient indication of the shape of the town, and that calculating the shape index will do nothing to explain why towns are of a particular shape'. He adds that some sections of the book read more like a mathematics than a geography textbook, and many readers will recognize the experience of calculating 'Nearest Neighbour' statistics or working out the correlation between the population size of settlements and their place in the shopping hierarchy.

Though Graves criticized the new geography because it seemed more interested in methods rather than value of the techniques, he did not reflect on the wider implications of the geographical knowledge that was being offered to students. Johnston, in a reflection on the purposes of geography education at school and university, noted that, in schools:

> the 'new' geography of the 1960s is taking over, but the unreality of rank-size rules and matrix manipulations of transport networks are not subjects for budding geographers/social scientists/young citizens: we can surely do better than technology for technology's sake.
>
> (Johnston 1977: 9)

He argued that school geography, like university geography, has been linked to the notion of training in the solution of empirical problems. This is reflected in 'decision-making' exercises that suggest the best location for a facility or the management of valued environments. These are forms of applied technical knowledge. The problem is that they do not explore or explain the basis of the society that produces these problems. Geography thus becomes a training ground for a cadre of experts. This explains Harvey's (1974) comment that listen to a discussion among geographers and quickly you will hear the 'voice of the expert', somebody who claims to know a lot more than ordinary people. In short, some critics argued that the new geography was elitist, and was largely confined to the 'best schools'. School geography, then, opted to follow the 'royal road to science', with the result that it lost touch with some of the wider currents of culture. For example, Lee (1977) described the new geography found in schools as representing a 'top-down' geography. He argued that the new geography represented a methodological rather than an epistemological break, and that future attempts to reform school geography should emanate from the 'blackboard jungle' rather than the 'ivory tower'. These questions about the relevance of school geography came to the fore in the 1980s.

The geography of the 1980s

The previous section argued that the 'new' school geography, represented by the Schools Council Projects, can be seen as a response to wider social and economic changes. However, the representations and explanations they offered of the world were increasingly challenged by the experience of growing up in an increasingly socially divided society. In this section, we argue that school geography experienced a 'crisis of representation' in the 1980s, and that this was likely to have been felt by all geography teachers. The crisis of representation is literal, because the assumptions on which geography teaching had taken place before had been shattered by processes of economic, social and cultural change.

The post-war consensus that had shaped Britain's economic and political landscape broke down in the 1970s, and the end of the decade saw the election of a Conservative government committed to radical change. This involved abandoning the notion that the role of government is to regulate capitalism, rejecting the idea of a social contract with organized labour, and seeking to withdraw the state from economic and social intervention. In the 1980s nationalized industries were privatized, failing industries (so-called 'lame ducks') were allowed to fail, trade union power curtailed and effectively broken in the decisive industrial dispute of the decade, the Miners' Strike of 1984–5. In line with a belief that the market offers better solutions on how to live, council housing was made available for private purchase (the 'Right to Buy'),and private heathcare was encouraged. Public spending on health, education and welfare was squeezed, although the overall size of public expenditure was the same, but redistributed to areas such as defence, law and order, and providing unemployment benefits for the four million unemployed. The medicine was tough, but the Conservative government could point to the fact that, following the deep economic recession of 1979–82, Britain experienced an economic boom, based on the growth of financial services and foreign investment. However, this was a period of deep social division, marked by mass unemployment, riots in many large urban centres, rising crime, homelessness and increased poverty. In effect, the notion that governments should seek to redistribute wealth was rejected, and replaced with the promise that increased wealth would eventually 'trickle down' to the poorer sections of society.

A divided society was reflected in a divided geography. These economic tensions led to social divisions, and the 1980s was marked by the concerns about urban violence and inner-city decay. The politics of race was a significant force in these accounts, once more rendering the older models of urban structure difficult to take seriously. Rural geography, once concerned with the agricultural economy, the location of settlements and, in its modern version, the management of land-use conflicts, came to stand in for a deeper divide between urban and rural Britain. These changes brought about significant shifts in social theory and geographers increasingly looked to ideas in political economy, sociology and cultural studies to understand them. In this context, geographers produced a series of accounts that pointed to the fact that the Conservatives inherited a country divided by class, gender, race and location, and pursued policies that exacerbated these divisions. Many of these accounts amounted to what Mohan (2001) calls 'cartographies of distress' because they mapped in detail the existence of a social and economic crisis.

Table 1.1 lists the contents of some of these representative texts, and indicates the political nature of the subject matter.

Table 1.1 Contents of selected geographical texts that mapped the impact of Thatcherism

---

Lewis and Townsend (1989) *The North–South Divide*
Owner-occupied housing: a north–south divide
The growth of financial centres and the location of non-financial HQs
The geography of ill-health and healthcare
The privatization of education
The division in voting patterns

Mohan (1989) *The Political Geography of Contemporary Britain*
Nationalism in a disunited kingdom
The crisis of local government
Deindustrialization and state intervention
Changing geography of trade unions
The politics of race and segregation
Women in Thatcher's Britain
The political geography of housing
The geography of healthcare
Policing the recession
Environmental politics and policy in the 1980s

The contents reflect a concern with four main areas. First, they highlight economic changes in the form of deindustrialization and manufacturing decline, which is only partly compensated for by new types of employment. Second, there is a focus on the changing internal relations of the British state. Third, they focus on the social divisions along axes of gender and race that accompanied these developments. Finally, the environment is recognized as an important area of political tension and conflict (see Box 1.2 for a discussion of this theme)

In the face of this 'geography of division', it was inevitable that the question of *whose* geography is taught in schools would surface. In other words, the content of the curriculum became a political issue. As Huckle argued:

> While the majority of school geographers were preoccupied with the 'new' geography, others were employing humanistic or structuralist philosophies to design lessons on such topics as environmental issues, global inequalities and urban redevelopment.
>
> (Huckle 1985: 301)

These arguments caused real problems for geography teachers seeking to provide students with an understanding of the forces shaping a changing geography, since they were simultaneously facing demands to purge their subject of political content. However, we suggest that, without a strong and robust analysis of the role that the subject plays in understanding social and spatial relations, school geographers were unable to offer students the type of critical understanding of the relationship between society and space, and there emerged a 'gap' between the way that geography was taught in schools (largely focused on empirical patterns and offering spatial explanations for phenomena) and how geography was studied in universities (drawing on post-positivist approaches and linked to social theory).

Box 1.2

THE CHALLENGE OF THE ENVIRONMENT

In the 1980s and 1990s the 'environment' emerged as an important focus of political concern. This represented a challenge to geography as a school subject since, for most of the post-war period, school geography reflected the belief that society was on a trajectory of development and progress and that nature was experienced as a set of opportunities and constraints that could be overcome through the application of technology. School geography textbooks as late as the mid-1980s reflect what, with hindsight, appears as an era of steady growth, social harmony and rising prosperity, and political consensus (see Morgan 2003 for a discussion). Where environmental issues are mentioned, it is usually to provide resource inventories and discuss how to maximize the supply of them. From the mid-1960s, geography in schools was likely to be divided into 'physical' and 'human' aspects. Physical geography, which ostensibly focused on the environment, was taught in terms of physical processes. However, the development of an environmental critique meant that some teachers and students questioned the representations of environmental issues in school geography. Books such as Carson's ([1962] 2000) *Silent Spring*, Schumacher's (1973) *Small is Beautiful*, and the Club of Rome's (1971) report on *The Limits to Growth* provided a context in which environmental issues were reflected in calls for environmental education.

Radical geography provided the basis for a critique of society–nature relations. For example, in an analysis of the London Board's A Level examination syllabus and papers, Pepper (1985) argued that the physical geography papers did not allow pupils to set knowledge within the context of human society and problems. The physical environment was not seen as a part of a system that also contains human society. The questions split knowledge into little information 'bits', such as how stream load and discharges are related, or the 'five stages of coastline development'.

Pepper asked the question 'Why teach physical geography?' and concluded that without a *social* purpose, there is little justification to teach physical geography. The London examination discussed by Pepper 'fosters an uncritical, atomistic and functional approach to the physical environment which is quite divorced from its socio-economic context' (1985: 69). The physical geography described by Pepper is derived from dominant models of science education that fail to address the societal context in which decisions are made.

By the late 1980s it was difficult to entertain the idea that society and nature could be separated. This was reflected in curriculum developments of the period, such as the Schools Council 16–19 Project whose first 'knowledge principle' stated: 'People are an inseparable part of the global system within which physical and cultural systems are closely inter-related'. The idea that geography is concerned with 'people–environment' relationships is now at the centre of most contemporary geography curricula.

The case of environmental issues is an excellent example of the way in which school geography reflects broader arguments about the nature of society. Education for Sustainable

Development is now an important theme in the National Curriculum, and many geography teachers would see geography as an important vehicle for teaching about environmental issues. However, there are dangers in this approach. Critics such as Williams (2008) argue that the curriculum is being used for political purposes to promote moral values, and serve to promote an anti-progress view of Western models of economic development. Meanwhile, more radical critics argue that school geography tends to offer simplistic and unrealistic accounts of environmental issues that do not pay sufficient attention to the idea that nature is a social construction (e.g. Huckle 2009). Environmental problems are portrayed as global problems and attributed to such common causes as overpopulation, resource scarcity, inappropriate technology, overconsumption or overproduction. For Huckle this type of teaching fulfils an ideological role because it fails to relate issues to the different social settings in which they arise and fails to explain how population, scarcity, technology, consumption and production are structured by economic and political forces.

Geography teaching in 'new times': 1989–2009

> Not only in the universities, but also in the media and in private encounters, virtually everyone, everywhere, became increasingly conscious of the problem of creating meaning in situations in which so many of the parameters of economic, political and social life had shifted.
>
> (Shurmer-Smith 2002: 1)

Shurmer-Smith draws attention to the way in which the economic changes of the 1970s precipitated fundamental changes in the ways in which people experienced and understood society. If, in the 1980s, many geographers had been concerned to understand the processes by which the seemingly 'solid' geography of post-war Britain had been eroded, in the 1990s others began to explore the new spaces and places produced by the shift towards a post-Fordist society.

It is widely argued that the economic regime of mass industrial production and capital accumulation began to fail in the 1970s, and that out of this crisis there emerged a new and invigorated global capitalism that originated in Britain and the USA. Three factors underpinned this revival. The first was the development of new information and communications technologies that began to transform traditional manufacturing and distribution systems. The second was the influence on economic policy of neoliberal ideas, which emphasized the primacy of markets. The third was the emergence of counter-cultural values among the middle classes that gave rise to post-materialist values associated with identity, ethics and belonging.

We would argue that much of the human geographical literature of the past two decades can be read as an attempt to make sense of these changes to the economic, social and cultural landscape. In particular, the political-economic approaches that dominated human geography in the 1980s have been challenged by the development of the so-called 'new cultural geography'. In the rest of this section, we seek to outline some of the important shifts that have occurred in the latest phase of capitalist modernization and explore different interpretations of these changes.

Economies

As suggested above, it is widely argued that advanced economies such as Britain have made the transition from Fordism to post-Fordism that involves a shift from an economy dominated by manufacturing to one dependent on services. In the sphere of production, advances in technology have facilitated a shift from mass production to small-batch production, and less stockpiling of goods in the light of 'just-in-time' production and distribution. These changes were prompted by the long downturn of the late 1960s and early 1970s and have led to a weakening of trade union power as transnational corporations sought to shift production to sites of cheaper labour overseas. In response to this, governments sought to change the rules of accumulation. They did this by attacking the institutional strength of labour movements and moving away from the arrangements for state intervention that had prevailed in the post-war period. The effect was a reduction in the real level of pay, but this was insufficient to restore profitability, and, in the face of this, influential economists argued that a radically new approach was needed; one that drew on the tenets of classical forms of economics – neoliberalism.

These changes have had important implications for the nature of work. Whereas an earlier regional geography was based on the predominance of skilled and semi-skilled male workers in primary or secondary industries, the archetype is now the white-collared worker employed in offices. The growing internationalization of the economy has meant that large transnational corporations have shifted manufacturing jobs to the 'developing world'. This process of 'de-industrialization' and its associated occupational shift are represented in movies, such as *The Full Monty* and *Brassed Off*, which document the fortunes of the male working class in industrial towns and cities. At the same time there has been an increase in the number of service jobs, there is reduced demand for traditional skilled manual workers and increased participation for women. The cultural associations of work have also changed, with a growth in flexible working; long hours' culture and the reported shift from bureaucratic to flexible organizations, mimicked in television shows such as *The Office*, based in a firm supplying stationery in a 1960s-built office in Slough. Despite relatively low rates of unemployment nationally, there remain stubborn rates of unemployment among male and ethnic minority groups, growth of the informal economy, and growth in the number of people disconnected to the labour market.

Within economic geography there have been important developments in seeking to understand these processes of change. The restructuring of the 1980s revealed the limits of the older models of industrial location and the need to understand spatial changes in location as linked to shifts in the nature of capitalist production and organization. Increasingly, economic geographers pay attention to the differentiated nature of the labour force and its role in shaping processes of production (Hudson 2001; Lee and Wills 1997; Massey 1984).

Consumption

For those in work, there have been new opportunities to consume in an economy which, in order to maintain high levels of profitability, seeks to harness people's desires through advertising and spectacle. This has led to the rise of shopping culture – and the physical rise of new temples of consumerism – the shopping mall – has been one of the key stories of the past two decades. It is argued that consumption is part of the way in which we define ourselves as men and women. Global brands such as Nike and Benetton offer visions of desirable ways of living, and while this is perhaps not a new development, its scale and intensity has increased. This is, in many respects, a reflection of the intensification of economic activity in the aftermath of the long downturn in capital accumulation from the 1960s. In response to a fall in the rate of profit, policies of marketization and commodification led to increased turnover of goods and services. These were facilitated by advertising that sold people images of themselves. The result was a shift in identities from production (what work you did) to consumption (you are what you buy). Of course, not all people and all places shared equally in these developments, but few were exempt from their symbolic representation in television, films and communications. Whereas, in the 1980s, many geographers, following in the traditions of critical theorists such as Adorno and Horkheimer, saw the cultural industries as promoting 'false consciousness', the advent of the cultural turn has seen geographers examining the complex ways in which people use consumption to fashion their identities. In many ways, this work is optimistic, since it offers new ways of understanding how people make sense of the world.

Social change

It is common to argue that post-Fordist economies are characterized by flexibility and mobility, and that this is reflected in how people experience the world. For instance, sociologists such as Anthony Giddens (1991) describe the process of 'de-traditionalization' in which former stable identities based on 'traditional' assumptions about gender, age and class have been loosened, and Bauman (2000) argues for the increased 'liquidity' of economic and social life, as opposed to the former 'heavy' qualities of the Fordist period. The result, it is argued, is that people are increasingly free to decide how to live their lives. This is reflected, for example, in discussions of the de-traditionalization of gender identities (McRobbie 2009), the 'decline of Christian Britain' (Brown 2001) and proliferation of sexual identities (Weeks 2007).

These changes were reflected in the types of place studied by geographers. For example, cities were traditionally sites of public investment; new roads and housing and public buildings. They grew in response to economic development. However, processes of de-industrialization in the 1980s led to the crisis of the inner cities, with policies aimed at regeneration. They were primarily about production. In light of economic change, geographers have come to study cities as sites of consumption. The consuming city is a response to patterns of de-industrialization, with the waterfronts of large cities that are seen as opportunities for investment. Another significant area for study is the process of gentrification, which is seen by many city leaders as heralding new life and prosperity for former declining urban spaces. There are important questions about how far these developments benefit the wider population of towns and cities, as often they are targeted at wealthy and affluent groups. Critics talk of the ways in which these premier sites effectively become gated communities that exclude undesirable groups who are subject to heightened surveillance, and indeed the geographies of crime and fear are disproportionately experienced in the excluded neighbourhoods. This is reflected in the concerns that we live in an increasingly polarized society.

Geographies of exclusion and inclusion

While there is much work that explores the new cultural developments that are associated with a more flexible consumer capitalism, many geographers have pointed out the existence of structural inequalities that limit the opportunities of many people to share in the new times. Geographers who study the continued existence of places of exclusion or those that are 'off the map', and those who draw attention to the continued inequalities in access to the products of a consumer society provide an important corrective to accounts of 'postmodern consumer society'. They also point to an important aspect of the argument in this chapter, which is that geographical knowledge always entails a response to processes of modernization.

Although, in the space available, it is impossible to do justice to the rich variety of work produced by geographers, we hope that this section is suggestive of the ways in which the spaces of modernity have been reworked in the past two decades. The result is that what it means to live and grow up in Britain in 2009 is very different than in 1989, and this is reflected in the geographical places and spaces we inhabit. Today's youthful generations will have to live their lives, not with the certainties of the Fordist period, but with the manifold uncertainties of life in societies that are in constant process of 'restructuring' and change. The stances adopted by geographers towards these changes vary. One approach is optimistic about the opportunities afforded by the new flexible capitalism. This is represented by Anthony Giddens and Scott Lash who argue that the processes of time–space compression lead to the 'de-traditionalization' of social categories such as class, gender, sexuality and ethnicity and heightened reflexivity in which people can renegotiate their personal identity. At the same time there are those who point out the continued existence of social structures that limit individuals' agency and choice. They point to the processes of exclusion and the emptying out of meaning for many people whose lives are at the mercy of the forces of capital. For geographers, one of the most significant changes has been the permission to shift from models of political economy to study processes of cultural production and consumption, and this has allowed a widening of the traditional remit of 'economy–population–settlement' that has dominated the subject. These new cultural geographies are tempered by an older concern to recognize the economic and social geographies that underpin them. These draw attention to spaces of exclusion and the ways in which certain groups are not invited to the party.

Conclusion

This chapter has argued that school geography should be seen as part of a continuing engagement with economic and social change. Geography teachers are charged with the task of representing complex social processes in meaningful and accessible ways to young people. The argument has at times been critical of school geography's failure to achieve this ambition. In the early post-war period, school geography operated with a class-based version of the subject geared to the experiences of the grammar school population. From the mid-1960s, school geography underwent a process of modernization that had the potential to engage with a range of economic, social and cultural changes. In practice, the curriculum projects of the 1970s and early 1980s adopted a consensual model of society that favoured the role of geographer as 'technocrat', fixing the problems of industrial society. These models were not flexible enough to handle important questions of social and cultural change around, for example, gender and race. The failure to develop its own distinctive theories of curriculum change meant that school geography relied for its innovation on developments in academic geography, and, in the face of economic and social change, capitulated to demands for a 'restorationist' geography during the late 1980s and 1990s.

We argue that one of the reasons school geography was unable to respond to these developments was that it tended to be socially selective. It found it hard to address the question of 'whose geography'. In a sense, this book is the product of two authors who have been socialized in a particular intellectual milieu. We were both profoundly affected by the changes of the 1980s and the limits to school geography's responses. The models did not work, and school geography has not developed a robust and intellectually defensible alternative. In this book, we seek to develop an approach to geographical education that is able to do justice to what Lee (1985: 211) called 'societal geography', which incorporates 'the idea and the reality of the connections between the social and the material conditions of life that are central to the making of history and geography'.

This is a challenging agenda, but it is one to which this book seeks to contribute. As Lee concludes:

> Looking at the world from the perspective I have advocated will be uncomfortable in both personal and social terms, difficult to understand, and difficult to teach ... it will insist upon a materially and socially grounded ecological analysis of development, and it will necessitate the specification and accurate description of the society through which people engage with nature. But the approach must not be bound by disciplines; it will not be marginal and must force itself into any sustainable 'core' curriculum.
>
> (Lee 1985: 215)

2 The place of geography in schools today

The previous chapter provided an account of how, in the post-war period, geography teaching has responded to and reflected wider changes in economy, society and environment. This chapter focuses more closely on the contemporary moment, one in which a 'new' National Curriculum has been introduced in response to the challenges of living in the 'knowledge economy'. It argues that the National Curriculum is underpinned by a particular 'geographical imagination'. This imagination has two components: first, the idea of a global knowledge economy in which capital, goods, ideas and people flow with increasing velocity; second, the idea that these forces threaten the sense of 'community' for many people. Schools are urged to respond to these changes. Having described this 'geographical imagination', the chapter analyses it in more detail, raising questions about its veracity. The chapter closes by posing the question of the role of geography in the current educational context.

Shift happens

In 2007 a presentation called *Shift Happens* was being presented to schools and teachers at a range of conferences and training events. Shift Happens was originally produced in the USA, and later a UK version was posted on the Internet. The message of *Shift Happens* is that there is currently a major transformation taking place in population and economy, which is being driven by technological development, and which means that education systems are not equipped to deal with the new types of student who enter formal education. The presentation starts with statistics about the growth of China and India's population, which raises the spectre of a large, cheap and highly educated workforce to compete with countries like the USA and the UK. The next section talks about the idea that there is no such thing as a 'job for life' and that in the future there will be a need for people who are flexible and prepared to live with uncertainty. The presentation suggests that what drives these developments is the exponential growth of technology (especially through the Internet and networked computers), which means that new information is being created at ever-faster rates. Children in schools and entering colleges today are comfortable with this new technology as evidenced through the use of Google, My Space and handheld video games. In educational terms, *Shift Happens* suggests, we are preparing children who can solve problems that we do not even know exist that will require technologies that have not yet been invented.

The question posed by *Shift Happens* is whether the type of education we offer students today is adequate preparation for a fast-changing, networked and technology-rich world. This is an important question. However, before we start to think about the educational implications of this analysis, in the next section we examine the assumptions that underpin the argument.

The rise of the digital economy

Shift Happens is based on the idea that there has been a fundamental change in the nature of the global economy. The basis of this is the development of what Malecki and Moriset (2006) call 'the digital economy', which represents the pervasive use of information technology (IT) in all aspects of the economy including: internal operations of organizations; transactions between organizations; and transactions between individuals, acting as both consumers and citizens, and organizations. They note that as IT has become cheaper, faster, better and easier to use, organizations continuously find new and expanded uses for it, so that digital applications become ubiquitous and central to economic and social activity. This increased connectivity has profound implications for economic geography, since the effect of technological convergence has been increased speed of access to, and processing of information, allowing organizations increased control over decentralized systems. Rather than shrinking space, telecommunications enables human extensibility to distant locations. Information and communication technology has permitted markets to be extended to the global level, as described by the economic geographer Peter Dicken (1998) in his book *Global Shift*. There is a fairly straightforward economics at work here, which involves overcoming the 'friction of distance' to allow for faster turnover of trade and further reach to markets elsewhere. This is the basis of the argument in Shift Happens: the world is increasingly networked and connected, and the rate of flows of information is increasing at an exponential rate. In such circumstances, survival will depend on fast and flexible responses.

The digital revolution is seen as simply the latest in a series of waves of innovation. Geographers are familiar with this argument in the form of the idea of *Kondratieff Waves* that describe the ups and downs of economic activity, in cycles of 50–70 years duration, over the past three centuries. Kondratieff was a Russian economist in the 1920s who studied historical changes in the price of grain. He identified a series of long waves of upturns and downturns in economic activity. Later researchers postulated that the upturns were coterminous with clusters of innovations. For example, the Industrial Revolution was precipitated by the development of steam power. It is widely argued that a Fifth Kondratieff Wave has begun or is about to begin, based on a new technological innovation: the microchip and biotechnology.

One of the problems with the idea of Kondratieff Waves and their links to innovation is that they appear to be based on ideas of technological determinism or the idea that it is only a matter of time before new inventions arise to bring about social change. Indeed, this is one of the problems with the analysis found in *Shift Happens*: it is never explained what drives these processes other than the presence of new technologies.

Education and the knowledge economy

How does this discussion about global shift and the digital economy relate to current debates about education and schooling? The arguments in the previous section about the existence of a new phase of economic growth fuelled by IT and based on the competitive global market are accepted by most governments and seen as the backdrop for educational policy-making. However, the terms of this argument are drawn rather more widely to embrace the idea that we are currently involved in the shift to a 'knowledge economy'.

The phrase 'knowledge economy' was coined by the economist Peter Drucker in 1969. He distinguished between manual workers who work with their hands and produce 'stuff' and knowledge workers who work with their heads and produce or articulate ideas, knowledge and information. Drucker's argument was that in the latest stage of economic development information and knowledge are replacing capital and energy as the primary wealth-producing assets, just as capital and energy replaced land and labour during the Industrial Revolution. Technology and knowledge are now becoming the key factors of production, and what is significant about these is that they can be instantaneously transported around the world.

In the light of this argument, many commentators assert that education systems that were designed to meet the demands of the industrial age are no longer geared to the requirements of a knowledge economy. In the post-war period economies were organized around Fordist mass production, and the role of the state was to manage the economy to maintain productivity and social welfare. Educational policy responded to this. However, the economic crisis of the 1970s was revolved through increased international mobility of capital, which meant that the state was no longer able to maintain high levels of taxation without risking capital flight. In this competitive global economy, states seek to provide cost-effective public services that directly contribute to the production of 'human capital'. Thus, there is a 'reschooling' of society in the face of economic and cultural change. Education's place within (and contribution to) the 'disorganized' conditions of a globalized, post-Fordist world is harder to define than in 'advanced industrial society'.

Increasingly, in policy terms, there has come to be a widely accepted view of the role that schools play. Education is currently considered by governments across the world to have particular importance because of the development of a 'global knowledge economy'. With the decline of traditional manufacturing (or at least its outsourcing to growing economies in China and India, for example), countries such as the UK are looking towards the production and trade of knowledge to secure economic prosperity. Special importance is therefore being given to education because the nation's economy depends on having a future workforce able to produce and trade in knowledge by mobilizing the power of information and communication technology. It is asserted that education systems must be reformed to ensure children can prosper and also to secure national prosperity. This entails moving away from what is often assumed to be a 'factory floor' model of schooling to one more suited to a technologically rich, 'always-on' era.

According to this analysis, there has been an epochal shift in the nature of economy and society. Although the terms used to describe this shift vary (they include: industrial to post-industrial society, Fordist to post-Fordist, organized to disorganized capitalism), what they have in common is the sense that what it means to live and work in the contemporary world has undergone qualitative change, and schools are seen to lag behind in responding to these shifts. These types of epochal analysis tend to take a critical view of the role of contemporary education policy, which, they suggest, is based on a concern for 'raising standards', traditional teacher-led pedagogy and a focus on testing of content. This is seen as a narrow agenda that acts with an impoverished model of individual students. The focus is on academic success (defined by examination scores) as opposed to personal and social development, which is not conducive to producing a productive citizenry needed to face the challenges of the twenty-first century.

In this type of analysis, there is a move to reimagine the future education system as one in which technology is taking on enhanced importance and, simultaneously, where individuals are required to take increasing responsibility for themselves and for their use of public services. Thus, the work of schools is to prepare a future workforce capable of contributing to and prospering in a knowledge-based economy as well as a future citizenry enabled to exert their own self-control and self-discipline.

As a result of this, Ball argues that contemporary education policy faces two ways:

> towards an imaginary past of a British heritage, traditional values and social order and authority, within which social boundaries are reinforced, and an imaginary future of a knowledge economy, high skills, innovation and creativity and a meritocracy within which social boundaries are erased. The first rests on a set of fixed national and social identities, the second envisages a post-national, post-social, but connected world that is flexible and fluid, within which identities can be continually remade.
>
> (Ball 2008: 205)

It is worth pointing out that Ball thinks that the 'empirical evidence for the knowledge economy is still weak at best' (p. 23), with the 'main areas of recent economic growth and expansion of jobs' resting 'not on knowledge but on "service"' (p. 24). This suggests that generalized assumptions about the pace of transformation at the present time need to be seen less as actual existing realities to which schools must respond, but imaginary scenarios to which policy aspires – policy blueprints for economic and educational rebuilding.

If we accept for now the assumptions on which this analysis is based, in these new economic conditions, education plays an important role. Here we consider one account that focuses on the role of education. In their book *Capitalism and Social Progress*, Brown and Lauder (2001) argue that advanced Western societies are undergoing a fundamental transformation in the operation of the capitalist market, and that education offers one way to respond to the attendant challenges. Brown and Lauder argue that the post-war 'Golden era' of Western capitalism was characterized by a situation of 'economic nationalism' in which nation states operated within 'walled economies'. Corporations produced goods and services and this arrangement offered the prospect of decent family wages to low-skilled (generally male) workers. Under these economic arrangements, large national corporations expanded to meet the demand for new consumer durables, along with a large public sector that created vast armies of white-collar workers. These provided predictable and stable career ladders to the middle classes and their children. In terms of social structure, this was a world anchored by the nuclear family. Brown and Lauder (2001) note that this economic arrangement was underpinned by a political settlement between the state, employers and workers. Governments offered a commitment to economic growth and full employment in return for wage restraint and political acquiescence.

However, this 'golden' era has given way to a new period of economic and social instability. This took the form of a series of shocks. Thus, in the early 1970s the oil crisis caused a rise in fuel prices that led to a fall in the rate of profit. This was in part the cause for a move away from walled economies to a highly integrated global market-place. The increased vulnerability to foreign competition meant it was unviable to build and rely on systems of national prosperity. Large companies have thus shed their national roots and become global operators. The political settlement was shattered as governments sought to reduce the power of trade unions to defend conditions of workers and maintain profitability for firms. A period of corporate 'downsizing' and a 'hollowing-out' of the state has had concomitant social costs in the breakdown of older stable social structures.

According to Brown and Lauder (2001), these changes pose major problems for nations in terms of maintaining their position in the global economy (through attracting investment and profitability) and at the same time securing social cohesion. They argue that the answer to this conundrum is new forms of 'collective intelligence': 'In an information-rich, knowledge-based society it is brains not brawn which will prove decisive in improving productivity and individual well-being. Hence the alternative to market individualism is collective intelligence' (p. 8).

Collective intelligence involves important changes in how we think about knowledge and learning. Specifically, it assumes that all are capable rather than a few; intelligence is multiple rather than a matter of solving puzzles with only one right answer; our human qualities for imagination and emotional engagement are as important as our ability to become technical experts; our ability to imagine alternative futures and to solve open-ended problems, and our interpersonal skills, should all be included in our definition of intelligence in the future:

> Collective intelligence involves a major change in the way we think about the relationship between the individual and society and consequently the way we organize our schools, companies, neighbourhoods, and government. This is because the pooling of intelligence, through the creation of social structures which enhance the capacity for intelligent action, offers the best prospect of prosperity, democracy and social harmony in the context of post-industrial development. Therefore, if the twentieth century has been dominated by the spirit of competition, the twenty-first century must begin in an attempt to create a spirit of co-operation.
>
> (Brown and Lauder 2001: 8)

Though we have focused on just one example of the type of argument that we are living in educational new times, there are others. We now examine how these ideas are increasingly influencing debates about the school curriculum.

Current policy agendas

These ideas about a global shift, the digital revolution and the knowledge-economy, have become very influential in debates about educational policy in the UK. In this section, we show how they are increasingly linked to arguments about the nature of the school curriculum and teaching and learning (pedagogy). These arguments have gathered pace in the face of criticisms of the National Curriculum. For example, Leadbeater argues that 'schools are out of kilter with the world children are growing up in':

> In a world in which everything seems to be 24/7 on demand, schools operate with rigid years, grades, terms and timetables. That might have made sense when most people worked at the same time, many of them in the same place, on the same tasks, their lives organised by the factory siren. But people increasingly work at different times and in different places. Schools are factories for learning in an economy in which innovation will be critical ... Traditional schools do too little to encourage individual initiative and collaborative problem-solving; learning is cut off from real-world experiences; teaching focuses too much on cognitive skills and too little on the soft skills of sociability, teamwork and mutual respect. Nor are schools necessarily the most important places where children learn ... Children spend 85 percent of their waking hours outside school: increasingly they learn from the games they play on computers and from the television. They organise their lives through their mobile phones and social networks.
>
> (Leadbetter 2008a: 147)

According to this analysis, schools tend to operate with an outdated view of knowledge. Thus, teaching proceeds on the assumption that knowledge is 'stuff' that can be stored in minds, books and databases. It is seen as being true and correct, which leads to demands to teach accepted facts and wisdom. According to this view, knowledge is something stable that accumulates slowly over time. It is built up by people, and people can 'possess' it, but it exists objectively, independently of people. Finally, there are different branches of knowledge, or disciplines, and becoming a knowledgeable person requires learning the accepted rules and methods of these 'subjects'.

This view of knowledge and learning is very different from how knowledge is understood in the 'knowledge age'. This alternative way of thinking about knowledge is summarized by Gilbert (2005) in her report *Catching the Knowledge Wave?* For Gilbert (summarizing a wide range of literature), knowledge is increasingly seen as a process rather than a product; it is performative in the sense that it is used to make things happen. In addition, knowledge is collectively produced rather than the possession of individual experts, develops on a just-in-time rather than just-in-case basis, is dynamic and changing, and resists being codified into subjects and disciplines, which are seen as imposing unnecessary limits on our thinking.

These 'new' ideas about knowledge and learning have significant implications for how schools are organized, the most important of which is that education should be less concerned with *what* and more concerned with *how*. This is reflected in calls for the development of 'higher order' cognitive skills such as problem-solving and thinking skills, and with ideas of meta-cognition or 'learning how to learn'. In addition, the collaborative nature of knowledge construction requires that students acquire a series of 'soft skills' such as teamwork, empathy and cooperation.

These ideas are increasingly influential in debates about curriculum and teaching, and currently there are a number of examples of projects that involve schools organizing learning in ways that downplay the importance of learning 'subjects' such as geography and history. One of the most publicized is the RSA's *Opening Minds* project in which teaching and learning is based around a series of 'competences' that are designed to provide students with the skills needed to thrive in the knowledge economy. These competences are largely concerned with the soft skills required to survive in the 'new culture of capitalism' rather than traditional curriculum knowledge. *Opening Minds* starts from the assumption that there is a growing divide between the current curriculum and the experiences and demands of the outside world – the content of the curriculum is fundamentally out of date, slow to react, fragmented and not suited to children's needs. The *Opening Minds* approach entails the realignments of subject areas and a focus on a set of competences that students will acquire through a range of experiences.

Clearing up after the economy

In the previous section, we suggested that contemporary education policy is underpinned by the view that learning in the twenty-first century needs to respond to the challenges of the knowledge economy. However, there is another dimension to recent arguments about schooling that centres on the role that schools play in promoting social cohesion.

For many commentators, the post-war dream of social democracy and equal opportunities has failed. In the last two decades of the twentieth century, governments pursued policies that sought to reverse the assumptions on which welfare policy had been constructed. Individual responsibility and choice were emphasized, and the idea was that if you were poor this was somehow down to the bad choices you had made. Post-welfare educational systems are organized around the principles of entitlement and choice, competition and accountability, and performance and personalization.

In 1997 a new Labour government was elected that was committed to placing the emphasis on education. It had twin goals of making Britain a competitive 'world class' economy and promoting social inclusion. Indeed, social inclusion was necessary to allow for a successful economy. However, a persistent criticism of education policy since 1997 is that it has not made for a more socially inclusive society. One of the important developments is the recognition that schools cannot be considered in isolation from the communities they serve. The Audit Commission argued that:

> Traditional school improvement activity has tended to concentrate on teaching and learning at individual school level. Critical though this is, by itself the approach is limited ...

> The strong relationship between parental socio-economic circumstances and children's attainment is long-standing, and clear at both school and pupil level.
> (Audit Commission 2006: 3–4)

This is a significant development in thinking about the work of schools, and led the Audit Commission to conclude that:

> School improvement and renewal are inseparable issues from neighbourhood improvement and renewal, particularly in the most disadvantaged areas. While

schools are profoundly affected by their neighbourhoods, they equally have a key role in promoting cohesion and building social capital . . .

(Audit Commission 2006: 3–4)

In October 2007, these concerns were echoed by Ofsted (the body responsible for measuring the quality of education provision in England) in its annual report. The report focused on three interrelated issues: improving the life chances of all children and narrowing the gap between them; the question of what it means to grow up in the twenty-first century; and preparing young people for the world of work.

The report generated a lot of media coverage, much of which focused on the report's identification of the gap in opportunities and outcomes that persists in the education system. HM Chief Inspector, Christine Gilbert, summarized this gap:

The relationship between poverty and outcomes for young people is stark; the poor performance of many children and young people living in the most disadvantaged areas is seen in the Foundation Stage Early Learning Goals, in National Curriculum test results, and in GCSE results. Participation in higher education continues to have much to do with socio-economic background.

(Ofsted 2007: 6)

In addition to measures to improve test scores and achievement in public examinations, it is widely argued that schools should pay attention to children's welfare and social needs. This is in line with the government's Every Child Matters agenda. In many ways this is the latest in a series of initiatives that are concerned with the health, welfare and upbringing of children. Every Child Matters was a direct response to the early death in 2000 of Victoria Climbie. One of the outcomes of the enquiry into this tragedy was that there was a lack of coordination between different agencies responsible for her welfare. The Every Child Matters document argued that there was a need for greater integration of a number of initiatives designed to tackle issues of child welfare. Schools were considered to be central to the success of Every Child Matters, and newly qualified teachers are required to meet a 'standard' relating to the policy.

Every Child Matters is the political expression of a growing concern that many children do not share in the general material prosperity of society, and reflects recent interest in the notions of happiness and well-being (e.g. Huppert et al. 2005; Layard 2005). This is related to the idea that economic growth and an increase in material well-being do not necessarily lead to greater levels of satisfaction or happiness. Rutherford summarizes the problems:

The penetration of market relations into the social fabric of people's lives has generated a set of 'post-material' social problems – widespread mental ill health, systemic loneliness, growing numbers of psychologically damaged children, eating disorders, obesity, alcoholism, drug addiction, compulsions to shop, spend and accumulate things, the breakdown of relationships and marriage. Thus, for example, the cost of mental health problems in the UK is estimated at £93 billion a year, in lost productivity, health care spending and reductions in the quality of life. Stress, anxiety and depression account for a third of all working days lost.

(Rutherford 2005: 10)

In the light of these concerns about community cohesion and social exclusion, the relationship between education and the 'good society' is posed with increasing urgency. In *Happiness and Education*, Noddings (2003) says that when she told people she was writing a book on happiness and education, some responded with puzzlement, stating that the two 'don't go together'. Noddings argues that: 'Happiness and education are, properly, intimately related: Happiness should be the aim of education, and a good education should contribute significantly to personal and collective happiness' (p. 1). She asks why it is that so many bright, creative people hated school, and why we continue to justify it with the excuse 'One day you'll thank me for this'. In a similar vein, the New Economics Foundation (nef) published in 2004 'a well-being manifesto for a flourishing society'. Its section on education reports a study of over 1000 young people in Nottingham who completed detailed questionnaires to measure their well-being. The results showed that students' satisfaction with their school experience plummeted between primary and secondary school, never to recover. The manifesto stated that the purpose of the education system 'should be explicitly to promote individual and societal well-being both now, and in the future. It should aim to create capable and emotionally well-rounded young people who are happy and motivated' (2004: 1). The manifesto made a number of criticisms of schooling, arguing that education policy must 'acknowledge that the best way of enabling people to realize their potential is to value them for who they are rather than their performance against targets. There is evidence to show that focusing heavily on testing can destroy learning, innovation, experimentation, and original thinking' (p. 1).

So, along with the arguments about the 'knowledge economy', educational policy and debates are simultaneously marked by a focus on a wide range of social concerns. For offer a few examples: schools are encouraged to attend to the emotional and social development of boys, who are widely seen to be falling behind; to promote children's healthy development through social education; and to attend to emotional literacy.

These issues are not straightforward, and the role of schools in 'solving' them is unclear. Thus, John Evans and colleagues (2008) have explored what they see as the rise of a modern 'child-saving movement' that centres around children's eating habits. This is part of a broader moral panic about children's health but they show how schools and teachers are increasingly required to monitor the behaviour of pupils in schools. Similarly, Matthews (2006) provides a thoughtful account of the need to develop students' emotional literacy in schools, and offers examples of this in practice. However, he suggests that there are a number of forces that are acting to reduce children's abilities to develop emotionally mature responses. These are: increased emotional anxiety (this is argued to be a feature of society as a whole, with influential psychologists such as James (2007) arguing that advanced capitalist societies are experiencing an epidemic of 'affluenza'); a decrease in people's ability to develop emotional attachments; increased surveillance; and heightened emotional control. Matthews suggests that there are currently developments in schools that are exacerbating these trends, with important implications for children's ability to develop emotional literacy.

This is the context in which the revised National Curriculum has been developed. In the rest of this chapter, we explore the role that school geography might play in future.

Widening the debate

So far, we have sought to describe and explain some of the discourses that are currently shaping debates about curriculum and pedagogy in Britain. We have argued that there is an appetite for innovation and change that many teachers will share. The vision of an education system geared to preparing young people to meet the challenge of living in a global knowledge economy is exciting and, in many ways, inspiring. However, we think that it is important to examine these arguments more carefully in order to map out some possible directions for geography education.

As we have argued in this chapter, contemporary educational policy is underpinned, implicitly, by a geographical imagination. This geographical imagination is that of a global capitalist economy in which goods, services, images and people circulate at an ever-faster rate. In order to compete in this capitalist economy, nation states must prepare young people to work and live in responsive and responsible ways. At the same time, there is another aspect of the geographical imagination at work, which is that economic change brings with it costs to individuals and communities. Indeed, the flow of capital into and out of places threatens to undermine a sense of place. In the face of this, schools can provide a way to support people's sense of self and make them feel that they belong as active citizens. At this point, we should record our view that neither of these approaches seems to offer much of a role for a *critical* geographical education. In the first, geography will at best provide a way of developing the skills and competences required for life in the global economy. There will be little room for geographical knowledge, since the important emphasis is on developing flexible workers with the right mix of 'learning dispositions' for life in a precarious economic system. In the second, the focus will be on developing within students the 'correct' attitudes and values to play their part as good citizens. Here, too, as Ecclestone and Hayes (2008) have argued, the approach will be one of offering therapy to students and moral injunctions to get fit, save the planet, do kindly acts and so on. The rest of this chapter explores ways in which applying critical perspectives sampled from the wider subject offers alternative ways of conceptualizing the place of geography in schools.

Deconstructing the knowledge economy

In this section, we explore the question of whether the model of economy and society that informs contemporary curriculum thinking is valid. In order to do this, we look at some recent accounts provided by economic geography.

The first thing to note is the widespread acceptance of the need to understand changes in the economy from a global perspective. Thus, Knox and Agnew (1998) state that: 'The rapidly increasing interdependence of the world economy means that the economic and social well-being of nation, regions and cities everywhere depends increasingly on complex interactions that are framed at the global scale' (p. 1).

Similarly, Dicken has produced an influential text that examines the nature of the 'global shift':

> The nature of the world economy has changed dramatically, however, especially since the 1950s. National boundaries no longer act as 'watertight' containers of the production process ... Each one of us is now more full involved in a global economic system than were our parents and grandparents. Few, if any, industries now have much 'natural protection' from international competition whereas in the past, of course, geographical distance created a strong insulating effect.
>
> (Dicken 1998: 2)

One of the important contributions of economic geographers to our understanding of this global shift is their insistence on the uneven development of the global economy. They highlight that the process of globalization takes place at different rates and that the ways in which these processes impact on places, regions and localities is not predictable. Instead, the global and the local are interrelated in complex ways, something which has led some geographers to talk of the process of 'glocalization'. In this way, geography matters.

However, other geographers have made important criticisms of these arguments about globalization. The first is that this analysis risks giving the impression that the processes of globalization are one-way and inevitable. In addition, accounts of globalization largely start from the concerns of large transnational corporations, with the result that labour is mostly absent from these accounts. In response to these criticisms, geographers have attempted to provide alternative accounts of contemporary economic geography. An example is Castree et al.'s (2003) *Spaces of Work*, which explores the way in which production is organized. The authors suggest that the dominant story about the world economy is based on a series of 'myths'. These include:

- first, that we live in an increasingly 'borderless world';
- second, globalization is an irresistible force that stands over and above people and places;
- third, globalization signals the demise of the nation state;
- fourth, the myth of worker vulnerability;
- fifth, the myth of cheap labour.

Castree and colleagues argue that there is an element of truth in every one of these myths, and that taken together they suggest that globalization is everywhere transforming the world. However, in the subtitle of their book, they insist on using the term 'global capitalism'. This is important because it draws our attention to the specific way in which social relations are organized. Capitalism has not existed in all times and in all places. The term 'global' denotes the fact that capitalism is the dominant way of organizing production, but it is not a globalized capitalism. They suggest that we should pay attention to the politics of using the term 'globalization', citing Harvey's (2000) argument that we should pay attention to who is using the word, for what purposes, and who stands to lose and gain from globalization. This is similar to the idea that economists often refer to the market economy, when in fact the economy is much more complex. Drawing attention to the term 'capitalist' is crucial:

> Indeed, as capitalist social relations have penetrated into new areas and become more firmly entrenched during the past three decades ... it is of utmost importance to stress that we live in a world in which capitalist social relations are dominant, the rationale for production is profit, class and class inequalities do remain, and that wealth distribution does matter.
>
> (Hudson 2001: 2)

These arguments about the 'constructedness' of economies is important, because they highlight how the economy is the product of human activity rather than something that we are born into and have to accept. The effect of using terms such as 'the knowledge economy', 'globalization' or 'the market' without exploring who is using them and how is to suggest that these are natural and overarching concepts. Similarly, Herod concludes his book-length analysis of the 'geographies of globalization' with the observation that:

> much of the rhetoric concerning globalization emerged in those places – particularly the manufacturing economies of the global North – which experienced significant deindustrialization and disruptions in the 1970s and 1980s in how their economies had been historically ordered and which saw the rise of right-wing governments enamored of 'free markets'.
>
> (Herod 2009: 232)

Herod is not claiming that 'globalization' does or does not exist, but is drawing attention to the way that the 'economy' does not exist separately from the language we use to talk about it. The 'trick' of the last 20 years has been to persuade people that there is no alternative to the inevitable triumph of the global market economy, something that has become increasingly hard to sustain during the period we have been working on this book.

In this context geography teachers might look to draw on recent work in economic geography that offers alternative ways of thinking about economic space. For example, Gibson-Graham (1996) highlights the 'performativity' of concepts in economic geography, by which they mean that the concepts and theories we use in explaining the world do not simply reflect that world, but actively help constitute it. In *The End of Capitalism (as we knew it)*, they note how, in representations of economic life, both supporters and critics of capitalism tend to speak of it as a monolithic and all-powerful structure. In this way, capitalism is seen to colonize all aspects of social life. For example, we might speak of life in 'the capitalist family' or that we live in a 'capitalist culture'. For Gibson-Graham, the effect of this way of thinking is to obscure the possibility of thinking about non-capitalist spaces and practices. This leads us to ignore the fact that, for most of the time, most of us live our lives in social relations that are decidedly non-capitalistic (we act out of love, do things for fun, give our time freely and so on).

A similar approach is developed by Leyshon, Lee and Williams (2003) in *Alternative Economic Spaces*. The essays in this collection take up Gibson-Graham's idea that we should 'think and perform the economy' otherwise. The political importance of this task is clearly identified. At a time when the rich and powerful routinely announce the hegemony and inevitability of capitalist way of organizing economic and social life, the essays seek to show that there are already existing alternatives to the mainstream of global neo-liberalism. The book consists of a series of empirical studies of 'actually existing' alternative economies. These include: credit unions, Local Exchange Trading Systems, 'retro-retailing', informal work, employee-ownership, the social economy and 'back-to-the-land' migration. Colin Williams, one of the co-editors of the collection, has subsequently published *A Commodified World? Mapping the Limits of Capitalism* (2005). Williams sets out to survey the data to support the claim of the 'commodification thesis' that is defined as the belief that goods and services are increasingly produced and delivered by capitalist firms for a profit under conditions of market exchange. He suggests that even though there may be disagreement about the desirability of this development and debate about the speed at which this is occurring, there is widespread acceptance of the thesis among business leaders, politicians, journalists and academic commentators.

Williams presents data to suggest that significant and increasing amounts of time are spent in subsistence work, non-monetary and not-for-profit activities. In addition, the geography of commodification is uneven, and varies for different socio-economic groups. Once we move beyond the idea that economic space is dominated by commodity exchange, Williams argues, we are able to imagine different ways of organizing economic space. For example, economic policies might be designed to build on people's existing networks of provision, and there could be attempts to foster plural economies. Though both books recognize the challenge involved in realizing sustainable alternatives, their contribution is to alert readers to the possibility that 'another world is possible'.

Deconstructing the community

Just as many geographers would be dissatisfied with the rather uncritical view of 'the economy' that underpins current educational thinking, so others would be unhappy with the explanation that schools and communities should be linked without understanding the ways in which 'communities' are understood. In educational policy terms, poor places are seen as suffering from a lack of social capital. The aim of a policy that seeks to connect schools and communities is to increase the levels of social capital and thus reduce social exclusion. The idea of social inclusion is a relatively recent one. It emanates from the concerns of the New Labour government elected in 1997 to tackle issues of unemployment, poverty, crime and lack of involvement in mainstream society. However, whereas previous Labour governments developed policies to alleviate poverty through policies of redistribution, the new Labour government framed the issue in a new way. Social exclusion refers to a form of life that is outside of the mainstream of society. The political task, therefore, is to draw this excluded underclass back into the mainstream. Of course, waged employment is one part of this, but it also involves the excluded changing their family life, public behaviour, community participation, attitudes to the self and involvement in politics – this is about cultural as well as economic transformation. Within this, communities are to bear the burden of change. Thus, the oft-heard claim that 'poverty is no excuse'.

This way of understanding the problems of communities represents a significant shift. As geographer Ash Amin (2005: 612) has argued: 'Twenty-five years ago, few policy makers in the advanced economies would have expected localities facing sustained economic hardship to sort out their own problems, especially through the route of rebuilding local community'.

Instead, there was an understanding that urban and regional fortunes were linked with the wider economy. It was important to develop local approaches that would provide people with a place in the waged economy, but ultimately, if the market did not provide work, there was a belief in the role of redistribution of wealth. As Jamie Gough and colleagues (2006) argue in their work on the spaces of exclusion, poverty was regarded as a misfortune occasioned by the vagaries of the economy. It was widely accepted that a safety net of basic benefits should be provided by the state. Under the terms of a Keynesian welfare settlement, there was a national commitment to full employment.

This changed dramatically in the 1970s and 1980s. Neo-liberalism portrayed the previous welfare regime as expensive and wasteful, sapping individuals' enterprise and independence and limiting their choice. Communities and individuals needed to learn to stand on their own two feet, and if jobs were not available where you lived, because the industries had gone, then it was a case of being prepared to be flexible. In the event, this did not occur. Poverty increased dramatically. Some communities became cut off from the mainstream. The urban poor were increasing represented as a dangerous 'underclass'. These were places on the margins, literally 'off the map'. As Prime Minister Tony Blair stated:

> We inherited a country where hundreds of neighbourhoods were scarred by unemployment, educational failure and crime. They had become progressively cut off from the prosperity and opportunities that most of us take for granted. Communities were breaking down. Public services were failing. People had started to lose hope.
>
> (Blair 2001)

One of the important developments in debates around geography and social policy from the 1970s was that the social and the spatial are not automatically linked. Thus, area-based policies were seen as inappropriate in solving problems of poverty and social inequality. However, as Amin shows, recent moves have sewn the social and the spatial together, so that it is particular place-based communities that are seen as having the characteristics of social exclusion. Amin argues that it is strange that at a time of increasing connections and flows between places linked to the diverse geographies of globalization we should think of place as 'somehow spatially enclosed'. Of course, it is *only some types of place* that are thought about in this way. Other places are seen to be connected in healthy ways combining the cohesion and local rootedness of *gemeinschaft* with the openness and connectedness of *gesellschaft*. But for less-favoured and hard-pressed places, 'the rich tapestry of the social conceded to other spaces is conjured away'. The lack of community is blamed for local degeneration.

If the focus on communities as lacking in the required levels of social and cultural (not to mention economic) capital risks the pathologizing of particular places, then educational policy also tends to focus on the ways that individuals are rendered vulnerable and prone to misfortune. It is the job of schools and teachers to make good these deficits through ensuring that 'every child matters'. In texts written to support schools in developing the relations between schools and communities, there is very little evidence of an understanding of the wider geographical and social contexts in which schools operate, and little attempt to examine critically the notion of 'community' or social capital (this issue is discussed further in Chapter 9).

The ways in which these deficits are to be made good is to provide students with sources of support and guidance, when it could be argued that what is required is access to knowledge and perspectives that can allow them to make sense of their own lives and place in the world – the types of knowledge that geography (and other subjects) can offer. However, there is a danger that they are offered schooling as a 'therapeutic enterprise', which seeks to make life that little bit more comfortable.

Evidence of such palliative approaches to the problems faced by children is offered by the focus on 'emotional intelligence'. While among the intellectual elites emotional intelligence is seen as a way of improving one's ability to engage successfully in the 'new capitalism', in terms of schools facing the challenges of social cohesion, there is a risk that it is used as a way of managing 'unacceptable behaviours' (this is reflected in the ways in which particular groups of students are offered courses in 'anger management'). While for some children there may be opportunities in developing 'emotional capital', McWilliams and Hatcher (2004) argue that a focus on emotions within schools can be used to manage and control teachers and students.

This may sound overcritical at a time when there is a widespread concern to help students deal with the problems that are thrown up by living in a rapidly changing society. At a time of economic uncertainty and where the bonds of the social are increasingly strained, moves to involve schools and teachers in forms of social and personal education are to be welcomed. However, a major problem with this approach is that learning is conceptualized within individualist models. Thus, concerns about pupils' eating habits and calls to develop a healthy life are focused on what they can do to improve their lives rather than examining the wider social factors that shape individual behaviour. Many geographers will be unhappy with discussions of lack of healthy exercise that do not address the structural inequalities in access to opportunities to exercise. Similarly, decisions about healthy eating cannot be divorced from wider economies of food production and consumption (e.g. social geographers point out the problems that people have accessing fresh vegetables in the poorest areas). Most importantly, teachers will be aware of how children are targeted by corporations and advertisers that promote versions of what it means to be a happy and healthy person; namely, one who consumes in the appropriate way. These wider social and structural factors cannot be ignored in classrooms, and as the chapters in Part 2 of this book seek to show, subjects such as geography provide a set of critical frameworks with which to start to raise these questions.

Conclusion

The question we wish to ask, having provided an account of the geographical imagination that underpins educational policy, and having provided a brief critique of this imagination using the work of contemporary geographers, is: how should geography teachers in schools respond?

In this chapter, we have suggested that contemporary education policies are underpinned by two main drivers. These are preparation for life in a global knowledge economy, and the goals of a cohesive and happy society. Schools and teachers are to play their part in meeting these goals, and school subjects such as geography are to be welcomed to the extent that they contribute to these goals. This explains the position of school subjects in a recent representation of the 'big picture' of the curriculum produced by the Qualifications and Curriculum Authority. The aims of the curriculum have been set as producing 'confident individuals', 'successful learners' and 'responsible citizens'. School subjects such as geography feature only as 'vehicles' through which these goals are to be realized. In such circumstances, curriculum planning in school geography is unlikely to be based on a strong and principled analysis of the way the subject can contribute to an understanding of the making and remaking of society and nature.

This may be a depressing conclusion, but the rest of this book is an attempt to show how school geography can be refigured in ways that are intellectually defensible. Writing in 1986, Johnston argued that school geography 'fails to explore what it is that produces society, other than variation in the physical environment': 'By not seeking to understand societies, only describe them, however sophisticatedly, it fails to educate people, fails to help them see what it is that governs their lives' (p. 159).

We suggest that the same might be said of school geography in 2009. As the analysis in this chapter has suggested, school geography is increasingly seen as a vehicle for maintaining the status quo, rather than as a means of potential transformation.

3   What does it mean to be a teacher of geography?

This chapter argues for teacher engagement. As we point out, this in itself is not in any sense a challenging idea, for how can a teacher not be engaged – with the craft of teaching, with the students and with what they are trying to teach? However, we are interested in a particular aspect of engagement, following the context we have provided in the previous two chapters. Put crudely, we hope teachers are not satisfied with teaching geography simply because 'it is there' (on the National Curriculum or as a timetable slot). What geography, for whom and for what purpose? These are questions which are vital to keep in mind if teachers are to see themselves as more than merely the delivery agents of someone else's agenda. We make an argument therefore for the subject discipline to be understood as a resource. That is, not as a list of contents to be covered, but as a means of making sense of the world in a special way. This requires a particular kind of intellectual engagement with the subject. At the very least, we argue, teachers as 'curriculum makers' need to grapple from time to time with the conceptual underpinnings of the subject. One reason why this is important is to guard against students' experience at school being driven by short-term expediency or short-lived fads.

Introduction

> All relationships that can influence learning matter, and so do all the settings in which those relationships operate. Peer-to-peer, parental, family, social relationships may matter as much, if not more, than a pupil's relationship with a subject teacher.
>
> (Leadbeater 2008b: 23)

This book is concerned with geography *in education*. The opening two chapters have provided an account of geography as a discipline and field of enquiry, and thus a back-drop for everything else that follows in this book. The crucial theme concerns the relationship between geography and something more particular called school geography: that is, the purpose of geography and its contribution to the school curriculum.

As we have seen in Chapter 1, school geography has over the years drawn from the discipline to contribute significantly to a narrative of Britain in the world, what we have termed the story of modernization. Geography in UK schools has been a significant subject and distinctive in this regard. Furthermore, with its traditions of fieldwork and the comparative readiness of geography teachers over the years to embrace change, both in the curriculum and pedagogy (see Walford 2001), geography has frequently been perceived to be a source of curriculum innovation in schools. During the last two decades, however, the picture has become less certain. Stories of geography's decline in schools, traced by falling GCSE and A-level take-up, mask a deeper set of issues: the impact of post-modernism in the academy, in a post-industrial world where the post-subject school curriculum is increasingly being articulated, geography's identity and its contribution to education is less clear cut.

Chapter 2 focused on the present and showed that far from being irrelevant in the 'knowledge economy' and 'information society', geographical perspectives help provide a means of understanding contemporary process more fully. Also drawing directly from the products of geographical enquiry, we have shown some of the limits and potentials of some prominent debates in schools on matters such as child health, happiness and community cohesion.

This chapter goes on to address the teaching of geography in schools. What does the analysis we have provided mean for the teacher of geography? What implications does it have for professional identity and the ways geography teachers address their work? From the outset we are mindful that teachers operate in various and mostly complex settings. Charles Leadbeater, quoted at the start of this chapter, is very clear about this and indeed prefers to put his emphasis on learning rather than teaching. His portrayal of successful learning emphasizes healthy 'relationships for learning', in which children:

- actively *participate* in their learning;
- are *recognized* and valued as individuals;
- are *cared for* and feel safe;
- feel *motivated* to learn with high levels of confidence and increasing capability (see Chapter 4).

The stress that Leadbeater makes here is helpful. This chapter also examines relationships, albeit for teaching, on the understanding that teachers also need to form relationships in order to undertake their work productively: with young people, with other teachers and adults and with the subject. The last in this list is the one that is often overlooked. And yet it is of profound importance. In what ways can teachers work with their subject specialism in a way that contributes to 'twenty-first century learning'?

Schoolteachers as engaged professionals

It is commonplace to hear teachers described, with approbation, as being committed or engaged (see Lambert 2009a for a broader discussion on 'professionalism' and geography teaching). But what is meant by teachers as 'engaged' professionals? School teachers are certainly among the most committed professionals possible to imagine. Engagement is in part a measure of such commitment. The disengaged teacher is unlikely to find much enjoyment in the classroom. After all, it is to engage children and young people in productive activity that lies at the heart of teaching, and most teachers seek to do this by engaging with students.

However, and equally obviously, productive educational transactions need to have 'content'. In the recent past this has often been specified as aims and outcomes expressing the development of knowledge, understanding, skills and values – the so-called 'elements of learning'. In the new era of collective intelligence and knowledge-as-process outlined in Chapter 2, there is a fresh emphasis on 'learning': learning holistically, learning with each other, learning-to-learn. Does this mean teachers abrogate all responsibility for *what* is learned? Or more precisely, what we should attempt to teach? Our argument is that within the context of education[1] to focus on the teaching is at least as important as learning. Thus, when we advocate teachers as engaged professionals, we are taking as read engagement with children and young people as learners. In this book we are emphasizing engagement with the *subject*: with what is being taught.

However, a challenge with geography is that it carries so many different meanings. Geography in the popular imagination is dominated by 'facts' and maps – and quiz questions that often valorize the 'vocabulary' of the subject, especially place names and features such as rivers, mountain ranges and natural regions. Schoolteachers of geography usually try to promote a far broader idea of geography and often resist the 'pop' version. But the 'grammar' of the subject, by which we refer to the concepts and perspectives on which the subject discipline draws, and which affords us a means to understand and make sense of the world, often remains elusive to students, parents and even the school leadership team. Indeed, we might be tempted to argue that the diverse and adventurous subject discipline of geography is in some ways ill-disciplined in its grammar, leading for example to that often heard all-embracing definition of geography: 'geography is what geographers do.' The significance of Chapters 1 and 2 is therefore precisely in the *narrative* we have attempted to provide. There are stories in geography. It has tasks to perform. We argue that the subject is therefore able to make an important contribution to education. This chapter therefore links the subject to its role in education. The link is embodied in schoolteachers themselves who, as educators, need to be engaged at some level with the discipline.

But which discipline? Here's how Sarah Holloway and her colleagues put it in the opening lines of their influential undergraduate text *Key Concepts in Geography*:

> Defining the core of geography is harder than one might expect. Sociologists have society, biologists have living things, economists the economy and physicists matter and energy. But what is at the very core of geography? What are its key concepts?
>
> (Holloway et al. 2003: xiv)

To some extent, this is a false question. We need to be careful not to worry too much over a non-problem. Biology has living things (etc.), it is true. But geography has the world. It is, as has often been said, the world subject (e.g. Taylor 1993), or as Johnston (1985: 6) succinctly put it, the 'study of the earth as the home of mankind'. Of course, this does not get us closer to what we have called the 'grammar' of the subject, in the form of its key ideas, but then neither does the identification of 'living things' get us closer to how biologists do their work, nor the kinds of understanding they seek. Let us not fall into the trap, therefore, of believing that geography in the popular imagination is any more difficult to define than other subjects. It is perfectly straightforward to do so, but all definitions leave a lot out.

To get the idea of a subject at work, that is, the subject discipline in pursuit of particular ways of seeing, we need to grasp what it is trying to understand and how it is setting out to do this. The reason 'key concepts' are useful (discussion of which fills most of this book) is because they allow us to glimpse at how the discipline tries to see the world, and the nature of its gaze. Not fully, because there is still more to think about; for example, the methodologies and procedures its practitioners use. But a list of key concepts certainly indicates the subject's architecture, or to revert to our earlier metaphor, its 'grammar'. This in turn captures at least part of the subject's discipline.

Certainly, Holloway et al. (2003) do refer to the 'discipline of geography' but are at pains to point out that the concepts they choose to expand on in their book are not self-evident: ' . . . the concepts are not stable and bounded but, like geography itself, open, temporary and mobile. Rather than being problematic, this is what makes geography a dynamic and fascinating discipline' (p. xv).

'Dynamic and fascinating' – we can all agree with that! But 'temporary and mobile' are perhaps more difficult aspects to live with, at least if you are a schoolteacher of geography with lessons to teach tomorrow. This is what this book tackles full on, and explains why we are at pains in these opening chapters to trace the development of geography in its social, economic and political contexts. Just as we live in a rapidly changing world, we need disciplines such as geography to be dynamic and adaptive in schools – to keep up, as it were, and to help interpret change not as inevitable but as the product of people – environmental interplay. But what are schoolteachers to make of this? What is their role in keeping the subject dynamic and adaptive in schools?

The challenge for teachers to 'keep up' with the subject is nothing new. Often this means ensuring that the teaching materials selected are contemporary and up to date. While we acknowledge that for geography teachers this is a considerable matter in its own right because the world changes constantly (albeit made a lot easier to manage with the help of digital technologies), our emphasis in this respect is not so much on keeping the 'vocabulary' current, but with the 'grammar' of the subject – its key concepts and ideas on how to make sense of the world. Another way of expressing this is to stress the importance of teachers being in possession of a robust theoretical basis for geography in the school curriculum. This helps them make decisions about what to teach, but also to clarify how this may contribute to the curriculum and its wider aims. During times when new flexibilities are being encouraged in schools, where subjects are likely to occupy a less 'given' space in the curriculum, such disciplinary thinking has never been so important. And yet it has never been more challenging, for there has been a qualitative shift in the way the discipline of geography can be delineated. When Graves (1979) wrote about curriculum planning in geography, he saw the key division as being between scientific and regional geography. What we can now see is that both these 'paradigms' of geography were understood to create accurate, mimetic reproductions of the world. Today's proliferations of geography and geographical thought often challenge this assumption, adding substantially to the challenge facing the teacher in deciding what to teach and how to teach it.

The importance of the big picture

In much the same way as school geography has been modified in the face of changing socio-economic and political contexts, as Chapters 1 and 2 have shown, teachers' work is not a fixed entity; that is, there is a history of geography teaching, and it is helpful to acknowledge this in order to appreciate fully the present discussion about what it means to be a geography teacher in the current times. How teachers respond to new opportunities for more flexibility in the school curriculum depend heavily on how teachers understand their work.

Readers interested in a detailed historical account can consult Walford (2001), who provides an account of the emergence of school geography in the nineteenth century to its position in the National Curriculum at the end of the twentieth century. For much of Walford's narrative, the story is one of key individuals and groups wielding influence and at no time period is this more evident than during what has been referred to as the golden age (see Jones 2003) of teacher autonomy in the late 1960s to the beginning of the 1980s. This was the period that saw the birth and the historically rather short-lived Schools' Council – a government-funded quasi-autonomous body devoted to teacher-led curriculum development. In geography three influential projects[2] resulted, whose impacts can arguably be felt to this day. However, as Jones (2003) shows, histories can also be written in ways that reveal the social, cultural, economic and political circumstances that limited or at least shaped human actions. As we have already seen in Chapter 1 geographies are shaped in this way. It is interesting to examine the nature of geography as projected by these projects, not least the perceived variance between 'academic' geography in the Bristol Project and the more applied or 'relevant' geography for (less academic) young school leavers in the influential 'GYSL' project, but also the expectations on teachers. Though each project had a strong frame, and produced many excellent exemplar materials, it was the teachers who were judged to be in the curriculum driving seat.

Jones (2003) shows that if there was a grand narrative to educational policy in the latter half of the twentieth century, it could be characterized in terms of successive governments responding to persistent 'failure' and 'crisis'. This can be portrayed as a struggle over the curriculum. Following the Schools Council experiment, the government eventually took more direct control, and in so doing substantially reduced the autonomy of teachers, as described in, for example, Lowe (2007) in *The Death of Progressive Education*.

Following the so-called 'great debate' in education, launched by James Callaghan in 1976 (itself predicated on perspectives of economic failure), the government of the day finally 'bit the bullet' and introduced a National Curriculum to England under the 1988 Education Reform Act. By 1991, a statutory curriculum for geography had been set down in detail, initially for all children between the ages of 5 and 16 years.[3] Although this was seen at the time by many as geography 'finding its place in the sun' and a considerable achievement, it was also noted at the time that the way the curriculum had been framed was possibly not propitious for the continued development of the subject in school (Graves et al. 1990a; 1990b). This is not the place to replay the arguments, for they are well documented (e.g. Rawling 2001). But the introduction of the National Curriculum marks the beginning of a period of accelerated divergence between the continuous development and recreation of the wider discipline, and a bureaucratized school geography laid down by statute by the government's curriculum agency with its emphasis on 'delivery' and implementation.

The result is that teachers in secondary schools have for a generation been inducted into a more restricted form of professionalism than was previously the case, at least from the point of view of curriculum ownership (but arguably not in other ways: teachers have a sharper understanding of pedagogy and assessment, for example, than in earlier times).

During this period, the education system has expanded enormously and has received unprecedented levels of funding. Governments have therefore been under pressure to show value for money, and like at no time before teachers have in turn been required to perform against measurable targets and standards. Examination results have improved almost continuously throughout this period.

These changes, driven by the economic imperatives, have been controversial from the start and remain so. In some ways it is not just a struggle for the curriculum, but a struggle for the very idea of education itself in a modern globalized world. All teachers are caught up in this argument, although such is the power of the 'performance culture' that now pervades schools, it may not feel this way: so long as the next target is reached, the next innovation implemented the sense of 'improvement' may be continuous. Educationists have attempted to respond constructively by reconceptualizing teacher professionalism in various ways. For example, Hargreaves (1994) has linked teacher development and institutional development and emphasizes the teacher as 'researcher'. Wenger (1999) has opened up the powerful idea of communities of practice where practitioners who share common concerns within an identifiable domain (say, geography) can support and learn from each other. What has happened is that we can see teachers in far more complicated terms than perhaps was the case in earlier times. Delivering a centralized policy agenda, based on notions of 'what works' is not a straightforward matter across 5000 secondary schools in all manner of different social and economic circumstances.

Notions of practice communities and professional development emphasize relationships that lie at the heart of education and have to be made and remade almost every day in schools. Teachers are now advised, even by central policy-makers, to be creative and innovative (e.g. Qualifications and Curriculum Authority's work on curriculum futures: www.qca.org.uk/futures). Some inside the profession urge colleagues to 'take risks' in their teaching (e.g. Garner 2008: 10 reported a headteacher explicitly urging more risky teaching). But all this depends on refashioning a concept of teacher autonomy fit for the current times, a challenging idea indeed if we pause for a moment to consider the implication in a society in which trust (e.g. between government and public; or between public and professionals) is said to have broken down (Sennett 1999; see also Groundwater-Smith and Sachs 2002). Judyth Sachs (2003a) of the University of Sydney, perhaps demonstrating that the currents and influences on teaching outlined in the above paragraphs have a global reach, has proposed one version of new teacher autonomy, calling for an 'activist profession' in which teachers take responsibility for matters such as curriculum and mobilize in order to re-establish trust with parents, young people and communities. Reflecting on her book *The Activist Teaching Profession*, she writes:

> I am more convinced of its need, especially as a strategy to re-instate trust in the teaching profession by the community at large and to counter the de-skilling of teachers by governments who want to control teachers and the teaching profession.
> (Sachs 2003b: 3–4)

To summarize, teachers as professionals are subject to regulation in the same way as any professional group. This operates to limit the autonomy of individuals in the group, and society is perfectly reasonable in its expectation that this is so. However, there are legitimate matters of debate as to what is controlled by the state and its agencies, and for what purpose. Sachs is perhaps provocative in her chosen terminology, but is correct in arguing that to be truly effective teachers need to accept and take responsibility for key aspects of the role.

However, discussion of the curriculum – what to teach – is decidedly absent in this analysis. In this book, therefore, we focus this point on what we call *curriculum-making* (page 50) in which teachers form productive relationships not only with young people but also with their subject. It is the latter that can drive a rigorous and challenging educational encounters with young people. As Sachs observed, 'Obviously the beginning point is to get a group of like minded people together whose common goal is to improve the quality of education and student learning outcomes. This could be said to be a ' "big picture" group' (Sachs 2003a: 15). To facilitate their creation could be the crucial role and contribution of subject associations such as the Geographical Association (www.geography.org.uk).

And back to geography

In Brooks's (2007) analysis of 'expert' geography teachers, she discerned teachers operating within a constellation of influences on their practice. In Wenger's terms, we might say teachers belong to several 'communities of practice'. Each of these influences was considered in Brook's research to be a 'culture' in its own right, although all cultures interleaved and interacted with each other. For example, teachers operate within a school culture that may to some extent be governed by, or very different from, the national education culture expressed by law and regulation. Part of the mix was the subject culture of teachers which, she found, varied greatly in strength and articulation between teachers. However, what she concluded was that all the teachers she studied exhibited what she called 'synoptic capacity' in the subject. This term, taken from Rice's (1991) work on the scholarship of teaching (in higher education settings), denotes the capacity to think across the subject in terms of its big ideas and how they link, and their meanings and purposes. One of the reasons why synoptic capacity is vital is that it helps practically in classroom settings: to have a clear view of the architecture of the subject, its principles and perspectives is of great importance when responding to students' contributions, difficulties with certain ideas or what some authors have referred to as 'misconceptions' (e.g. Dove 1999). Also, synoptic capacity helps plot a progressive geography curriculum, driven by worthwhile goals derived in part by the teacher's understanding of the subject's educational potential.

Finally, synoptic capacity provides the basis for a 'strong interdisciplinarity' in schools. By this we imply it is the synoptic view of the subject that helps to ensure rigour in the content selection for thematic teaching in a skills-led curriculum, whether oriented by a 'learning to learn' motif, 'competence' or 'preparation for life in the twenty-first century'. By means of a concrete illustration of this, we could cite a number of cross-curricular themes such as climate change or migration, to which geographers might reasonably be expected to contribute. But it is important to have a view on *what* exactly geography brings to the table in each of these cases, so that sensible interdisciplinary thinking can be undertaken. In 2007, Doreen Massey provided the *Today* programme with a three-minute essay examining climate change using a geographical perspective (Box 3.1) and in doing so successfully illustrated this point; for example, drawing particularly strongly on 'interdependence' as a key idea. A scientist, or a historian, drawing from different disciplinary perspectives and standpoints, would produce different mini essays. Hopefully, they would be complementary, bringing different insights and perspectives to a complex problem.

Box 3.1

GEOGRAPHICAL PERSPECTIVES

There is an argument – about climate change – that goes like this.

- ' ... the UK's contribution to global emissions of greenhouse gas is only a small percentage.'
- ' ... there's not much point in taking responsibility for our own place when India and China are growing as they are.'

Now, I might have found that a comforting argument. But it seems it is a totally *inadequate* geography.

What that 'small percentage' counts is the greenhouse gas emissions from the UK directly. In that sense, it treats the UK as an isolated entity.

But it is not.

Firstly, that calculation, it seems, misses out the effect of all the things we import from elsewhere (many of them indeed from China). We demand those goods but we do not count as our own the pollution of producing them.

Secondly, that 'small percentage' does not take account of the role UK companies in production around the world. It has been estimated, for instance, that something like 15% of global carbon emissions derives from companies listed on the London Stock Exchange. Our economy is said to benefit from those companies. So what responsibilities do we, as UK citizens, have towards them?

I could go on. The point is this. That 'small percentage' is meaningless in an interconnected world. We cannot pretend that because all that greenhouse gas emission doesn't happen *here* it doesn't happen *because* of us ... that we are in no way implicated.

But surely, might come the reply, we *are* improving. The UK *is* on course to meet its Kyoto target.

Indeed it is. But why?

It is largely because:

- we have allowed our manufacturing to collapse
- we closed the mines and dashed for gas
- we opted for an economy based on services and, especially, finance.

It is not so much that we are behaving better, as that:

- we have exported our pollution
- and we have reshaped the UK's role in the global economy.

That reshaping has also reshaped the geography of the UK itself, as

- manufacturing regions have declined
- the north–south divide has widened
- our economy revolves more and more around London's financial sector.

Forget that comforting geography of small percentages. *These* are some of the other geographies that lie behind responsibilities for climate change.

Source: Professor Doreen Massey in a broadcast by Radio 4 *Today* programme on 1 January 2007 and reprinted with permission. See also www.geography.org.uk/news/bbctoday programme/.

We are arguing for geography teachers in schools to be engaged with the subject in a way that extends and refines their synoptic capacity. In Chapter 2 we encountered some of the reasons why many teachers may *not* see this as a priority: the policy environment is, as we have seen, dominated by a 'shift happens' culture, with its attendant pressures of performativity and personalization, all of which pull schools to imagine new formations that do not necessarily include subjects. Furthermore, there are additional structural reasons why engaging with the subject, at least in the manner we advocate, can be easier said than done. One of the backwash effects of the National Curriculum, first introduced to England following the 1988 Education Reform Act, was to lay down 'statutory orders' for each subject including geography. This gave the impression that subject content was a given (see Rawling 2001), and under the direct control of the government and/or its agencies. In effect what happened was that teachers surrendered a crucial aspect of their identities – or, some would prefer, responsibilities – ceding to the state decisions about what to teach. Teacher energy has been redirected to assimilating ever more complex requirements and guidance on pedagogy and assessment. There is relatively little incentive to engage with the subject. Even the Teacher Training Agency (now the Training and Development Agency (TDA) responsible not only for teacher preparation but also professional development of teachers in England), when introducing teaching 'competence' assessment for the first time in 1995 merely required new teachers to have a 'secure' knowledge of what they had to teach, severely devaluing the spirit of intellectual enquiry and indeed the contents of their undergraduate degree courses. Revised TDA Professional Standards make stronger demands on subject knowledge, perhaps reflecting National Curriculum reforms in 2008, which have stripped away much of the *prescribed* content from the subject statutory programmes of study.

During roughly the same time frame, geographers in universities have been required to focus on research assessment and on securing funded research for their institutions. Many academics have therefore been less inclined over the years to think of geography in its educational (or at least school) contexts, leading Goudie (1993) famously to write about the 'chasm' growing between school and university geography. This observation was made at a particularly crucial time, when the school curriculum had just become set in bureaucratic aspic, as we have seen. While the expansion of the higher education sector was gathering pace both in student numbers and its research productivity, the schools sector had new pressures to contend with. This has left subject knowledge issues relatively low on the list of priorities of most teachers and at the same time fewer opportunities for academics to engage in dialogue with teachers.

Our response to this crisis, and the argument we are making in this chapter, is in part to apply fresh thought to school subjects: what is meant by 'subject knowledge' in teaching? We focus on:

- the relationship that teachers have with geography as a *curriculum resource*;
- the role of teachers in *curriculum-making*.

In Chapter 4 that follows, we take this discussion as a basis for exploring geography's contribution to a 'capability' approach to education.

Geography as a curriculum resource

Time was when 'subject matter' in schools seemed all important. Goodson (1983) argued convincingly that school subjects, in order to win status and acceptance in the curriculum, have to become 'academic' with the support and influence of university experts. The old grammar school caricature of the expert authority figure lecturing his pupils with little sensitivity to their diverse needs (if it ever really existed) has long gone. The school curriculum is no longer the preserve of, nor even dominated by, subject disciplines. What seems to have happened is that more 'pedagogic' concerns have become influential, driven by the 'corporatization' of schooling. Subjects are just one of a range of social, educational and organizational matters that school teachers also have to incorporate in their planning. For example,

- examination results and 'value added';
- assessment for learning;
- the need to demonstrate 'progression';
- Every Child Matters;
- social inclusion and community cohesion;
- enterprise education and creativity initiatives;
- thinking skills;
- global dimension;
- language and learning;
- effective pedagogy;
- education for sustainable development;
- Using information and communication technologies (ICTs);
- learning outside the classroom;
- raising achievement.

Furthermore, school leadership teams, which set down the 'rules of engagement' for teachers, are often results-driven and encounter many other initiatives and priorities, from 'healthy' and 'sustainable' schools to remodelling KS3 to become the best preparation for new 14–19 diplomas. The point is that deciding what to teach in geography lessons and how to arrange this is not as simple a matter as perhaps it once was, or at least seemed.

According to the historian of education and geography educationist, Bill Marsden, the place and role of subject disciplines has always been in tension with competing priorities, but by the 1990s it was possible to see the unfolding process of how geography was being taken out of geography education. A decade earlier the question, as Walford (2001) and others have described, was how to secure a space for geography as a National Curriculum subject. By the 1990s, the issue was more subtle, namely the place of the discipline in influencing curriculum debates *within* school geography – and Chapter 2 provides the social, political and economic backdrop for this. It is interesting to note a couple of signifiers or outcomes of this: for example, school geography textbooks are now written by schoolteachers, not academic geographers as had been the case in the past. And the leadership of the professional association for geography teachers, the Geographical Association (GA), once dominated by leading academics, was by the 1990s far more in the hands of teachers, teacher educators and local authority advisers; indeed, in one year the President was neither a teacher nor an academic, but an educational publisher.

Marsden was interested in three dimensions of curriculum influence:

- geographical distinctiveness;
- educational value;
- social relevance.

He shows that 'geographical distinctiveness', itself a matter of some contention from time to time as the nature of geography is challenged and evolves (as we saw in Chapter 1), can be submerged when either or both the other dimensions – Brooks (2007) might call these 'cultures' – come to dominate practice. Furthermore, although he is certainly not arguing for a return to grammar school principles, he suggests that there are costs incurred if geography ceases to play a significant role in influencing what is taught and learned. An appropriate balance needs to be struck within the constellation of influences on the teacher and the curriculum.

In the contemporary educational world, it appears the orthodoxy is one that stresses educational value. Thus, one of the leading teacher unions states: 'ATL proposes a national curriculum model which starts with pupil needs and interests and is designed in terms of the skills and attitudes that we want pupils to acquire and develop' (ATL 2006: 1).

The pamphlet from which this comes appears to propose that subjects lack relevance and educational value, not least in its title – *Subject to Change*, Marsden's (1997) paper predates the ATL pamphlet by a decade, showing that its thinking is far from new: 'In general, educational theorists (have always) strongly favoured integration, dismissing subject-based syllabuses as mere social constructions and/or historical accidents' (p. 247).

An overemphasized concern to integrate knowledge for the supposed benefit of the learner carries the danger that the pedagogic adventure can come to dominate classrooms: the simulation game, the mystery, the card-sorting, the speech-making, the letter-writing ... all perfectly respectable teaching and learning techniques, but with severely reduced educative power if not driven by a clear sense of what is being taught and learned – the content. As Marsden (1997) helpfully stated, content is 'defined not as a collection of facts but as the state of the art conceptual frameworks of the subject' (p. 242). The problem here is not to say that secondary teachers can only teach from a narrow specialist base: clearly an absurd notion. It is that a distinctively geographical perspective is likely to be lost, for as we have seen, it is not given very easily to the generalist to adopt a "synoptic" understanding of geography and to accommodate its ever developing conceptual frameworks, ideas and perspectives.

When it comes to social relevance, Marsden traces how 'good causes' of various kinds have exerted influence ever since geography found a place on the school curriculum: indeed, it is possible to argue that geography became an established school subject (before its widespread presence in higher education), *because* of the imperialist imagination it promoted, albeit through jingoistic and what we can now see as racist underpinnings to international understanding. The British Empire needed to be mapped and described to children and Britain's place in the world reaffirmed: as central, dominant and in many ways superior. It is not difficult to substantiate this concern to use geography to teach children a 'correct' way of seeing the world: there are examples from virtually any school geography textbook written in the nineteenth and early twentieth centuries (see Hicks 1981; Marsden 2001; Wright 1979). Thus, the problem with social relevance is that 'good causes tend to generate inculcation and indoctrination rather than genuine education' (Marsden 1997: 244). Here, it is taken as read that education is a process that encourages and promotes independent and critical thought. It helps young people achieve this partly through its acceptance of conflict and dispute arising from alternative perspectives, and any subject discipline's profound confidence in the power of argument and process. In other words, 'genuine education' attempts to introduce young people not only to knowledge (i.e. some of the *products* of scientific, historical, or geographical enquiry) but to knowledge-making (derived through the application of a subject's 'state of the art conceptual frameworks' *and methods*).

Some contemporary 'good causes' that may distort geography's contribution to genuine education today, and which have been discussed at length by Standish (2009) include:

- citizenship (incorporating 'Britishness');
- sustainable development (incorporating climate change);
- global dimension (incorporating the 'war on poverty')

Standish argues that since the 1980s, school geography has experienced an 'ethical turn' that removed the modern, objective-scientific version of the subject that had become established in schools during the post-Second World War period. In each of the above, the danger lies in teaching geography for a 'better' world (according to those who wield sufficient influence to promote a particular view – often the government). Polemics can easily replace constructive and sometimes challenging or uncomfortable argument. This is not to say that geography cannot or should not contribute to each of these, merely to say that it should only do so through educational engagement. On the other hand, we may reasonably believe that the productive 'genuine education' of children and young people may well contribute to a better world, because they acquire knowledge, understanding and skills that extend their capability as individuals and active citizens.

However, maintaining such an ideal is itself challenging. By way of illustration, we can compare geography education with a recurrent dispute in science education. To what extent, if at all, should teachers of science address creationism in the classroom? *The Guardian* newspaper (2008) ran a headline 'Teach Creationism, says top scientist', as a summary of advice published by the Royal Society. This was eye-catching, but misleading. The scientist in question wrote:

> Your headline ('Teach creationism, says top scientist') misrepresents the views of myself and the Royal Society. The Society believes that if a young person raises the issue of creationism in a science class, a teacher should be in a position to examine why it does not stand up to scientific investigation. This does not put it on a par with evolution, which is recognised as the best explanation for the history of life on Earth from its beginnings and for the diversity of species.
>
> Evolution is rightly taught as an essential part of biology and science courses in schools, colleges and universities across the world. Creationism, which has no scientific validity, can be discussed in a science class if it is raised by a pupil, but in no way be seen as comparable to evolution or any other scientific theory backed up by evidence.
>
> (Professor Michael Reiss, Director of Education, Royal Society)

This case illustrates the difficulty facing teachers as genuine educators holding the line on education against a host of pressures and what Marsden called 'a debilitating anti-intellectualism' (2001: 249). More recently, others have made similar critiques suggesting that the contemporary school curriculum has been 'corrupted' by social relevance (Whelan 2007). Marsden, Reiss and Whelan are diverse in their subject backgrounds and positioning, but are united in their concern that the disciplinary perspectives, frameworks and methods for investigation can so easily be disregarded or misunderstood. Whelan even writes: 'Over the past two decades the school curriculum has been estranged from the challenge of educating children' (Whelan 2007: 1)

Geography, we argue, is one of the subject disciplines that has a distinctive role in the school curriculum. It has particular ways and the potential to help us critically to understand the real world. It is through achieving this that enables the subject to contribute to citizenship education.

Curriculum-making

Who is responsible for designing the school curriculum? Whatever the answer to this question, we can be sure that the curriculum *as experienced* by children and young people in the classroom is, at least in part, the one that has been made by teachers. Teachers are the curriculum-makers. And as we have seen from the previous section, subjects are not the only influence in play. Teachers have quite a balancing act to perform.

Figure 3.1 captures the meaning of curriculum-making. It is not quite the same as curriculum planning (e.g. Graves 1979) or curriculum development (see also Rawling 2008), both of which need to take place on a number of levels in and beyond the school, and which guide the practical business of curriculum-making.

It is also not the quite the same as lesson planning, which is a highly specific activity referencing particular materials and learning resources, and possibly even particular learning objectives achievable over one or two 40-minute periods, or lesson sequence. Figure 3.1 shows three competing zones of influence on the teacher as she grapples with

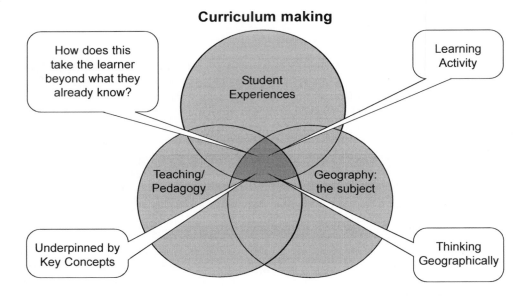

Figure 3.1 The three pillars of curriculum-making as expressed in the Action Plan for Geography (www.geographyteachingtoday.org.uk)

the 'in-between' work of translating a curriculum plan, which may scope out several years' work in geography (and is presumably driven by some broad aims or goals), into lesson sequences. The purpose of curriculum-making is to show an internal coherence representing something more than simply an accumulation of short-term objectives. It is also to hold in balance the *various* influences that might be brought to bear. The three zones of influence in the figure may also be thought of as sources of energy that feed educational encounters in schools. They are the resources for curriculum making:

- The young people themselves bring curiosities, ingenuity and often individual interests that the teacher may choose to find out about and use. Young people also experience the world in many different ways, through their activity spaces and through communication channels opened up by the world wide web, film, music, and so on, which means they already have geographical behaviours, perceptions, skills and knowledge. In a modern-day geography classroom it is not only good sense, but necessary to 'connect' in some way to this energy. (For an exploration of this, take a look at the Geographical Association's Young People's Geographies Project: www.youngpeoplesgeography.co.uk[4]).
- Teachers have a range of knowledge, skills and understanding on which to build a teaching repertoire. For example, what if the students do not display overt levels of 'individual interest' in the subject matter? The teacher can deploy a range of strategies to generate 'situational interest' (Trend 2008) instead. This is in the knowledge that, once societal and resource levels are allowed for, motivational effects are perhaps the strongest determinant of learning outcomes.

- The subject matter is the key resource that students and teachers use. The previous section explores the significance of subject disciplines as resources.

Figure 3.1 shows that the teacher needs to keep these zones of influential energy in some kind of balance. If the subject was the *only* real source of creative energy (and students were thought to be passive recipients of what the teacher, literally, had to tell them), then we return to the often caricatured grammar school ways of the mid-twentieth century. On the other hand, if the curriculum is made entirely to serve students' interests, and is entirely 'child-centred', it risks taking them nowhere new in their learning and could be as deeply unproductive as the previous option. Finally, if the teachers were only really interested in their own performance and the 'pedagogical adventure' they can provide, the curriculum risks being emptied of meaning, overly driven by 'skills' at the expense of knowledge and understanding.

Thus, despite all the complexities of teaching in today's schools and the competing demands placed on teachers, drawing from the subject, though not the teacher's only concern, remains a key. It is not possible to expect teachers of geography to 'keep up with' all the developments that have taken place in the wider fields occupied by academic geographers. It is also wrong-headed to imagine that school geography may be left in peace as a stable entity and immune to much change, as we have already seen. So what are teachers to do? We have now said a great deal about the nature of the teacher's relationship with the subject discipline. The rest of this book explores this further in order to underpin disciplined curriculum-making in various, local curriculum contexts.

Conclusion

To finish, let us return briefly to Leadbeater (2008b) whose work in the early years of this century has been influential. In stressing 'personalization' as a means to respond to the widespread view that state education has in some ways run out of steam in England – it has certainly failed to reduce the persistent attainment gap and the long tail of under-achievement – he advocates an innovatory mindset that would turn schools and the school curriculum into flexible institutions. For instance, the places where learning happened would vary (e.g. more opportunities in the community), the spaces for learning would evolve (e.g. to become much more flexible social spaces), the timetable would become more flexible with shorter and longer slots, and sometimes no subject slots at all (e.g. themed weeks) and the pace would vary (e.g. skills testing 'when ready'). This focus on personalized learning is at odds with much of what we have been discussing in this chapter. It is worth noting therefore the sociologist, Richard Sennett's, analysis of what may really underpin this new flexibility and why teacher groups may wish to be cautious adopters of recommended innovative practices. He asks:

> How do we decide what is of lasting value in ourselves in a society which is impatient, which focuses on the immediate moment? How can long-term goals be pursued in an economy devoted to the short term ... These are the questions about character posed by the new, flexible capitalism.
>
> (Sennett 1999: 10)

Sennett goes on to make the important observation that 'if change occurs it happens on the ground, between persons speaking out of inner need . . . ' (1999: 148). We translate this to teaching in a way that is perhaps now self-evident: teachers working with each other and young people need to clarify their goals and purposes in order to drive the creation of meaningful educational encounters in geography.

Notes

1   It is worth emphasizing what we value in the idea of education. What we showed in Chapter 2 was the potential for deepening the critical understanding of ideas such as globalization or community with geography. To paraphrase Peters (1965), this is not necessarily to lay down fixed positions or facts, but to enable students to 'travel with a different view' – words used by the Geographical Association in their 2009 'manifesto' (see also Slater 1992 and Lambert 2009b).
2   The Geography for the Young School Leaver (GYSL), also known as the Avery Hill project, the Geography 14–18 Project, also known as the Bristol Project and the Geography 16–19 Project, based at the Institute of Education, London.
3   The curriculum was later 'disapplied' post-14 years for non-core subjects like geography and history, reverting to their earlier status as 'optional subjects' to GCSE.
4   The Young People's Geographies Project was funded by the Department for Children Schools and Families from 2006–11 as part of the Action Plan for Geography (www. geographyteachingtoday.org.uk).

4 A 'capability' perspective on geography in schools

This chapter argues for fresh ways of articulating geography's contribution to education. After restating the importance of aims and the need for teachers to engage with questions of purpose, we present an analysis of geographical knowledge and understanding for the school setting – distinguishing intensive and extensive knowledges and advocating an approach that centres on an education for understanding. This includes the important notion of students as knowledge producers and the notion that knowledge is often contingent, not least on what the learners bring to the task of knowledge production. We then use this discussion as a platform to introduce the helpful idea of education for capability. We suggest that there may be something worth exploring under the guise of 'geo-capability' that would centre on the capacity of children and young people to use the key, organizing concepts of geography (such as scale or interdependence) in their enquiries and endeavours to make sense of the world.

Introduction

> Misconstruing education as the simple transmission of information from one party (teachers) to another (students), these partners can fail to see the true importance of pedagogy ... (E)ducation is always life changing for students – whether they realize it or not ... (T)he knowledge that students assimilate is not simply 'added on' to fully formed characters – like icing on a cake or an extension to a house. Rather that knowledge helps to mould students into certain kinds of people. Formal education cannot, in short, fail to shape the character of those who experience it.
>
> (Castree 2005: 245–6)

The overarching theme of this book so far has been the relationship between geography the subject discipline and geography teachers, or more precisely, the purpose of geography and its contribution to the school curriculum. In Chapter 3, we looked at some implications for those teaching geography in schools, emphasizing their role as 'curriculum-makers' and the profound importance of developing a big picture of geography and its place in curriculum-making.

This chapter takes us one step further. Castree (2005) follows his 'sober recognition' of the significance of educational encounters (quoted above) with the realization that this is liberating for both teachers and students. He goes on to say, and we certainly agree, that 'there is no one "correct" set of things that students should know; there is no one "proper" way of learning; there are no "self-evident" goals of education. Instead, there are only ever *choices* about what to teach, how to teach and to what ends' (Castree 2005: 246, original italic). This is, as bell hooks (1994: 206) once wrote, an 'awesome responsibility'.

Here we advocate deeper thought about the purpose of geography in the curriculum and how it serves wider *educational* goals or aims. Thinking geographically contributes to cultural, spiritual, social and moral understanding, which is why, for example, geography teachers may develop with students their argumentation skills, strategies to address moral dilemmas and awareness of the ethical dimensions of topics, themes or issues. In a sense therefore it is not at all difficult to see how geography serves educational goals. However, this is a very broad set of claims and so loose that it offers some dangers to the unwary or ill-equipped. Teaching 'carelessly' (Morgan and Lambert 2005: pp. 62–65; see also Lambert and Balderstone 2009) needs to be avoided and Chapter 3 has shown the importance of balancing various competing priorities in order to minimize the risks of 'curriculum corruption' (Whelan 2007) as described in Chapter 3 of this book (see also Lambert 2008). Our argument is that careful thought about educational goals and purposes is essential and we are particularly concerned to do this in relation to knowledge and understanding in geography. Later in this chapter, we describe a framework for this using a 'capability' approach. Capability is an important synthesizing idea. It concerns the growth and development of the individual *per se*, but also contributing to the building of 'social capital', meaning here the dynamic and developing intellectual resources from which society as a whole can draw in addressing choices of how to live.

Aims and purposes, knowledge and understanding

It is difficult to overemphasize the significance of aims. Geography (or indeed any other subject discipline in school) may no longer be a sufficient end in itself, if ever it was. Subject disciplines, contributing to the selection from the wider culture that the curriculum represents (Lawton 1989), have a justifiable place in the curriculum only because they serve, and can contribute to, a range of educational purposes in particular and significant ways. What this means in a complex 'knowledge society' (see Chapter 2) demands a sophisticated response. Subjects connect us to a range of intellectual traditions (Chapter 1), and are shot through with arguments and disputes about how to make sense of the world. School subjects are a product of these traditions. We have seen (in Chapter 3) that teachers are crucial in making the curriculum drawing from the subject as a resource. But we now need to say more about subject knowledge characterized in this way. This section addresses aims, knowledge and understanding. We show that young people can become more capable as individuals through *using* some of the products and methods of disciplines such as geography.

The original (1988) National Curriculum for England and Wales was essentially aimless (White 2004; 2006). However, enthusiasm for an aims-based curriculum has grown apace in recent years. A growing number of schools are following new programmes at Key Stage 3 such as the Royal Society of Arts *Opening Minds* project (RSA 2005) based on a number of core 'competences' needed for life in the modern world. In such schools subject teaching is played down in favour of cross-curricular learning, often based on themes. In this context John White, a philosopher of education, has observed:

> Society-watchers on the look-out for changes in national zeitgeist should take note of what is happening at grass-roots level in schools and in major

educational agencies and pressure groups. The 1988 settlement is now widely rejected. While government may be cautiously reluctant about radical change for fear of being accused of flirting with the soggy progressivism of the 1960s, professionals are increasingly taking things into their own hands.

(White 2006:6)

What White (2006) appears to show is that teachers in schools are prepared to challenge certain taken-for-granted aspects about school education and specifically the assumption that it should be based on a 'traditional range of school subjects'. Fundamental questions are in the air such as:

- What is school education *for*?
- What should be its aims in a society like our own?
- How can these aims best be realised in the timetabled curriculum and in the wider life and ethos of the school?
- How can we best assess to what extent pupils are receiving an education in line with these aims?

As we have seen, a fully conscious, autonomous teaching profession can make a vital contribution to answering these questions, alongside other 'stakeholders' such as parents, employers and government. When they do so, it helps them in their work. They use the subject in a manner that is guided by their concept of educational purpose. However, as we have also seen, this engagement with 'philosophy' is never straightforward. The school curriculum can be understood to be the vehicle for arranging the introduction of coherent educational encounters and experiences for young people, but as we have been at pains to point out in this book 'the curriculum', understood ideologically and politically, is not a 'pure' nor neutral vehicle. Thus, although we have a settled set of aims for the secondary curriculum in England (Box 4.1), supported by statements about curriculum purposes and underpinning values, there is still a lot of interpretation yet to do, especially for teachers in their curriculum-making role. An ever present danger is that certain ideological or political ends dominate at the expense of others, for there can never be an ideology-free curriculum. Teachers, who interpret the curriculum, need to be conscious of this.

Box 4.1

NATIONAL CURRICULUM AIMS

Education influences and reflects the values of society, and the kind of society we want to be. It is important, therefore, to recognise a broad set of common purposes, values and aims that underpin the school curriculum and the work of schools.

Clear aims that focus on the qualities and skills learners need to succeed in school and beyond should be the starting point for the curriculum. These aims should inform all aspects of curriculum planning and teaching and learning at whole-school and subject levels.

The curriculum should enable all young people to become:

- **successful learners** who enjoy learning, make progress and achieve
- **confident individuals** who are able to live safe, healthy and fulfilling lives
- **responsible citizens** who make a positive contribution to society.

Source: www.curriculum.qca.org.uk/key-stages-3-and-4/aims/index.aspx.

Arguably, as we have shown, the contemporary school curriculum in England has been shaped by the growing dominance of economic purposes, preparing children and young people for the world of work and to enable the nation to compete successfully with the rising economic might of eastern Asia, India and Brazil. The groundswell that White observes, leading to innovative curriculum solutions as noted above, is all very well: but whose aims and purposes are dominant? Designing a curriculum based on 'competences needed for life in the modern world' is beguiling and in a sense could be risky, particularly if the notion of competence is aligned too closely to work-related 'skills'. What is the role of knowledge and understanding? It is possible to imagine young people who have been successful learners, who feel confident as individuals and who possess a positive disposition to responsible citizenship, but who are still ill-prepared for life in the modern world, either because of a knowledge deficit or an inability to apply understanding to new situations and encounters.

It all depends on what we have in mind with the idea of education, and indeed, what we imagine are the challenges that young people will face during their lives. Let us take as read that in order to respond intelligently to environmental, economic and social change some knowledge and understanding is essential. But knowledge of what? And more tellingly, what is it for and in what *way* is knowledge essential?

Extensive knowledge

For some, a key component of education and the sign of an educated person is literacy in its broadest sense. This includes a knowledge dimension, particularly in its influential form of 'cultural literacy' – 'a limited educational goal . . . that needs special emphasis today' (Hirsch 1988: xi). In his book, subtitled 'what every American needs to know', Hirsch distinguishes cultural literacy from 'literacy to a specific task' by comparing it with 'world knowledge'. He shows how world knowledge is essential in the development of various functional skills, and is therefore empowering. Books, newspapers and other media he argues assume a common readership: 'that is, a person who knows the things known by other literate persons in the culture' (p. 13). This does not have to be in-depth knowledge – Hirsch uses the phrase 'vague knowledge' (p. 15) – and it is in some ways similar to our use of the term subject 'vocabulary' (e.g. on page 39). It is knowledge that gives access to contemporary culture, society and economy. Hirsch refers to this as a person's 'second' or national culture and without access to it, and the possibility to engage with it, a person is trapped in their first or local culture. A young person, say from a socially deprived setting or from a minority group with a strong sense of self-identity, is diminished in their capacity to succeed outside their local 'first' culture if they reject the national culture – or are denied access to it, for example, by the nature of the curriculum they are given, which avoids the knowledge question altogether and focuses on life skills or overemphasizes notions of personalization and local 'relevance'.

A simple example to illustrate the idea of cultural literacy, which draws from geographical knowledge, may be helpful at this point. Reread Massey's mini essay on climate change (page 44): what knowledge references are necessary to comprehend this piece? Here is one list:

- global emissions;
- greenhouse gas;
- India;
- China;
- goods;
- carbon;
- UK stock exchange;
- financial sector;
- dash for gas;
- manufacturing regions;
- north–south divide.

The cultural literacy argument would be that 'vague knowledge' of these matters is essential for an intelligent reading of Massey's essay. Such knowledge ought to come out of what Hirsch (1988: 127–30) called the 'extensive curriculum'. World knowledge learned through the 'extensive curriculum' supports deeper, more intensive study that may aim for deeper, critical understanding (see below), but it is also is required to gain access to society wide conversations and discourse. Some items on the above list may emerge at young ages and some at a later stage of education – knowledge builds up over time. While some of the items on the list are self-evidently 'geographical' vocabulary, all the items *may* emerge from geography lessons, possibly in the form of world knowledge. This we might assume to be one of the resultant *residuals* of a geography education; for example, a mental 'sketch map' of the UK space characterized by a general concept of its regional shape and economic geography.

To summarize, the geographical knowledge contribution to cultural literacy enables people to engage with national debates, some of which, like climate change policy, are crucial. Or, more prosaically, it enables people to watch the television news more intelligently. Hirsch himself uses a famous remark from Thomas Jefferson:

> Were it left to me to decide whether we should have a government without newspapers, or newspapers without a government, I should not hesitate a moment to prefer the latter. But I should mean that every man should receive those papers and be *capable of reading them*.
>
> (Hirsch 1988: 13, our emphasis)

World knowledge, or cultural literacy, is important. But this is, in the end, a fairly restricted view of knowledge. For a start it equates knowledge mainly with what is known, giving little sense of knowledge creation. It may also seem to overemphasize the delivery of 'facts' and says relatively little to teachers about what subject knowledge *they* need. As always, there is a need for teachers as curriculum-makers to keep notions of cultural literacy in balance with other priorities.

Intensive knowledge

As we have seen in earlier chapters, the role of knowledge in education is the subject of great current interest. To cite yet another contribution to the international debates that continue to impact on schools, Doerr and colleagues open their article on the changing nature of knowledge in education with this:

> In a speech given at the National Education Summit on High Schools, Bill Gates (2005) declared, ' ... America's high schools are obsolete ... training the workforce of tomorrow with the high schools of today is like trying to teach kids about today's computers on a 50-year-old mainframe. It's the wrong tool for the times.' His sentiments echo a growing trend among the business world: education is not preparing students to be productive members and workers of the new Knowledge Age.
>
> (Doerr et al. 2007: 279)

The attitude to educational aims and knowledge expressed in this quotation certainly suggests some other priorities to sit alongside cultural literacy. Almost certainly Gates would support cultural literacy, but preparing young people to become productive members of society in the knowledge age requires a lot more besides, including a sense of the *intensive* exploration and use of knowledge as well as the *extensive* acquisition of knowledge implied by cultural literacy.

Following a useful discussion and overview of several ways in which knowledge in education has been classified over the years, drawing from classic and influential texts from the likes of Bloom (1956) and Popper (1972), Doerr and colleagues describe working with a teacher on a view of subject knowledge as a 'resource' (our term – see page 46). The teacher uses the subject discipline creatively with students in a manner that captures both teacher and students as 'knowledge workers'. They show that in addition to knowledge as facts that can be learned and 'possessed' (e.g. of the physical world) and knowledge that is essentially personal and subjective (e.g. of the world of opinion and conjecture) there is a third 'world' of knowledge consisting of:

> ... theories and ideas (as) workable and improvable artifacts. These artifacts, which can consist of anything from a blueprint to a recipe, are termed *conceptual artifacts* by Bereiter (2002b). He proposes that the new classroom should create and improve conceptual artifacts. Students' endeavors in the classroom involve the formation of conceptual artifacts by understanding knowledge as creatable, something that can be worked with and improved upon. For this idea to take hold, students and educators need to shift their understanding of knowledge as facts stored in their individual minds to ideas that are out there in the world, independent of them.
>
> (Doerr et al. 2007: 283)

Thus, teachers are not simply knowledge communicators, and the subject is not just a store of content to be delivered. As we saw in Chapter 3, teachers need to work with the discipline's evolving *ideas*, developing their synoptic capacity of the subject to do so. They should expect their students to be able to pick up and use these ideas too.

Doerr and colleagues continue with a reprise of what they claim is a 'new approach' to knowledge:

> To help students become the new knowledge workers, Bereiter and Scardamalia (1998) suggest that educators adjust their view of knowledge and educational practice to one that allows students to work with and improve knowledge. They also believe that students and educators need to begin to see knowledge as something outside of themselves that they do not own or *possess*. The idea that students do not possess the knowledge learned in school can be a dramatic shift in understanding.
>
> (Doerr et al. 2007: 283)

Such a 'new approach' to knowledge is not supposed to replace other approaches to knowledge such as cultural literacy. Its usefulness is that it helps us conceptualize not only the nature of subject knowledge teachers (and students) need, but the nature of classroom encounters. Some will be teacher-led and possibly 'extensive' in nature while others will be more intensive with students more agentive and using the subject in a different way. As the teacher remarked in Doerr's research 'It doesn't matter what I say. It matters what sense the students make of what I say . . . ' (p. 296). It is exactly at this point that the subject discipline is useful, for the sense (the understanding) that students make is deepened through the use of those structures and ideas that lie outside of themselves and beyond their immediate, direct experience. Thus, understanding is not just a personal view or opinion. We can again use the Massey example (Chapter 3, page 44) to illustrate this point. It needs a certain amount of world knowledge to read this piece intelligently, but what she also provides in this passage is a conceptual framework, a disciplined way of seeing, broadly based on the idea of interdependence. It helps us *understand* the UK in the context of global climate change, perhaps in a new way: it challenges our possibly 'inadequate' geographies. It is important to realize that the example being described here is not quite the same as 'scaffolding' the student's understanding in a Vygotskyian constructivist sense. What we are advocating here is using the subject to challenge maybe taken-for-granted or common-sense understandings, rather than simply deepen or extend existing conceptual understanding.

Understanding

Howard Gardner, the founder of the theory of multiple intelligences (Gardner 1999), has written extensively on education for understanding. While recognizing the limitations of school curricula designed only to 'cover' extensive lists of content, he has expressed the importance of disciplines and understanding in forthright terms: 'We find the disciplines to be indispensable in any quality education, and we urge individuals not to throw away the "disciplinary baby" with the "subject matter" bathwater' (Gardner and Boix-Mansilla 2006: 145).

Before closing this discussion on aims, knowledge and understanding, it is worth just noting what Gardner means by understanding because it may be useful to us before moving to the idea of capability. Few educationists would resist the goal of 'teaching for understanding' and Gardner gives it pride of place in his work. But there is no shadow of a doubt that to achieve deep understanding is extremely demanding, and if we take the new approach to knowledge expressed in the previous section as the starting point (which we could characterize as 'knowledge-for-understanding'), it is easy to see why this is so. Gardner writes:

> In our own work we define 'understanding' as the capacity to use current knowledge, concepts and skills to illuminate new problems or unanticipated issues. So long as one is drawing on such knowledge only to illuminate issues that have already been encountered, it is not possible to tell how much genuine understanding has been achieved. But one can with some confidence conclude that genuine understanding has been achieved, if an individual proves able to apply knowledge in new situations, without applying such knowledge erroneously or inappropriately.
>
> (Gardner and Boix-Mansilla 2006: 145)

There are many reasons why teaching for understanding is often hard to find in schools (see Gardner and Boix-Mansilla 2006: 157–8). Among them are the legacy of curriculum as 'coverage' and what has been called the 'correct answer compromise' between teachers and students governed by externally controlled syllabuses and high stakes tests. There is also what Gardner calls the 'teacher's fallacy' – which assumes that because a fine lesson was taught the students therefore understood. However, we think that teachers who adopt the role of curriculum-maker as expressed in Chapter 3, and armed with the perspectives on aims, knowledge and understanding outlined in this section, are in a strong position to use geography to deepen understanding. One way to illustrate this is to imagine how geography can be used to address with children and young people the kinds of question below. Gardner (2006: 149) calls these *basic* questions: ' . . . articulated by young children, on the one hand, and seasoned philosophers on the other; they are addressed by the disciplines created by the scholars . . . '. Box 4.2 provides an abstract taken from a longer list of questions grouped into broad conceptual domains. Our abstract, slightly amended, is limited to four such domains, all of which have at least the potential of being addressed productively though geography:

Box 4.2

BASIC QUESTIONS ABOUT OURSELVES IN THE WORLD

Identity and history: Who am I? Who is my family? What is the group to which I belong? What is the story of that group? Who are the people around me, and in other parts of the world? How are they similar to and different from me? What do they do? What is their story?

My place in the world: Where do I live? How did I get here? How do I fit into this world? How do I feel about it? How is it changing? How do I want it to change? What regularities and patterns are there in the world? How do they come about?

The physical world: What is the world (and this place) made of? What do we know about the water, the air and the rocks? Why do things move? What becomes of things? How are humans related to the world of plants and other animals?

The human world: Who decides on who gets what, where and why? What is fair? How do communities, nations (and other groupings) handle differences of opinion and conflict? How do people treat each other? How are decisions affecting people's lives taken – who is 'in charge'?

These questions are useful on a number of levels. For example, they may offer a means of defining geography in schools through identifying the kinds of question that geographers have, at different times and in different ways, attempted to address. They evoke the kind of understandings and geography can provide. It would be a useful task for the reader to imagine how some substantial concepts that help shape the discipline – like space, place and scale, as well as interdependence, diversity, nature and culture – not only help identify basic questions to ask, but provide particular purchase to the questions identified in Box 4.2. To illustrate, 'who is my family?' will suggest different avenues of enquiry to the sociologist, biologist, historian – or geographer. Thus, the questions can be *put to use* by geography teachers designing and making a curriculum, possibly in collaboration with others (as we have noted, geography is not the only discipline that can address these questions). In a curriculum geared towards understanding, it should, arguably, be possible to relate any topic and/or sequence of classroom activity to the questions that inspired it, and to the long-term goal of achieving a sophisticated understanding of it.

Summary: the role of disciplines

We have in these sections stressed the role of subject knowledge and understanding in education, and how important it is for teachers to be involved in deep thought about aims and purposes. Certainly, there are several additional important practical and technical matters to take account of in curriculum-making, including making judgements about the age, readiness and other characteristics of the learners in question, what they have already experienced, what options lie ahead, and so on. However, these are subsidiary to the need for clarity about aims and purposes that the subject discipline, described as more than 'bodies of reported fact and information' (Carr 2007), is able to provide.

The Universities Council for the Education of Teachers (UCET), a body charged to represent the views of those engaged with teacher preparation and in particular preservice training, has usefully captured the crucial role of subject knowledge in teaching. We quote this at length, for it offers a broad perspective that brings together much of the discussion in Chapters 1–3 and our current analysis of knowledge and understanding:

> There are those who look upon subject teaching as the transmission of slabs of content for no worthier purpose than examination success, and the subject teacher, operating within a highly restricted pedagogical range, as having no loftier ambition than to crowd pupils' heads with facts. Of course, such characterisations represent an absurd caricature of subject teaching. Properly conceived, however they differentiate and coalesce over time, subjects constitute the available ways we have of exploring and interpreting the world of subjective

experience, of analysing the social environment and of making sense of the natural world. It is through subject study that learners acquire historical, scientific, mathematical and other forms of understanding; and it is through subject study that learners develop the capacity to engage in the distinctive modes of investigation and analysis through which human experience is differentiated and extensions of human understanding are achieved. That rationale does not by any means imply that knowledge can only be mediated through subject specific teaching; nor does it discount the value for particular purposes of combining knowledge that is drawn from discrete disciplines. Clearly, for many, including early years and primary teachers, that integrated approach is the preferred mode of knowledge engagement.

Moreover, subjects are communities of debate and argumentation, of exploration and criticism, of conjecture and refutation; they are pursuits in which knowledge, in due recognition of its provisionality, is open to continuous reconstruction. As such, subjects are educational resources of remarkable power, offering unlimited scope for realising an enormous range of educational purposes for enquiry and reflection, for hypothesising and the interrogation of evidence, for adjudicating between the valuable and the meretricious; for the use of the imagination and creativity; for the examination of human motive and the improvability of the social condition; for coming to terms with the responsibilities of citizenship; for promoting personal, social and environmental competence; and much else besides.

(Kirk and Broadhead 2007: para. 39)

Capability

In the extended quotation above, Kirk and Broadhead (2007) emphasize knowledge and understanding that is derived through subject teaching, and also the significance of introducing young people to the world of knowledge-making, echoing our earlier discussion distinguishing a necessary balance between extensive and intensive curriculum experience (see pages 56–59). They also finish with reference to wider educational goals, as we have been advocating throughout, using the notion of personal, social and environment 'competence'. Their take on competence is clearly deep and broad, and as such probably equates closely with the idea of 'capability' that we now wish to explore.

The idea of 'capability' derives from the conceptual framework developed by the economist Amartya Sen (Sen 1985) and the US philosopher Martha Nussbaum (Nussbaum and Sen 1993) in the field of human welfare and development economics. There is clearly not the space here to expand on this in any detail, save to say that the capability approach has become a widely accepted means of applying a broad set of criteria to such matters and an effective counter to 'one size fits all' measures of well-being such as gross national product (GNP) per capita. Many readers will be aware of the 'human development index' and use it in their teaching of welfare geography. This has been shaped by Nussbaum's 10 capabilities which, apart from fairly obvious matters to do with the right to life and health, include items such as:

- *Senses, imagination and thought*: Being able to use the senses, to imagine, think and reason – and to do these things in a 'truly human' way, a way informed and cultivated by an adequate education, including, but by no means limited to, literacy and basic mathematical and scientific training.
- *Practical reason*: Being able to form a conception of the good and to engage in critical reflection about the planning of one's life.
- *Affiliation*: For example, being able to live with and toward others, to recognize and show concern for other human beings, to engage in various forms of social interaction and to be able to imagine the situation of another.
- *Control over one's environment*: For example, the political – being able to partici-pate effectively in political choices that govern one's life; having the right of political participation, protections of free speech and association.

Thus, capability is not a simple measure of material possession and access to services. The framework emphasizes human *functioning* or what are called 'substantial freedoms' such as the ability to live to old age, engage in economic transactions, or participate in poli-tical activities. Thus, poverty is understood not in terms of low income but as capability deprivation, meaning lack of choice and ignorance as much as lack of financial resources. This approach to human welfare, with its stress on freedom and choice, diversity and human possibility or potential, clearly has an educational dimension. But it is also pos-sible to see quite readily how educationists, working in both richer and poorer countries, can apply a capability perspective to the education process itself, in terms of capability-building of both individuals and societies. Some educationists have begun to explore this (e.g. Hinchliffe 2007a, 2007b).

In this book we limit ourselves to the idea that geography education can contribute to developing the capability of young people. This chapter has provided the basis for making such a case. This is to argue that the value of geography in education, through its contents and driven by its aims, is its contribution to the enhancement of human cap-ability in particular ways. The main point of making such an argument is to provide a conceptual basis for expressing an idea of education that is ambitious, sophisticated and multidimensional, and which has its roots in the notion of human potential – to become self-fulfilled and competent individuals, informed and aware citizens and critical and creative 'knowledge workers' (see page 58).

Although capability refers to what people are able to do, it is worth repeating that it does *not* equate exactly with the narrower notion of skills (or what are sometimes called competences in skills-led curricula such as the RSA's *Opening Minds*). Capability certainly includes skills, but a lot more besides, enhancing people's individual freedoms, particu-larly with regard to making choices about how to live. Rather than discrete skills, cap-ability rests on acquiring and developing a range of 'functionings' (Hinchliffe 2007a) that contribute to human autonomy in thought and action. Part of the appeal of this approach is the realization that people with similar capabilities may derive these from different sets of functioning. Furthermore, whereas skills are often said to be value-free, capabilities are value-laden, emphasizing what lies at the moral heart of teaching: tea-chers in our view cannot abrogate or subcontract the responsibility for thinking through their aims and purposes. Teachers can infer from this that capability draws not only from 'knowledge' in an extensive curriculum sense, but from some engagement with the chosen epistemological roots of the subject discipline also. In other words, what is learned, and how it is learned, matters. Teachers as the curriculum-makers are in a position to make choices about what to teach, and why.

School subjects like geography are often understood in a more restricted way than this however. When this is so, it is hard to imagine their contribution to young people's developing capability in anything more than in a fairly modest way. In the case of geography, this is sometimes reduced to a partial description of the world and some rudimentary knowledge of a selection of human and physical processes. This may be one reason why currently it is so easy for some influential voices to dismiss subjects altogether – as being nineteenth-century constructs that have now outlived their usefulness in a post-disciplinary world. As we noted in Chapter 3, this restricted view overemphasizes the 'vocabularies' of the subject and rather underplays the 'grammar', or in the terms used in this chapter, the extensive curriculum at the expense of the more intensive curriculum for understanding. Capability in geography requires both. When an appropriate balance is struck, geography in schools can help young people not only to see the world anew but with a means to engage with basic questions (see Box 4.2 page 60) about the world, their place in it and conversations about possible futures (Hicks 2007).

In conclusion: towards geo-capability?

Many years ago in his discussion about the future of geography Johnston (1985) showed that '. . . there is general agreement as to its purpose. Literally defined as "earth description", geography is widely accepted as a discipline that provides "knowledge about the earth as the home of humankind" . . . such knowledge is considered desirable in a well-educated society' (p. 6). He also remarked that ' . . . it must be accepted that there is no necessity for a discipline of geography . . . Geography is a human creation' (p. 5). Although he was writing at a different time and for a different purpose, these sentiments form a golden thread through this chapter, for we have tried to show that geography consists of both extensive and intensive knowledge without which individuals and society may be considered educationally impoverished. The idea of capability has been useful in describing the nature of such 'impoverishment': it lies in a form of capability deprivation. Having created this thing called geography, which is a particular way of seeing and investigating the world and addressing a range of basic questions, it is up to teachers and educationists to use it in such a way that it contributes to young people's capability.

To be specific and final about this is perhaps risky. More research is certainly required, and talk of 'geo-capability' maybe premature. However, with suitable health warnings and tentativeness, we could speculate on how such an idea may be developed. That we should try is underpinned by the advantages that may accrue from placing aims and purposes so strongly to the fore. For it is this that is achieved by adopting a capability perspective: capability provides a framework for clarifying the education goals.

If capability involves the development of young people's capacities to function effectively in the world, then we can (with regard to notions of educational aims cited earlier in this chapter) devise a threefold framework:

- capabilities concerned with enhancing individual freedoms (autonomy and rights);
- capabilities concerned with choices about how to live (citizenship and responsibilities);
- capabilities concerned with being creative and productive in the 'knowledge economy' (economy and culture).

Each of these contains a full range of learning elements; that is, of knowledge, understanding, skills and values. Some examples, purely for illustration, of how geography lessons may contribute to young people's functionings in these ways are:

- handling and communicating geographic information, looking for spatial patterns, shapes, distributions, flows and relationships, increasingly confidently and critically with the use of GIS technology. The power of persuasion and the need to maintain a healthy scepticism may therefore be part of the rubric that underpins geography lessons, possibly arranged around the notion of 'decision-making' and the human occupation of space;
- understanding that place context is significant in understanding and interpreting human processes; for example, in response to 'natural hazards' or 'global' processes, such as climate change or the 2008 credit crunch. It is risky to generalize about how these universal processes play out locally or assume uniform or easily predictable impacts across the world. Geography lessons may therefore encourage us to keep an open mind and to be aware of the importance of context;
- realizing the pulling power and significance of 'home' on a number of scales, and learning how to live with difference and diversity. How people see the world (and each other) depends on their perspective and circumstances. Geography lessons may focus on developing the capacity to empathize with people and places, both near and far.

Using these examples (you will be able to think of more), readers may like to relate their contents to Nussbaum's capabilities (pages 62–63) *and* the 'basic' questions we encountered on page 60. We are not, of course, claiming that geography is the only subject that can support the development of capability through an orientation to basic questions. But we are suggesting that teachers of geography with a synoptic capacity (Chapter 3, page 43), for thinking about the subject and its educational potential, may find this way of curriculum thinking useful and productive.

Overall, a capability perspective on geography in education evokes a subject that can contribute to young people's:

- 'world knowledge';
- their relational understanding of people and places in the world;
- their propensity and disposition to think about alternative social, economic and environmental futures.

It would be expected that such learning will be achieved through teaching strategies that emphasize the application of geographical understanding, often in realistic decision-making contexts (see p. 138–139 in this volume).

This chapter makes a bold claim about the significance of teaching geography for understanding, thus giving young people opportunities to apply a range of key ideas and ultimately to make judgements about particular issues or themes. The rest of this book examines in some depth a range of the big ideas that are often claimed to lie at the basis of geographical thinking.

PART 2
RECONSTRUCTING CONCEPTS

5 Space

Social and cultural theory has recently undergone a 'spatial turn': this is found in political theory, history, literature and psychology. This has culminated in the critical acclaim for Doreen Massey's (2005) For Space, *a major statement of the importance of the geographical imagination in social theory. It is odd then that there has been little critical reflection on this concept in geographical education. This chapter seeks to provide an analysis of the different ways in which space has been conceptualized and the implications for curriculum-making.*

> Those in the 'discipline' of geography have for long had a difficult relation to the notion of 'space' and 'the spatial'. There has been much head-scratching, much theorising, much changing of mind.
>
> (Massey 1985: 9)

Introduction

This chapter is concerned with the concept of *space*. The aim is to provide an overview of how space has been used by geographers in Anglo-American human geography in recent decades, and to discuss the implications of different ways of conceptualizing space for curriculum-making in geography. The method used in this chapter is to provide a chronological account of the concept of space, showing how shifts in understanding have occurred as a result of argument and debate within the subject. While this approach risks giving the impression of the unfolding of a linear process, it is necessary to do this in order to develop the argument about space in this chapter. The key argument we make in this chapter is that debates about space within contemporary human geography must be seen as part of the tradition of critical social science. This has significant implications for geography teachers.

The science of space

We start this discussion of space with the development of spatial science in the 1950s and 1960s, since this represents the point where school geography began to take seriously questions of theory. Some of the ideas in this section were seized on by geography teachers to argue for a more 'scientific' approach to geography teaching. The impacts of this are still evident in examination specifications and the textbooks that are used to support these.

Spatial science emerged as a reaction to preceding forms of descriptive, regional geography. It originated from key university geography departments, mostly on the west coast of the USA. Its proponents were convinced of the need to develop new approaches:

'At stake was little short of the status of geography as a rigorous science' (Gould and Strohmeyer 2004: 7). Gould and Strohmeyer identify a number of important figures in the development of this 'quantitative revolution'. The first was Walter Isard at the University of Pennsylvania. Isard was an economic geographer who had become dissatisfied by the aspatial aspects of economics. He wrote a book entitled *Location and the Space Economy* (1956) that revived a generation of earlier German economists including Johann Heinrich Von Thunen, August Losch and Walter Christaller. These works provided a body of spatial theory demonstrating that there were more intellectually demanding ways of describing geographical phenomena. The second set of figures identified by Gould and Strohmeyer worked at the University of Washington and were responsible for developing methodologies for the new spatial science. They included: Brian Berry who became influential for pioneering work in central place theory; William Bunge who published a volume entitled *Theoretical Geography* (1966); and Richard Morrill, who pioneered quantitative work on transport networks.

These spatial science approaches were taken up by a generation of British geographers, most notably Peter Haggett and Richard Chorley. They developed and popularized the new approaches, most significantly in a series of lectures to geography teachers in the 1970s at Madingley Hall in Cambridge. It is important to note that the 'new geography did not go unchallenged'. For instance, Haggett was accused by Professor Steers of Cambridge of 'bringing the discipline into disrepute'. While the pioneers of the spatial science were labelled the 'space cadets', those who looked to develop the approaches in schools have been dubbed by Walford (2001) as the 'New Model Army', and it is remarkable the extent to which these ideas permeated and transformed the teaching of geography in schools. Geographers were interested in creating models of spatial structures that could generalize settlement patterns, urban structures or industrial location. At the same time, they adopted 'scientific methods' of hypothesis-testing. In addition, the laws that geographers produced often adopted scientific language (e.g. gravity models to predict flows of commuters between settlements). These views were popularized in a series of textbooks, written for sixth-form students, called *Concepts in Geography* edited by John Everson and Brian Fitzgerald. The introduction to the first book stated the problem and the solution:

> Teachers are beginning to realise that much of what is taught in our schools is purely repetitive and lacks intellectual challenge and stimulus to the student. Basic to these changes, we feel, is an ability on the part of the student to appreciate fundamental concepts in geography: those concerned with space, location, and interactions through time.
>
> (Everson and Fitzgerald 1969: ix)

In the second book of the series, *Analytical Human Geography*, Ambrose (1969) stated that 'spatial analysis is now emerging as the focal point and the organising framework for much geographical research' (p. 291). There were three elements to this: (1) to disentangle the basic regularities that occur in urban and rural land use patterns; (2) to analyse the processes that bring those patterns about; and (3) to use the knowledge gained to predict their future development. Thus, there are three key ideas: *spatial pattern regularity, process analysis and prediction*. The scope of this approach was enormous, amounting to nothing less than geography's legitimate claim to deal with the whole range of phenomena on the earth's surface. This was possible because all these features have certain vital features in common; they all have location and they all form spatial patterns:

> In fact location and pattern are two of the fundamental attributes of any terrestrial phenomenon and it is the human geographer's task to study these fundamental aspects, to develop techniques to measure and analyse them and, by understanding the processes that bring them about, to make predictions about how they will change.
>
> (Ambrose 1969: 291)

Though Ambrose recognizes that these approaches are not fully developed within geography, he was hopeful that it may soon be appropriate to define human geography as 'the science of the location and spatial distribution of man and his works'. At the heart of this approach is the development of a series of spatial concepts that provide a framework around which geographical work can be organized, 'much as a modern high building is organised around its steel framework'. The four that Ambrose singles out for discussion are 'gradient', 'network', 'least-cost location', and 'cumulative causation'. What these concepts have in common is their universality of application and their progressively increasing complexity. Thus, it is argued that people everywhere are concerned to save money by wise use of crops or wise location of factories. People everywhere form parts of networks. In addition, each of these concepts can be made intelligible at the level of complexity required to suit the reader. Thus, examples of the working of each concept could be found for those in primary education, in the early years of secondary education, or in doctoral theses.

This is an attractive manifesto for human geography, not least because it appears to solve the problem of too much content associated with the subject. The facts become meaningful in the light of concepts, and Ambrose's argument was that it was spatial concepts rather than the 'region' that made these facts more intelligible.

The limits of spatial science

The spatial science discussed in the previous section has had a profound influence on the field of geographical education. In fact, it may be seen as the main episode of theoretical work and is evident in the writings of those who have engaged with curriculum development. It is found in the work of Graves (1979), Marsden (1976) and Hall (1976), all of whom published influential texts on curriculum planning in geography. It also heralded a 'golden age' of textbook writing in geography, most notably Everson and Fitzgerald, Bradford and Kent, Tidswall and so on. Most importantly, perhaps, it was reflected in revised examination specifications that were based on the 'modern' geography. However, there were limitations to the development of geography as a spatial science, and other approaches to space became influential in human geography. These have not been so fully discussed in relation to geographical education, and one of the main aims of this chapter is to examine their implications for geography teachers.

Looking back, it is notable how many of those involved in the development of the so-called new geography saw it as the solution to the perceived fragmentation of geography. For example, Haggett's (1980) *Geography: A Modern Synthesis* predicted an era of harmony and stability in the discipline as it focused around the concepts and methods of spatial science. However, this unity was short-lived, and, again by way of example, Dicken and Lloyd (1981) felt the need to correct their earlier text *Location in Space* with *Modern Western Society* (which was subtitled *A Geographical Perspective on Work, Home and Well-being*). They note that the revolution of the 1960s in human geography was the parallel of the British Prime Minister's Harold Wilson's 'white heat' of technological revolution. Both looked forward to the modern, efficient post-industrial society of the future. But this climate of economic optimism was short-lived and along with it came a re-evaluation of the gains of the quantitative revolution. Dicken and Lloyd noted that that research atmosphere of the 1980s was substantially different from that of the 1960s.

In addition to the shift away from mathematical techniques and models as ends in themselves, there was now more focus on the processes that create the human geography of 'the world in which we live'. Alongside this, there was more attention to the social, economic and political problems that these processes generate. Geography was still concerned with space, or 'with the location and spatial organization of human activities on the earth's surface, with the similarities and differences between places as the habitat of mankind', but it was increasingly recognized that spatial patterns cannot be explained by spatial processes. Instead, spatial patterns are related to aspatial processes, and these aspatial processes require geographers to have 'considerable understanding of other relevant disciplines'. For example, whereas the spatial science associated with Ambrose and others might have explained the pattern of ethnic segregation in cities in terms of the desire for people of similar backgrounds to concentrate together for reasons of cohesion and safety, the geography of the 1980s would seek to explain those patterns through ideas about economic and social structure.

Modern Western Society was set within a problems approach or what has come to be known as a 'welfare approach' (Smith 1974). The book is concerned with describing and explaining spatial patterns. As such, it is a classic geography text filled with tables of figures, maps of distribution and models of processes. The empirical devices are used as the basis for explanation. The authors are keen to point out that space and the social are interconnected, that social processes do not take place on the head of a pin, but that aspects of location or accessibility also influence those processes. Reading the book in 2009, it is striking how far the explanations of social processes were framed within mainstream economic and social theory. The basic assumption is that society as it is organized is effectively sound, but that problems result from unequal access to the 'goods' and 'bads' that these processes create. The exact relationship between society and space is not theorized. The classic statement of that argument came from Massey (1984) in her text *Spatial Divisions of Labour*.

In order to grasp the significance of Massey's argument, it is important to recognize the changed context she was seeking to explain. This was the breakdown of an older spatial division of labour that had been characterized by regional specialization by industry and the decline of older 'heavy' industries alongside the growth of newer 'hi-tech' industries. In the UK, this was leading to heightened regional divisions which, due to the nature of the workforce, were centred on class. This pattern was accompanied politically by a breakdown in the consensus that held that governments should seek to maintain full employment and minimize regional spatial inequalities. In other words, for Massey the assumption that capitalism was basically able to provide well-being for all was flawed, and in this context space became a way in which capitalism could 'fix' the problem of accumulation or declining profits.

Massey argued that new spatial divisions of labour emerged as space was actively used by capitalist enterprises to restructure the labour process and labour relations. 'Command and control' functions were focused around London and Southeast England, whereas manufacturing was taking place in the peripheral regions of the UK and, increasingly, overseas. Research and development functions were separated from manufacturing or assembly and relocated in the 'sunrise' belts of the M4 corridor west of London and 'silicon fen' around Cambridge. At the same time areas such as South Wales became 'screwdriver' assembly plants, using standardized components produced elsewhere to make consumer goods. Much of this work was done by 'green' labour that had the advantage of being non-unionized (or at least part of single union agreements) and in many case dominated by female workers who were brought into the labour force to supplement the family wage in the face of high rates of male unemployment as a result of the collapse of traditional industries such as coal and steel. Massey showed how capital was not only producing new spatial patterns but was achieving this by actively using space to secure profitability.

The deeper theoretical significance of Massey's (1984) argument in *Spatial Divisions of Labour* was that space and society are mutually constituted, something that was reflected in the rather glib phrase that 'geography matters'. What Massey did so well was to show how precisely and in what ways geography matters, and this was something that was taken up and developed by geographers in the 1980s and beyond. This position is summarized by Gregory and Urry (1985) in their introduction to the edited book *Social Relations and Spatial Structures*: 'Spatial structure is now seen not merely as an arena in which social life unfolds, but rather as a medium through which social relations are produced and reproduced' (p. 3).

There were some attempts to develop the implications for geography teaching of this way of conceptualizing space in the 1980s. For example, in a series of articles Lee (1985a; see also Lee 1985b) advocated a 'societal geography' that explored the relations between spatial patterns and social process. He provides two questions that should underpin and structure teaching and learning: what makes history work? What makes the real geography of our daily lives? Answering these questions involves defining, exploring, and explaining the bases of historicity: the specific and reproductive qualities of the societies about which we teach. Lee argued that this would require 'nothing less than a rewrite of the curriculum'.

The important point here is that geographers such as Massey, Lee and Gregory were arguing that spatial or geographical patterns cannot simply be explained as the result of geographical factors or spatial processes. Instead, there was a need to understand how space is structured by social processes. If this sounds rather abstract, it is useful to consider the following example provided by Sayer (1985) in a review of the University of London's 16–19 Geography Project. Sayer suggested that the syllabus was based on 'systematic mystification' because it obscured the nature of the social relations of production. One of the examples he provides is the case of plantation systems of agriculture in pre-revolutionary Cuba. He notes that the main landowners owned more fertile land than they actually cultivated. This was because it meant that peasants were forced to farm less fertile mountainous land where they could support themselves for only part of the year. In this way landowners were able to secure a reliable supply of labour.

Sayer (1985) pointed out that both the landowners and the peasants were involved in the transformation of nature but that the way they did so was dependent on the social relations between plantation owners and peasants. These social relations were embedded on historical relations and served to reproduce two social classes with subsistence crops and a seasonal wage for one group and profits from the sale of sugar for the other. The point that Sayer makes in relation to the geography syllabus is that teaching would focus on the 'impact and productivity of agricultural systems' and the 'impact on the environment', along with perhaps the different 'values' or 'perceptions' of the various actors. The problem is that teaching is less likely to focus on the social relations of production or the 'structures' that shape these relations. Rather than accept terms such as 'subsistence farming', 'cash crops', 'peasants' and 'landowners' at face value and seek to measure or describe them, there is a need to 'problematize' them and understand them as the result of historical and social processes.

We have been discussing the various ways in which space has been conceptualized in geography and its implications for geographical education. It is worth reminding readers of why this is important: the revised National Curriculum for geography is based on a series of key concepts around which geographical study is to be organized. While this represents something of an opportunity, it raises important challenges because, when we start to examine concepts such as space, place and scale, it becomes clear that they do not have a fixed meaning and embody distinctive traditions of geographical study and thought. Rather than impose meaning on these terms, we argue that a productive approach is to undertake a genealogical exploration of the concepts. This will allow geography teachers to understand what is at stake in using these concepts and make 'disciplined' decisions about how to construct curriculum experiences in classrooms. In this section, we turn our attention to debates about space in geography in the 1990s, focusing our argument around some influential texts published in 1989.

1989: The reassertion of space in geographical education?

An important part of the argument we are making in this chapter is that the concept of space is contested and that this is a consequence of attempts by geographers to understand and explain the changes that are taking place in the world. Times of economic and social change are accompanied by intense struggles over how to interpret the changes. Shurmer-Smith (2002: 1) states this very well in arguing that 'as people have become increasingly aware of the radical changes inherent in late modern society, there has been a growing desire to find new ways of thinking in order to reach new modes of understanding'. These changes were the oil crisis in 1973 and the ensuing wave of neoliberal globalization that were felt not only in the economic and political order, but 'permeated into the recesses of ordinary people's lives'.

The 1980s were a period in which the human geography of Britain was fundamentally transformed. The decline of heavy industry led to large areas of dereliction in cities and in coalfield areas, newer 'sunrise' industries grew up in the south and east of England.

The 'north–south divide', a perennial and recurring historical problem, reasserted itself. These changes brought with them social divisions, reflected in the levels of wealth and consumption available to different classes. Rural areas increasingly became home to the 'service class'. In all of this, old social structures and ways of living and thinking began to change. It is widely argued that it is these changes that have led to an increased recognition of the importance of 'space' in understanding aspects of society.

The first text we consider here is Jackson's (1989) *Maps of Meaning* which was subtitled *An Introduction to Cultural Geography*. We start with this text because Jackson's work drew on and developed out of the rich tradition of work on society and space that followed Massey's (1984) *spatial divisions of labour*. In the acknowledgements to *Maps of Meaning*, Jackson notes that the book was a development of an earlier text written with Susan Smith (*Exploring Social Geography* 1984). That book was concerned to explore the implications of different traditions of social theory (positivist, interpretive, Marxist) to spatial problems. Following a review and discussion of these approaches, the final chapter 'applies' these to the question of ethnic segregation. *Maps of Meaning* sought to show how space is 'fundamental to the very constitution of culture'. As Jackson (1989) states: 'If social processes do not take place on the head of a pin, then we need to take spatial structure very seriously, not least in the production and communication that we call culture' (xi).

At the centre of *Maps of Meaning* is the notion of cultural politics where meanings are negotiated and relations of dominance and subordination are defined and contested. The book was written towards the end of a long decade of Conservative rule in Britain in which questions of culture were prominent, and the reformulation of cultural geography should be situated in its political context:

> What is there about the current politics of fiscal retrenchment, privatization, and economic recession in Thatcher's Britain or Bush's America that might be relevant to a revival of interest in cultural studies? Why have phrases such as 'enterprise culture', 'Victorian values', and 'moral majority' gained such sudden salience? Is the age of the yuppie and corporate culture, of urban heritage and rural nostalgia, of football hooliganism and inner-city rioting, a response to national economic decline? Or does it not also represent the growing confidence of the 'consumption classes' and the increasing alienation of the impoverished and despairing underclass, each with its own distinctive geography?
>
> (Jackson 1989: 5)

Jackson's answer, developed through the examples and case studies throughout his book, is that an understanding of contemporary culture requires an appreciation of changing political and economic contours. Whereas certain Marxist commentators saw culture as the reflection of economic structures, Jackson drew on approaches that stressed how the cultural, political and economic could not easily be separated and this made space for individual agency and social interaction. The important thing is that these meanings were contested and negotiated in actual spaces, and that an understanding of locality and context were essential to cultural geography. This was a theme that became more influential as the 'postmodern' turn developed in geography throughout the 1990s and beyond.

Finally in this section, we turn to Soja's (1989) *Postmodern Geographies*, a book that has been influential in shaping debates within geography over the past two decades. It is important to remind ourselves that the subtitle of this text is *The Reassertion of Space in Critical Social Theory* and that it was published by Verso, a press that specializes in 'New Left' thought. Once more, this reminds us that arguments about space in human geography must be seen as part of a political debate and therefore do not rest easily with dominant ways of thinking about geography education in schools.

For the past century, Soja argues, time and history occupied a privileged place in critical social theory; understanding the making of history was the primary source of emancipatory insight. Space or geography, on the other hand, was seen as inert and passive. Drawing on Foucault, Soja notes the tendency to treat space as dead, fixed, undialectical and immobile. Time on the other hand was richness, fecundity, life and dialectic. *Postmodern Geographies* signals the emergence of a 'far-reaching spatialization of the critical imagination': 'A distinctively postmodern and critical human geography is taking shape, brashly reasserting the interpretive significance of space in the historically privileged confines of contemporary critical thought' (p. 11).

Geography may not have replaced history, but new ways of 'seeing time and space together' are emerging.

Post-structural spaces

In this section, we want to provide a discussion of how space is conceptualized in post-structural geography. This is a notoriously complex area, and once more it must be seen as a development of critical social theory. However, given that geography education draws eclectically from the writings of geographers who work within these areas, it is important to know something about the origins of these debates in order to evaluate what is at stake in adopting their ideas to geographical education.

Post-structuralism developed in conversation with and against structuralism; therefore post-structuralist geography stands in relation to structuralist geography. In geography, structuralist geography became popular among radical geographers in the 1960s and 1970s, especially through the writing of Louis Althusser, a Marxist theorist. For Althusser, Marx provided a scientific perspective on societal development. At the heart of this method was the need to look beyond the actions of individuals and social movements to the determining structures that lie 'beneath' any social formation. In Marxist terms this meant drawing a distinction between the economic base of productive forces and the superstructure of political, social and cultural formations. The superstructure can make a contribution to the shape of any given society, but the economic base is determining in the 'last instance'. In analytical terms, any 'deep' explanation of society must be based on an economic account of social change. In geographical terms, writers such as David Harvey, Richard Peet and Neil Smith are examples of geographers who have consistently sought to recognize the value of this type of structuralist geography.

This approach was challenged in the 1980s, when human geographers developed approaches more informed by realism than Althusser's Marxism. Despite the differences, what these structuralist approaches have in common is that they tend to produce a geography of highly structured social spaces. Space is a surface configured by the play of underlying structures. The world is well-ordered and apparently stable. Against this, post-structuralism began to influence geographical thought. The initial move was to shift geographical attention away from the economy and towards culture. This can be seen in a number of areas of geographical study that have been influenced by the cultural turn. Post-structuralism emerged from the analysis of literary texts and geographers quickly realized how places and landscapes could be read in the same way. The idea that there was no single and final reading of landscapes opened up the idea that the meaning of landscapes was a negotiation between the text and the reader (of the Preface of this book). The result was that 'the closures and certainties of the objectivist tradition in human geography had become increasingly suspect'. (Gregory 1994: 75).

In the terms of Soja's (1989) postmodern geographies, the lifeworlds of individuals and social groups were now spatialized, and the result was that geographers sought out spaces that had been neglected by previous generations of geographers. The aim was to empower and give voice to social groups and focus on the forces that were dis-empowering and disenfranchising marginalized groups. The language of social theory was awash with terms like 'borders' and 'margins'. The result was that human geography came to engage with multiple perspectives, multiple spaces and sets of social relations. If people had multiple identities, then so could places. Geography with a capital G was replaced by geographies and the geographical tradition was replaced by geographical imaginations. As Murdoch (2006: 23) notes, this general form of post-structuralism soon found its way into geography: 'To begin with, post-structuralist geographers argued that there are many more spaces than those to be found in standard geography textbooks'. These spaces were linked to power and the way that some dominant versions of space (linked to dominant versions of identity) served to marginalize and exclude others.

Murdoch also identifies another element of post-structural geography, which was concerned to examine the nature of space itself. He starts from Harvey's (1996) argument in *Justice, Nature and the Geography of Difference* that space is not a container but is always dependent on the processes or substances that go into 'making it up' These processes are constituted of relations, and therefore any 'permanences' (structures) arise out of the connection of processes. Places can be seen as permanences, but however stable they appear, they are in the constant process of 'perpetual perishing'. So according to this view, space is not made by underlying structures but by diverse processes, and the relations between them. This view of relational space has been developed and expanded in Massey's later work. She seeks to go beyond a structuralist view of space because it has difficulties in accounting for the significance of space. She outlines three propositions that are intrinsic to the idea of relational space:

1   Space is a product of interrelations. These interrelations run through different spatial scales from the local to the global.
2   Space is the sphere of the possibility of multiplicity. Because all relations run through space all may come into being spatially.
3   Space is never closed, never fixed. Space is always in the process of becoming as relations unfold.

Space becomes a 'meeting place' where interrelations interweave and intersect. These arguments are developed in Massey's (2005) *For Space*, which draws together arguments from philosophy and geography to argue for a spatial politics. The approach is illustrated through a series of case studies in the Open University's book *A World in the Making* (Clark et al. 2006). The editors state that the title of the book may seem both 'strange and obvious'. Strange because we often imagine and act ourselves as living in the world as though it came to us ready-made. Obvious because of course the world is constantly being made and remade by a whole variety of forces. The chapters are structured using the geographical concepts of 'territory' and 'flow'. In the context of a globalized world, it is frequently asserted as a state in which all borders and boundaries have been dissolved and which flows of people, money, culture and communications flow freely. But at the same time there are attempts to fix and define territory. An important part of the argument is that both the human and the non-human are part of how we think about territories and flows that has implications for the traditional rupture between human and physical geography. In post-structural geography there are hydrid geographies of human and non-human natures. The making, unmaking and remaking of the world is a constant and ongoing process. It is taking place all around us, and on many different scales.

It is important to clarify the view of space that is being promoted in *A World in the Making*. It is relational space because it stresses the significance of networks, connections, flows and mobilities in the ongoing making of spaces. Space is a product of practices, trajectories and interrelations. In this version, relations are what *exist* and these relations create spaces. The world is always in the making as these relationships unfold. The world is in the process of becoming. In addition to the Open University book, there are other studies that usefully illustrate what this 'relational' view of space might entail. First, in *Consuming the Caribbean* Mimi Sheller (2003) demonstrates how a particular place – 'the Caribbean' – has been generated out of flows of plants, people, ships, material resources, foodstuffs, technologies, know-how and capital occurring over centuries. For Sheller, the essence of Caribbean life is movement. The modern Caribbean is tied together by shipping routes, airline networks, and communications infrastructure, and is the result of multiple, intersecting mobilities.

A second example of this type of thinking can be found in *Patterned Ground* that is subtitled Entanglements of Nature and Culture (Harrison et al. 2004). The text abandons all conventional notions of order and classifications. It comprises a series of short essays that focus on various objects. The editors employed a topological imagination in order to put the essays together. They start from the position that the delineation of landscape features and their placing on maps gives them more clarity than they have in the real landscape and in doing so, we separate the human and the non-human. These objects become stabilized or fixed, and the aim of the collection is to 'unsettle these ontological and epistemological assumptions', which of course is to question the 'we' who knows and produces that landscape: 'we are arguing that there is a "new geography", because it is important to appreciate that the world is now patterned by both human and non-human processes' (Harrison et al. 2004: 9–10).

Patterned Ground looks at elements in the world around us and seeks to (re)arrange them in unusual ways. In this, it follows a wider 'geographical impulse' to see patterns in the world. But it seeks to do so in ways that enable other, perhaps less visible patterns to emerge.

Case study: rural spaces

We have covered a lot of ground in this chapter, and at this point it will be useful to offer an example of how these rather abstract arguments about space are being played out in one area of human geography–the study of rural spaces.

In the early 1970s, Clout (1972) argued that from being at the core of studies in human geography prior to the Second World War, the countryside as a field of geographical investigation has been relegated to an inferior position. He explained this as the result of the pre-eminence of the study of urban geography. Geography from the 1960s became increasingly focused on towns and cities, encouraged by the scale and visibility of urban issues. The situation in very different in 2009, when rural geography, which is increasingly linked to the wider field of rural studies, is characterized by theoretical sophistication and takes its place at the cutting-edge of geographical debate. As such, the example of rural geography is useful in illuminating the implications of changes in how space is conceptualized.

Rural geography emerged in the 1950s as part of the development of 'systematic' studies that replaced the older 'regional' studies that had dominated the subject. Its object of study – rural space – was conceptualized in 'functional' terms. What this meant was the rural space was distinguished from urban space by differences in what happened there. Thus rural space is that which is dominated by extensive land uses, notably agriculture and forestry; contains smaller lower-order settlements which demonstrate a strong relationship between buildings and extensive landscape, and which are thought of as rural by most of their residents; and are based on a way of life that is characterized by a cohesive identity (e.g. village life). This functional definition allowed for the delineation of distinctive places that are labelled 'urban' and 'rural' and allow for the classification of space. In the light of the development of a positivist or scientific approach to space, rural geographers became increasingly concerned with developing measurements of rurality, applying models of land use and quantifying the changes to rural areas. The important thing to point out here is that rural space is a surface on which processes take place and that the focus is on finding order in the landscape. Settlements were 'explained' according to location models based on agricultural land use and economic rationale. Woods comments that:

> These models were essentially generalized cartographic representations of empirical observations, and not only did they fail to work when taken out of their original context, they also revealed nothing about the social, economic and political processes that produced the phenomena concerned.
>
> (Woods 2006: 19)

An important part of the argument that we are making in this book is that geographical concepts are not fixed and unchanging, but are changed and modified in the light of economic, social and cultural change. This means that it is important to understand the intellectual context in which concepts are shaped. As noted earlier in this chapter, human geographers responded to the criticisms that their spatial models lacked relevance and realism by seeking to understand the processes that were shaping rural areas. However, before showing how this happened, it is worth noting that the lack of attention to the social processes shaping rural space was not confined to geography. For instance, there was a distinct absence of rural sociology in the post-war period. Hillyard (2007) argues that while there a concern with the agricultural sector, the focus was on the strategic issue of food security, rather than the social changes accompanying industrial modernization. The post-war dream of increasing food output shaped the types of work academics undertook. Geographers now recognize this period as the 'productivist era' of post-war agriculture, and it was not until this era was challenged from the early 1980s that the focus shifted away from agriculture to the broader question of rural society. The relative demise of the dominant productivist paradigm in agriculture opened the space for a wider range of issues that focus on environmentalism and amenities, social clea-vages and in rural areas, leisure. Much of this work in rural social geography worked within a 'problem' or issues approach that meant it accepted the broad definitions of what rural society stands for and should be. However, in line with developments with critical social theory geographers increasingly came to adopt a more independent and sceptical attitude towards rural phenomena. Early research on rural restructuring focused on the economic relations surrounding agriculture, explaining the 'farm crisis' as the productivist era came to an end.

Whereas earlier work had tended to assume the existence of a distinct and separate rural space or spaces that could be studied independently, the search to understand the social processes that shaped rural space led geographers to recognize that rural space cannot be thought of as outside of the wider political and economic systems of which they are a part. In other words, the forces that shape events in rural localities may have their origins elsewhere. This point is made in the following passage from Marsden et al's.; (1993) *Constructing the Countryside*:

> We argue strongly that there is an urgent need to draw the study of rural areas and issues out of the margins and into the mainstream of social science, to reflect the contemporary economic and social salience of rural space. Crises of accu-mulation in capitalist societies necessitate the periodic and radical restructuring of production processes in order to establish new opportunities for profitable investment; one consequence is a reassessment of resources and spaces once considered unproductive or marginal ... We will suggest, for example, that from the point of view of production, rural space is often attractive to capital, being less encumbered by earlier Fordist labour processes and rounds of investment; offers many new and more pleasant places in which to work and live than represented by the modern city and suburbia; and has become more accessible as a result of improvements in telecommunications and transportation systems.
>
> (Marsden et al. 1993: 2)

We have quoted this passage at length because we want to highlight its similarity to Massey's (1984) argument in *Spatial Divisions of Labour*. It suggests that capital makes use of space to solve its contradictions in maintaining profitability. Rural areas take their place in the spatial division of labour. The important question is why this occurs at a particular time and this is explained by the shift from a Fordist to post-Fordist regime of accumulation. Political-economic approaches thus conceptualize rural space as simply part of economic space. This means that agriculture is seen as a capitalist enterprise; rural areas are seen as reflecting processes of class formation, rural economies undergo processes of change as the wider economic system shifts, and the state plays an important role in regulating these processes to maintain social stability and economic profitability.

One of the problems with this approach is that it seems to suggest that the distinction between rural and urban localities no longer seems to matter, since all are tied to the logics of the capitalist system. Indeed, it has been suggested that the rural does not exist as a distinctive category. However, it is clear that the 'rural' still holds an explanatory force both in everyday life and at the levels of policy and analysis. It will not do to abandon the 'rural'. Rural geography has undergone a 'cultural turn' that has paid attention to the different ways in which the rural is socially constructed. An example of this approach is found in an article by Thrift (1989) that explores the way in which culture is linked to wider questions of economic and social change. The argument is that rural areas are being colonized by the 'new middle classes' who, bolstered by high incomes, a degree of autonomy and discretion at work, and relative residential freedom, have sought to create space in its own image. Thrift argued that this social group has taken the countryside and heritage traditions most to heart, and this has allowed them to buy up old cottages and farm buildings, renovate them and develop a more 'natural' or 'green' aesthetic (Thrift 1989: 12–42). Other geographers have pointed to the way in which the English countryside serves as a reservoir of meanings about the 'nation' and 'ethnicity', suggesting that rural space gives off meanings about who does and who does not 'belong', and thus is an 'active component of hegemonic power'. (Neal Agyeman 2008).

In the mid-1990s rural geography was influenced by the emergence of social and cultural approaches that sought to 'put people back' in rural studies and to focus on the varied experiences of rurality. Previous geographical research had suffered from a modernist tendency to search for universal laws and represent the world through 'tidy' and 'abstract' concepts. Thus, Philo (1992) called for the study of 'neglected rural others'. He suggested that in the past there had been a tendency to steamroll the different stories of other people. As a result of this heightened sensitivity to 'difference', rural geographers have paid attention to the ways in which spaces are experienced and inhabited differently, and how certain groups can experience places as exclusionary. Cloke and Little's (1997) *Contested Countryside Cultures* explores a range of marginalized and neglected rural others. Much of this work is concerned with the question of representation and involves deconstructing what are seen as the dominant "rural idylls" found in literature and popular media.

In a later collection, *Country Visions*, Cloke (2003) points out that rural areas are not merely blank canvases on which to paint socially constructed meanings: 'To know rurality, to understand the countryside, full account has to be taken of the embodied practices of people in relation to the potentially transformative agency of animals, plants, weather and technology' (p. 5).

This comment reflects a more 'post-structural' approach to rural space in that it hints at the 'flows' of different materials, ideas, technologies and bodies through rural space. Murdoch and Pratt (1997) provide an interesting discussion that allows us to think through the implications of post-structural geography for the rural. They point out that there is a tendency to represent the rural as a distinctive zone, usually demarcated from the urban. Thus, they argue that academic texts have frequently portrayed the rural as a homogenous social space, one which seems in many ways to exist in some timeless zone where old-fashioned virtues and their associated forms of life still linger. They note that a much more critical stance is being adopted towards such dominant images of rurality, which stresses the conflictual, competitive and exploitative sets of social relations. Thus, the rural idyll is being deconstructed. But they also warn against an academic 'will to power', whereby attempts are made to tidy the messy complexities of the world. They argue that there is a need for reflexive awareness to permeate theoretical and methodological approaches. This is something that is of political significance. Murdoch and Pratt work on the premise that there is no single space, but a multiplicity of social spaces. This means that there can be no one unique and privileged vantage point, no one centre from which the rural can be captured or assessed.

Conclusion: space matters?

'Space' is one of the key concepts that underpin the National Curriculum for geography. However, as this chapter has demonstrated, sorting out what we mean by space is no easy task. As Massey says, space has prompted a lot of 'head-scratching'. This chapter has kept quite close to mainstream debates about space in Anglo-American human geography. These are not arcane academic debates, but are driven by arguments about why and how 'geography matters'. We would suggest that an intellectually informed geography education should engage with the arguments outlined here. It is interesting that the chapter started with a geography of spatial science that was focused around movement and mobility, and ended with a discussion of post-structuralist geography also concerned with flow and mobility. Cresswell (2006: 30) points out that 'One of the clearest absences in a spatial science approach is any sense of the values and meaning that get embedded in mobility', and it is this that is perhaps the key message of this chapter, the social construction of space.

6 Place

As a concept, 'place' is both simple and complicated. Starting from the injunction of human geographers that we should understand places as socially constructed, this chapter explores how any attempt to teach about places in school geography is based on assumptions about what makes a 'good' place. In this sense, there is a need to pay attention to the politics of place. The chapter explores a number of ways in which place is conceptualized in geography teaching, focusing on the widespread fear of 'placelessness', moves to develop more inclusive notions of place, and the idea that place is undermined by forces of globalization. Finally, the chapter argues for teachers to adopt an attitude of 'self-consciousness' in how they teach about place.

Introduction

> Human Geography is the study of places. It is, of course, many other things but it is, on an intuitive level, a discipline which has place as one of its principle objects of study. Students signing up for geography degrees and courses will often site their interest in different places around the world. Despite this general enthusiasm for the study of places there is very little considered understanding of what the word 'place' means.
>
> (Cresswell 2004: 1)

Cresswell argues that the concept of place is both simple and complicated. He concludes his own 'Short introduction' to the concept with a list of resources for further reading, noting that, 'the literature that uses place is endless' (he lists 27 recommended books for starters). Perhaps the most important thing to note about the way in which place is considered in human geography is that it should be seen as 'socially constructed'. Thus, to offer just a few examples, Bondi (1993: 99) argues that the 'geographical metaphors of contemporary politics must be informed by conceptions of space that recognise place, position, location and so on as created, as produced'. Harvey (1996) asserts that the only interesting question that can be asked is 'by what social processes is place constructed?', and McDowell (1999) summarizes: 'The commonsense geographical notion of a place as a set of coordinates on a map that fix a defined and bounded piece of territory has been challenged. Geographers now argue that places are contested, fluid and uncertain' (pp. 3–4).

This chapter is concerned with the challenge of teaching geography in the light of this argument that places are socially constructed. This has two implications. First, the need to acknowledge that places are constructed through the operation of a range of economic, social, political and cultural processes that operate at a variety of scales. Second, the need to recognize that in teaching about places, teachers are actively involved in the construction of representations of these places.

In this chapter, we focus on some of the possible ways in which geography teachers might teach about places. 'Place' is not a technical term that has a single and final definition. Instead, in this chapter we argue that teachers are likely to draw up more everyday uses of place in developing their teaching. The method that we adopt in this chapter is a form of 'critical cultural geography' that seeks to place the work of geography teachers in a social and historical context. The advantage of this is that it allows us to see the commitments and gaps that underpin teachers' 'geographical imaginations', and to identify something of *the politics of place*. In doing this, we seek to draw attention to what can be at stake in different ways of conceptualizing place and encourage a more self-conscious understanding of how teachers plan and teach geography.

Fear of a placeless planet

The idea of place often resonates strongly with geographers. Indeed, in conversation, many geography teachers often talk about the subject having the potential to develop in young people a 'sense of place'. This is unsurprising, since one of the reasons why people become geography teachers is their love of place. It is this experience of being in place, visiting places, spending time in a place that comes through time and time again in discussions with teachers, and perhaps explains their willingness to spend weekends and evenings to take students on field visits to valued places and landscapes. There is something about (certain) places that is valued.

In this section we argue that, in the past, many geography teachers have tended to adopt a stance that fears the loss of authentic and meaningful 'sense of place'. We suggest that underlying the desire to explore and celebrate certain places is a deep-seated concern with the threat of placelessness, of places that lack the required levels of authenticity and aura. In Britain (and especially England), this concern about 'placelessness' is part of a broader response to landscape change that has tended to view modern developments, such as roads, new ribbon development and so on as despoiling the landscape. For example, the writer and journalist J.B. Priestley's (1937) *English Journey* set out on a bus trip that took him the length and breadth of England. As he left London on the Great West Road, he noted how the road 'looked odd. Being new, it did not look English'. As a guide, Priestley took with him a copy of Stamp and Beaver's (1954) famous textbook *The British Isles: A Geographic Survey*. In *English Journey*, Priestley identified what he called three distinct Englands. The 'old England' was a land of cathedrals, minsters, manor houses and inns, of quaint highways and byways. The second is 'nineteenth-century England', of coal and steam, iron and railways, wool and cotton that had, for over a century, been the powerhouse of the industrial revolution. The third was the 'new England':

> arterial and by-pass roads, of filling stations and factories that look like exhibi-tion buildings, of giant cinemas and dance-halls and cafes, bungalows with tiny garages, cocktail bars, Woolworths, motor-coaches, wireless, hiking, factory-girls looking like actresses, greyhound racing and dirt-tracks, swimming pools, and everything given away for cigarette coupons.
>
> (Priestley 1937: 2)

In this statement, Preistley is trying to understand and make sense of the appearance of a distinctive 'geography of pleasure' in a country that was 'rapidly Blackpooling itself'. In the context of social reform that allowed for the reduction of the length of the working week, and increased mobility associated with the 'motoring age', the entertainment industry expanded, and was reflected in the growth of places for the public to 'let off steam' often in ways that challenged the decorum of polite society (smoking, drinking, gambling, screaming, kissing). These developments included cinemas, greyhound stadia, lidos, holiday camps and zoos (Peter, 2007).

This attitude to places is part of a wider cultural response to modernity, and has influenced geography teaching through the work of the local historian W.G. Hoskins, whose book *The Making of the English Landscape* (1955) popularized the idea that the landscape was a palimpsest, one in which generations of human activity have left their mark. However, it is significant that Hoskins could see nothing of value in modern landscapes or what he decried as: 'England of the Nissen hut, the 'pre-fab' and the electric fence, of the high barbed-wire around some unmentionable devilment: England of the arterial by-pass, treeless and stinking of diesel oil, murderous with lorries' (p. 299).

We think that this 'structure of feeling' came to influence how many geography teachers thought about places and landscapes and continues to influence the ways in which geography teachers teach about places. It is rooted in forms of English romanticism and based on an assumed empiricism that the best way to learn geography was to go out and get 'mud on your boots'. There are a number of features of this 'way of seeing':

- *Solitary experience* – understanding the landscape was a solitary experience, one conditioned by the physical activity of walking. Walking was a recurring theme in the inter-war years, and this is something that has continued in the way geography educators see fieldwork (mostly in emblematic physical landscapes) as the 'jewel in the crown' (Simmons 2001: 328). There is a celebration of direct above mediated 'experience' (p. 391). For instance, Simmons challenges the right of literary critics to talk of landscapes unless they have ever 'crouched out of the east wind behind the wall of a cow-byre eating fat bacon sliced off with a penknife onto greyish bread' (p. 328) (in a footnote he adds, 'And I have crouched with a farm labourer under the circumstances described: his name was Harold Smith') (p. 391).
- *Rooted in the gaze from above* – key to geographical experience was the act of examining and 'reading' the Ordnance Survey map and relating it to the patterns of landscape on the ground. It is also reflected in the importance of aerial photography and plans that allow a sense of perspective. Geography teachers will recognize the continued attachment to these techniques.
- *Aesthetic appreciation* – only by critically analysing and understanding its form and structure can we appreciate landscape – the focus is on experienced and knowledgeable observation, reading the clues to spot the bumps in the field that others never notice. The aim of this observation and analysis of landscape is a 'heightened sense of place'.
- *Translating landscape to text* – the landscape is there to be observed, interpreted and translated into textual form. The emphasis is on clear description and explanation. This focus is reflected in ideas about 'reading the landscape'. Many

geography teachers share Muir's (2007) view that: 'Landscapes are like pages printed in a special code. If you learn to read the codes then you can decipher the history of a wood, a field pattern, a network of lanes or ... a village' (p. 7).

- *Concern for the particular or genius loci* – the details and the particularities of a scene that give reward and pleasure. There is strong emphasis on the unique characteristics of a place or locality.
- *Observation as a method* – in this work there is no sign of Williams's (1976) point about nature being 'the most complex word in the language' (p. 219). There is a complete silence about how our views of landscape might be constructed. The method relies on standing and seeing – a deeply empiricist approach. The landscape speaks for itself without the need for theory.

Compare this with the way we introduced this book with the landscape photograph on page viii (which is also available as a download via www.geography.org.uk/ adifferentview). As geography teachers, we recognize the appeal of this way of knowing places and landscapes. The surprising thing is how this sensibility towards places was swept aside during the quantitative revolution in geography. Spatial science appeared to make everywhere seem the same as the complexity and sheer messiness of the Earth's surface was reduced to an 'isotropic surface' in the quest to determine laws of spatial behaviour. Places became simply nodes in networks of rationally determined flows of people, commodities and money. Daniels (1985) called this a 'geography without man' that is 'intellectually deficient'. There is little of the experience or meaning that is involved in dwelling in places. Though the influence of spatial science has lived on, geography teachers have sought to use more human-centred approaches. Huckle (1983) argued that the new geography brought personal costs in that 'it asked teachers and pupils to suspend feelings, intuition, and imagination, and to regard human environments as mere exemplars of scientific facts and theories' (p. 1). Against this there were moves to assert the importance of values. An important text in this regard is Relph's *Place and Placelessness*. Relph notes that:

> There is a widespread and familiar sentiment that the localism and variety of the places and landscapes that characterised preindustrial societies and unselfconscious handicraft cultures are being diminished and perhaps eradicated.
>
> (Relph 1976: 79)

The result is the development of a placeless geography, lacking both diverse landscapes and significant places. Relph suggests that inauthenticity is the prevalent mode of existence in industrialized and mass societies. An inauthentic attitude to place is essentially no sense of place, for it involves no awareness of the deep and symbolic significance of places and no appreciation of their identities.

Relph distinguishes between two types of inauthentic attitude to place. Unconscious inauthenticity involves the uncritical acceptance of mass values. Self-conscious inauthenticity is brought about by the application of technique to places, usually through planning. Thus, much physical and social planning is founded on an implicit assumption that space is uniform and objects and activities can be manipulated and freely located within it. Thus, Relph sees placelessness as resulting from two key aspects of modernity – consumption and planning.

An inauthentic attitude to place is nowhere more clearly expressed than in tourism, for in tourism 'individual and authentic judgement about places is nearly always subsumed to expert of socially accepted opinion, or the act and means of tourism becomes more important than the places visited' (Relph: 83) Relph suggests that for many people the purpose of travel is less to experience unique and different places than to 'collect' those places. This is forcing the 'active tourist frontier' into ever more remote and exotic corners of the earth.

For Relph, the forces creating this placeless geography are mass communication, mass culture, big business, central authority and the economic system. Mass communication is a central component in the construction of a placeless geography because it brings people into more frequent contact:

> Roads, railways, airports, cutting across or imposed on the landscape rather than developing with it, are not only features of placelessness in their own right, but, by making possible the mass movement of people with all their fashions and habits, have encouraged the spread of placelessness ...
>
> (Relph 1976: 90)

And these fashions and habits are the product of mass culture. They find expression in the tourist landscape, and in the rise of 'subtopia' – the same types of housing and road layouts so that 'it becomes virtually impossible to tell one locality from another, for they all look alike and feel alike' (p. 109). These placeless landscapes are the consequence of the activities of big business that, in the search for profits, have little interest in their use of the landscape. The shift from local and small businesses to standardization and brand names – the boxes or warehouses that are found on the edge of many towns or at the intersection of motorways lead to an indistinctness of place: 'the only possible consequence is a growing standardisation in the cultural landscapes of the world, both at the points of production and administration, and at the points of consumption' (p. 114).

Relph's discussion of a placeless geography is still relevant today, and is echoed in Ritzer's (2008) *The McDonaldization of Society* and Bryman's (2004) *The Disneyization of Society*. Ritzer's argument is that many aspects of our daily lives in the realms of health, education, sport and leisure are dominated by the logic that allowed McDonald's to successfully transform the 'fast-food' industry. These are efficiency, calculability, predictability and control. These allow for a standardization of the experience that allows for lower economic costs and that ensures customers know exactly what to expect. This standardization of product is also reflected in the landscapes of consumption, with each McDonald's having the same feel and appearance. Bryman (2004) has developed the idea of 'Disneyization' to suggest the 'process by which the principles of the Disney theme parks are coming to dominate more and more sectors of American society as well as the rest of the world' (p. 1). These principles are theming, hybrid consumption, merchandising and performative labour. This fear is reflected in the idea of 'clone towns', where the distinctiveness of places is being replaced by the same shops, with the same signage, on many High Streets.

One of the problems with this fear of placelessness, is the underlying distaste for the popular pleasures of what used to be called 'the masses'. Relph, for instance, is scathing in his treatment of the types of place inhabited by 'ordinary people' and bemoans the lack of ability of 'the masses' to appreciate places and landscapes in the correct manner. This type of thinking has a long history, and in educational terms is well represented by Leavis and Thompson's (1933) *Culture and Environment* where the pleasures of ordinary people are considered a form of a 'substitute living'.

It is interesting to reflect on the types of place that we as geographers (both as individuals and in our teaching) value. Geographers have, until relatively recently, been quite reluctant to study the landscapes of popular culture. Radical geographers have seen shopping malls and sporting landscapes as sites that reflect capitalist values, and humanistic geographers have been quite elitist in the paintings and literature that they have studied as examples of human consciousness. To what extent are these messages about what is valuable communicated to students in geography lessons? Do lessons on tourism, for example, promote the idea that there are 'better' or 'worse' forms of tourism? Or, is it important, through geography, to promote ideas about what is valuable in places and landscapes, and to encourage students to critique unwanted or 'ugly' intrusions in the landscape? Our point is that it is important to be aware of the persistence of particular ways of seeing places (see Box 6.1).

Box 6.1

A PREJUDICED VIEW OF PLACE?

To what extent is the 'structure of feeling' outlined in this section a fair reflection of how the idea of place is used in modern geography teaching? An interesting example is found in Rycroft's (1997) evaluation of the UK Land Use survey which involved children undertaking a survey of land use in 1000 1 km squares across England and Wales. Rycroft suggests that earlier land use surveys had worked within a project of post-war reconstruction and the vision of the modern citizen worked with the geographical idea that 'society and the environment must work in harmony to ensure efficient and aesthetically acceptable land use patterns'. In relation to the new survey, Rycroft detected a rural bias in the sampling procedure – 500 rural and 500 urban squares – which distorted the picture of Britain, where the population is predominantly urban. So from the start an educational activity that purported to understand the nation's geography seemed to equate the nation with the rural (or as Williams (1973) argued, uses the 'country' in both senses of the term). This tendency was reinforced by the 'national issues' that students were asked to identify in each grid square:

> Of the five national issues, not one is expressly urban. New housing, for instance, concerns the 'loss of countryside', in an echo of inter-war concerns for urban sprawl and the spread of urban intrusions into rural areas. In the 1920s and 1930s, urban intrusions did not simply refer to new housing but also to inappropriate elements in the visual environment, such as advertising or poorly designed street furniture. Similarly, this sentiment can be found in the fourth national issue, the existence of communication towers and pylons and this also applies to out-of-town retail developments.

(Rycroft 1999: 111)

Rycroft suggests that the selection of 'national' issues reflects a popular perception that the seat of national identity in Britain can be found in the idealized rural environment and that 'communities living in that environment somehow embody the ways of life and virtues to which, as a nation, we should aspire'. The message seems to be that: 'you do not *belong* to the nation as an active and conscientious citizen unless you can appreciate the nation's nature which is located in our countryside' (p. 111).

Rycroft's argument is that a particular landscape or environment was favoured by the survey – the rural/urban fringe. This landscape is highly contested in terms of land use and usually under intense development pressure. It is also the landscape that reflects the concerns and interests of the affluent middle classes and is expressed in attempts to limit this type of inappropriate development. More worryingly, this notion of the 'environment' was used as a blanket category that erased complex economic, social and cultural processes (p. 111).

Rycroft describes sitting at the top of a hill with a group of white middle-class students, looking down on the area they had just surveyed. There was a commuter village below, and he asked what the 'problem' might be with building new housing. The students' responses included that the architecture might not fit in with existing housing stock; that it may damage an ecologically sensitive area; and that council housing was always poorly designed. In addition, the problem of expanding the village would lead to 'more crime'. Rycroft argues that the 'environment' here was being used to express social issues or, more provocatively, hide social prejudices. He reports the same experience in a de-industrialized inner city area, where degradation of the environment (boarded-up shops, graffiti, vandalism) were related by students to the racial composition of the area; again, the 'environment' is being used to hide complicated and situated prejudices (p. 112).

Finally, Rycroft notes that the process of mapping squares serves to fix the local in space and time and to ignore the interdependence of localities in an era of economic and cultural globalization.

Whose place?

The previous section described a particular way of thinking and feeling about place that we argue has been (and continues to be) influential in geography teaching in schools. In this section, we argue that this sense of place has been undermined in the past two decades. This deconstruction of place has been most apparent in university geography departments, but, since it reflects broader ways of thinking in society, has invariably come to influence how place is conceptualized in school geography.

Within the social sciences and humanities, the period since the late 1960s has seen the development of 'theory'. In general, social theory has been critical of the direction that modern Western society has travelled, and has pointed to the exclusion of the perspectives of various 'others'. Many human geographers in Anglo-American universities were aligned with these currents of thought, with the result that there has been a 'normative turn' in geographic thought. This took place from the late 1960s in the context of political struggles in civil society. In geography this move is perhaps best signalled by the work of David Harvey who, in the 1960s, had been influenced by spatial science. He wrote his doctoral thesis on the cultivation of hops in nineteenth-century Kent and produced a book *Explanation in Geography* (1969), which set out the basis for the development of geography as a positivist science. However, by the time of the publication of his second book – *Social Justice in the City* – in 1973, Harvey had rejected this approach. In an interview published in 2000, Harvey explained that it was the experience of moving to Baltimore that made him reassess the value of much of this geographical theory.

Much of Baltimore had been damaged in riots after the assassination of Martin Luther King, and the anti-Vietnam war movement was in full force. For Harvey, the urban models studied by geographers seemed irrelevant and worse still, served to perpetuate the status quo. It is also important to acknowledge the role that feminist geography played in challenging the rather self-contained view of place held by many geographers. The development of social geography paid attention to questions of difference. This was supported by developments in wider social theory that became increasingly concerned with the differences between groups and identity politics. This was reflected in geography with important studies in the 1990s on the geographies of disability, sexuality, old age and mental health. These had the effect of challenging the idea that we can gain an objective view of place. Instead it became important to ask *whose place* was being represented here.

In all these accounts there is an acknowledgement of the ways that people may have radically different experiences of places and, importantly, that more powerful groups are able to define places and often exclude others. This prompts the question of whose place is being talked about in geography lessons. In the mid-1990s these issues were brought to the fore in three significant published accounts that explored the contradictions of place. These were Sibley's *Geographies of Exclusion* (1995), Cresswell's *In Place/Out of Place* (1996), and Shield's *Places on the Margins* (1992).

All these geographers stress how space is structured according to human processes of inclusion and exclusion. However, the authors differ in their focus and explanations. Sibley (1995) is one of the most influential accounts of the role that space plays in social inclusion and exclusion. His major contribution is to locate these divisions in the fear of otherness that is explained with reference to psychological processes. He provides a wide range of historical and contemporary examples of these processes. He draws on psychoanalytical theories of 'object relations' that are linked with notions of 'abjection' and the 'generalized fear of the other'.

Cresswell (1996) emphasizes the role that power plays in the drawing of boundaries between places. According to this analysis, powerful groups secure their position by promoting ideological ideas about how society should be organized. These become part of our common-sense understanding of how the world operates, and Cresswell shows how place and space are used to promote ideologies about who belongs and what is appropriate behaviour in a place. In this way, place is part of the moral order of society. Cresswell demonstrates these processes through a series of case studies. Part of the point of Cresswell's argument is that these ideas about place are not accepted by all groups, and people resist them, which leads to a concern with transgression, the breaking of powerful socio-spatial ideologies.

Finally, Shield's (1992) *Places on the Margins* has the subtitle 'Alternative Geographies of Modernity'. He is concerned with the place images that are attributed to particular environments. While this may seem similar to the idea of perception or mental maps that formed a part of school geography in the 1980s and beyond, Shields is critical of these approaches because they tend to adopt a disembodied approach that counts images and reduces their complexity. He develops a social and cultural analysis of four place images showing how the idea of marginal places is linked with the development of economic modernization.

In summary, the work discussed so far in this section has paved the way for more inclusive understanding of place. In terms of teaching geography, it suggests that we need to ask the question of whose place is being talked about here. It is important to remember that these developments have not occurred in isolation, and that moves to recognize difference are related to broader trends in the social sciences and education (see Chapter 9 for a discussion of the concept of 'cultural understanding and diversity').

In addition, there have been more positive evaluations of 'ordinary places'. This is associated with the so-called cultural turn in geography and more generally with the democratization of taste in society as a whole. As recently as the early 1990s, Warren (1993) noted the traditional neglect of 'landscapes of consumption' by geographers, and Jackson and Thrift (1995) pointed out that geographers had ignored many aspects of everyday consumption such as shopping, advertising and the media. A notable exception was an edited collection of essays *Geography, the Media and Popular Culture* (Burgess and Gold, 1985). In the words of the editors, this was an attempt to recognize that, 'Raymond Chandler is as valuable a source as Thomas Hardy and that the Daily Mirror has as much to say about the nature of places as the Geographical Journal' (p. 1):

> The media have been on the periphery of geographical inquiry for too long. The very ordinariness of the television, radio, newspapers, fiction, film and pop music perhaps masks their importance as part of people's geography 'threaded into the fabrics of daily life with deep tap-roots into the well-springs of popular consciousness'.
>
> (Burgess and Gold 1985: 1)

Since the mid-1990s geographers have produced a wealth of research that focuses on people's experiences of place, what might be called the 'geographies of everyday life'. These give the message that 'place is ordinary'.

Do places matter?

In this section we want to explore another example of how the concept of place provides a challenge for geography teachers in schools. Since the mid-1980s, in both academic and popular discourse, it has become commonplace to hear the argument that globalization is threatening the character of places and that the really significant forces that shape places are located 'elsewhere' in the spaces of the 'global economy'.

This way of thinking dates from the 1980s when it was increasingly recognized that an older regional geography with its solid geography of primary and manufacturing industry was being wiped out through processes of de-industrialization and economic restructuring. Lovering (1997) suggests that a 'simple story' circulates about these changes. According to this story, Britain's industrial regions, which were built on coal, the steel industry, engineering and ship-building suffered as a result of Britain's century-long decline from being the 'workshop of the world'. These industries have declined under the impact of technological change or moved to cheaper workforces elsewhere.

Newly industrialized countries, with cheaper labour and newer factories, have become the places where goods are made, and the global mobility of capital, encouraged by the development of transnational corporations, has exacerbated these trends. Britain's industrial regions have been in decline, and cities are no longer centres of production. These changes have dire implications for places, which have suffered from de-industrialization, and suffered from high rates of unemployment and social exclusion for certain groups of people. In this simple story, there is a consensus that little can be done to rescue these regions and cities from decline.

The 'simple story' contains a particular view of the relationship between global and local forces. The global is the space of autonomous economic change; the local is where the effects of these changes are felt and experienced. The global is the domain of world historical forces, whereas the local is the place of response, adaptation or resistance. This is a story that is familiar to us through the media and through the words of politicians; it is one where places are relatively powerless to respond to the forces that operate elsewhere. A good example of this is Massey's work which made clear that what was happening to companies was not attributable to the characteristics of place or the 'factors of location' but to social processes as part of a global economy. The first edition of Dicken's book *Global Shift* was published in 1982 and Johnston and Taylor's (1986) A World in Crisis? marked a recognition that the scale of social science had shifted from the nation to the global. The question then became how are the global and the local related.

Massey's (1994) *Spatial Divisions of Labour* was a landmark text, and developed out of a critique of the limits of geographical theories about the factors of production. These tended to offer 'spatial explanations' for spatial patterns, when in fact the key relation was between capital and labour, and this was a social process that operated in the economy. What happened to particular places and regions was therefore linked to the activities of firms who were operating across nation state boundaries. In the process of economic restructuring, some regions and localities fared better than others, and in the 1980s an important body of work was concerned with the effect on localities of economic change. The headline message of this work was that geography matters, and this has led to a focus on exploring how places are constructed and reconstructed as the result of processes that are simultaneously global and local.

Since Lovering (1997) wrote about the simple story, there have been significant changes in the way that places are thought about. In particular, it is argued that in order to compete in a competitive global economy places have to be innovative and market themselves in order to attract investment, visitors and residents. It is recognized that there will be winners and losers in this process. It is not possible to resolve once and for all the question of the relationship between the global and the local, and in many ways this is not the point. Instead, we are suggesting that geography teachers should be aware of what is at stake in representing places. The predominance of the 'global shift' narrative, which suggests that the 'real' action occurs in the sphere of the global economy and that places are left to respond more or less successfully to these developments, should give geography teachers pause for thought. As noted in Chapter 2, Castree et al. (2004) argue that globalization has been used as a 'tool to make people believe we live in a hyperintegrated world of ceaseless and irresistible flows' (p. 18). They identify a series of 'myths of globalization' that circulate in the business press and media and which tend to be reproduced in school geography texts (see Table 6.1).

Table 6.1 The myths of globalization and their acceptance in geography textbooks (*People, Production and Environment (PPE)* and (Copnall et al. 1999) *Geography in Focus (GF)* Cook et al.)

Myths of globalization	Examples
That we live in an increasingly 'borderless world'	'The global economic system affects every facet of human activity' (*PPE*) 'Globalization can be defined as the process in which national economies are becoming more and more integrated into a single global economy' (*GF*)
Globalization is an irresistible force that stands over and above different places and people	' . . . global action to provide solutions [to problems] has been only partial.' (*PPE*)
Globalization signals the demise of the nation state	'Governments and politicians cannot afford to ignore TNCs' (*PPE*) 'Globalization is about the challenge to nation-states posed by the activities of TNCs, and by the inability of nation-states to control the activities of the global economy' (*GF*)
Workers are increasingly vulnerable as firms are able to 'play off' workers as part of a divide and rule strategy	*GF* gives the example of Renault, who in 1997 announced their intention to close its plant in Vilvoorde, Belgium, while at the same time planned to build a new plant in Valladolid, Spain: 'There was widespread belief that Renault was playing the Belgian government and workforce off against the Spanish government and workforce'
The myth of cheap labour: firms with the capacity to choose between several possible production sites gravitate to places with the lowest labour costs	' . . . cheap labour can reduce the cost of the product so much it is cost-effective to transfer production thousands of miles to a new factory' (*PPE*)

These 'myths' all contain a grain of truth. However, according to Castree et al. (2003), they tend to be greatly exaggerated and as such serve particular social and political agendas. Castree et al. argue that concepts such as 'globalization' are never neutral, they have a material effect in that they influence how we see the world and act. The version of globalization that has dominated economic and political life in the last two decades is based on a 'neoliberal' understanding of economic space, which stresses that businesses are the main economic actors who increasingly operate on a global scale, roaming the world to seek out the best place to locate production. This process is characterized by high rates of mobility, so that the idea that individuals could stay in one place and have a job for life is replaced by the idea that employees need to be flexible. This is an influential and powerful view of economic space. However as Harvey (2005) insists, there is nothing inevitable about this, but should be seen as part of a concerted attempt on the part of capital to reduce labour's share of the economic surplus and accumulate wealth. Part of this strategy is to make existing social and spatial arrangements appear natural and inevitable – that 'there is no alternative'.

Conclusion

At the start of this chapter, we stated that we wanted to explore the implications for geography teachers of the idea that place is a social construction. We suggested that teachers should understand their own role as actively producing representations of place. The work of this chapter has been to explore the implications of different ways of conceptualizing place – what might be called *the politics of place*. We think it important for geography teachers to be 'self-conscious' about the types of representation of place that they produce in classrooms. An example of how we might reflect on the politics of place is provided by Simon Armitage's poem, *A Vision*, which is reproduced below.

A VISION

The future was a beautiful place, once.
Remember the full-blown balsa-wood town
on public display in the Civic Hall?
The ring-bound sketches, artists' impressions,

blueprints of smoked glass and tubular steel,
board-game suburbs, modes of transportation
like fairground rides or executive toys.
Cities like *dreams*, cantilevered by light.

And people like us at the bottle bank
next to the cycle path, or dog-walking
over tended strips of fuzzy-felt grass,
or model drivers, motoring home in

electric cars. Or after the late show –
strolling the boulevard. They were the plans,
all underwritten in the neat left-hand
of architects – a true, legible script.

I pulled that future out of the north wind
at the landfill site, stamped with today's date,
riding the air with other such futures,
all unlived in and now fully extinct.

(Armitage 2006)

Armitage's poem raises some interesting questions about how we come to understand place in the contemporary world. The overall tone of the poem is downbeat, making a distinction between cities or towns as they were imagined, and how they have turned out in practice ('The future was a beautiful place once'). It appears that this hoped-for future was the product of the planners' imagination, as referenced by the balsa-wood models, sketches, blueprints and artists' impressions. But how should we interpret the poet's loss of faith? One interpretation is that the poem is a comment on the failures of post-war state planning (it helps to know that Armitage studied geography at university in Britain). In other words, the modernist dream of 'building' out poverty and antisocial behaviour through rational planning is seen as having failed. More generally, the poem might be read in more general terms as representing a postmodern loss of faith in 'meta-narratives' of improvement and progress, or in more humanistic terms of the planning system's lack of attention to the lived experiences or meanings held by ordinary people.

Whenever we have used this poem with students, the phrase that seems to hold the key to understanding, and which therefore causes some difficulties, is 'And people like us at the bottle bank'. What does this mean? In line with the interpretation offered above, it could be a comment on the gap between planners' assumptions about how people could (and perhaps should) behave and how they do in practice (recycling waste, driving responsibly, cycling to work). However, the meaning of this phrase is questioned when we learn that Armitage's poem was included in a collection published to mark the thirtieth anniversary of the Commission for Racial Equality. This gives a whole new racialized meaning to the words 'people like us'. Indeed, when we have introduced this fact to students, their reading of the poem often shifts radically.

The poem is then read as a comment on the project of multiculturalism. Some students see it as highly problematic, since it seems to suggest that the poet regrets in some way the loss of the clean, bright and ordered city and town in the face of the presence of people who are not 'like us'. Other students offer interpretations focused on the possible environmental themes of the poem, particularly around the idea of the 'north wind'. In this interpretation, the 'people like us' is an implicit environmentally aware middle-class group. Further discussion leads to the idea that this is a particular perspective on this place (most students assume the writer is white, male, middle-aged), one that regrets the passing of the idea of progress, and that not all people may share this perception. Indeed, some urban and social geographers point to the excitement that the 'chaos' of the city affords people and how it allows them to find their own 'place'.

Of course, there is no final answer as to what Simon Armitage's poem 'means', and that is our point: in relation to teaching about places, the challenge is to pay attention to, and reflect on, the geographical imagination that informs our teaching in classrooms.

7 Scale

In this chapter we argue that scale needs to be understood in different ways. At its most straightforward, scale is a technical, operational matter, closely related to the idea of 'cartographic' scale and 'geographic' scale (the spatial extent of phenomena). Scale is therefore an essential and uncontentious component of school geography concerned with spatial distributions and patterns. What is also commonplace, is the use of scale divisions, such as local, regional, national, international and global, to organize geographical content, as if the purpose of scale was to operate like an enormous geographic filing cabinet. However, what we show is that geographers have theorized the idea of scale in recent years in a way that enables us to recognize its own agency. It is an idea, in other words, that can be applied for political or other reasons. Ideas such as 'local', 'national' and 'global' are not fixed therefore – and we need to study who uses these terms and for what purposes. Geography helps us to analyse the 'politics of scale' therefore, and for educationists critical perspectives on such taken-for-granted notions as 'global citizenship' may emerge. Having established the possibility of understanding scale as a social construction, the chapter stretches the idea still further, drawing from geographers who have explored scale inhabited in virtual world on the one hand (beyond the global) and the micro scale of home and the body, on the other hand which have tremendous possibilities for work with school students.

Introduction

> place ... includes far more entities than towns and cities, or even neighborhoods, homes and houses. Why not also fireplace, a favorite armchair or even another human being?
>
> (Tuan 1999: 105)

This chapter opens up the idea of scale. Few can doubt that scale is a core concept of geography, although it is, of course, possible to acknowledge from the start that the idea is not confined to geography. When we pose basic everyday questions such as what is big and what is bigger? (or what is long and what is longer?), we are immediately into applying measuring scales of some description – of say, time or distance. Mathematicians, chemists, historians, geologists ... probably all disciplines need to consider 'scale' in some way.

But how specifically is scale used in geography? What is its significance? Tuan (1999), in our opening quotation, is discussing place and identity. He invests some very small places such as 'a favorite armchair' with personal meaning, perhaps as a child does with their private space at home such as their bedroom. But what is interesting is that he explicitly links individual places like 'neighborhood' to a concept of spatial scales. Even in this short passage, we can see hierarchical relationships within this idea of scale and equally important, the difficulty in separating out scale from place and space. These are separate ideas but at the same time ideas that in geography are deeply related to each other.

Scale is one of the key concepts in the secondary National Curriculum and what we want to do in this chapter is survey the richness and significance of the idea. As we saw in Chapter 5, with Massey's (1985) comment about the related idea of space, 'There has been much head-scratching, much theorising, much changing of mind' and the same is true about scale (although in this case the head-scratching is more recent: e.g. see Marston 2000). Rather than take a chronological approach in an attempt to show the evolution of the concept in geography, we shall in this chapter survey ways in which the idea is conceptualized today. The key point of this argument is to show how scale involves significant choices; scale has a politics. Our aim is to discourage a taken-for-granted approach to scale, for the real strength of the idea is that it adds to the 'grammar' (see page 39) of the subject by providing meaning and significance that is not always self-evident.

The idea of scale in geography

An interesting observation about scale is that because it is such a basic concept, it is in some regards almost taken for granted. Marston (2000) added the following footnote to her article:

> Although scale is clearly of central concern to biogeographers, geomorphologists, climatologists and other physical geographers, I was chagrined to find when consulting the second edition of *The encyclopedic dictionary of physical geography* (Goudie *et al.*, 1994) for a definition of scale, none was there (in contrast to the *Dictionary of Human Geography* (3rd edn), where the definition takes up nearly two pages (Johnston et al. 1994: 543–45).
>
> (Marston 2000: 219)

Scale it seems is so well embedded in the work of physical geographers, it has escaped the notice of its practitioners! Alternatively, despite our protestations, maybe in physical geography the idea *is* simply self-evident. In this section we examine the idea of scale; first, in physical geography and then more broadly. We shall see that while scale is likely to be seen as a technical or operational concern in physical geography, in human geography there is more interest in the socially constructed nature of the idea. It is more relativist and an idea that is in a constant state of becoming – a powerful and useful thought in the context of teachers and students adopting the role of 'knowledge workers' as we discussed in Chapter 4 (page 58).

In physical geography questions about scale are of paramount importance. One reason for this is the realization that the *resolution* of an investigation or study is crucial to the nature of the questions being addressed. Larger-scale studies of an entire river basin for example require a coarser resolution in the data assembled than small-scale studies of, say, soil on a single slope. Thus, larger-scale studies – including those undertaken on a global scale – tend to rely on statistical description and analysis, while small studies are able to focus more realistically on particular process dynamics. A challenge facing physical geographers therefore is when there is the need to apply the results from one scale of analysis to different scales. Burt (2003) provides a very clear overview of this introducing the terminology of upscaling and downscaling. Because, he argues, that geographers have never confined themselves to any one scale alone; they are frequently faced with the issue of:

> ... upscaling of results from smaller to larger areas – for example, extending results from small catchment studies to large river basins (or) in some circumstances downscaling – for example, applying the results of general circulation models (global scale) to particular regions. It has long been known (Haggett 1965) that generalizations made at one level do not necessarily hold at another, and that conclusions derived at one scale may be invalid at another.
>
> (Burt 2003: 211)

The issue of 'scaling' described here is resolutely a technical issue rooted in a scientific view, although it requires from time to time interpretation and judgement. But the issue of resolution, which is a very familiar term in the worlds of remote sensing and GIS, where the technologies are defined by the greatest resolving power of the instruments in question (and their resolutions have been becoming ever more powerful of course), can therefore be equated with *operational* scale. Thus, when we have referred to larger- or smaller-scale studies in this section, we are in effect referring to the scale at which relevant processes operate.

Although this concept of scale is also applicable in human geography – for example, as we shall see, the 'lens' we select governs to some extent the nature of what we study – it is particularly germane in physical geography, and the source of an enduring tension between the need to understand the detail of particular process mechanisms and the need to understand how broader, very complex systems operate. To some degree this scale divide is increasingly bridgeable as researchers become more adept at modelling, aided by powerful computing. Although much of the research output is now through highly specialized journals rather than 'geographical' channels, it was nevertheless still the case that around 50 per cent of the 2008 'research assessment exercise' (the periodic process by which research funds are allocated to UK universities, based on the quality of research outputs) submission in geography was in 'physical' geography. This possibly reflects rising interest, at both ends of the scale spectrum, in the search for patterns, processes and functional linkages in the physical world.

There are other ways to conceptualize scale as it impinges on physical geography. Lam and Quattrochi (1992) offer a summary in which they distinguish geographic and cartographic scale from operational scale in the sense we have used it above. *Cartographic* scale is taught widely in schools and refers to the relationship between the distance on a map to the corresponding distance in real life, or 'on the ground'. *Geographic* scale denotes the spatial extent of a phenomenon or distribution, and in some ways is closest to the 'everyday meaning' attached to the word scale.

Extending the idea of scale

We have seen from the previous section that scale, like geography itself, has both more technical and popular everyday meanings. To a large degree, the more technical meanings outlined so far can be allowed to grow out of the more everyday understandings of scale that students bring with them to geography classrooms. The distinctions are fairly clear, and in all cases we can be fairly clear cut about how they relate. The significance of operational scale may be a little more challenging, but is nevertheless quite concrete. But let us now broaden our scope a little to incorporate the language of scale that was evident in our opening quotation and has already crept into our discussion in the previous paragraphs. The question we are now introducing concerns the orthodox and now ubiquitous scalar organization of public as well as geographic discourse into the following divisions:

- local;
- regional;
- national;
- global.

Geographers have generally come to accept these divisions for operational reasons cited above, and this framework has been adopted in school geography, almost without question. As Herod (2003) explains, the origins of the ready acceptance of such a matrix through which to study the social and economic world can be traced back to Kant's idealist philosophy. In other words, using these scales is simply to utilize a pre-existing system for making sense of the world. As Herod writes:

> As such, they are simply mental devices for circumscribing and ordering processes and practices so that these may be distinguished and separated from one another – a particular process or set of social practices can thus be considered to be 'local' whereas others are considered to be 'global' in scope. For idealists, the 'global' is usually defined by the given limits of the Earth, whereas the 'local' is seen as a spatial resolution useful for comprehending processes and practices which occur at geographical ranges smaller than the 'regional' scale, which in turn is seen to be anything which is smaller than the 'national' scale (which, for its part, is seen as the next smallest scale after the 'global' scale.
>
> (Herod 2003: 231)

The problem with this approach to scale is that it fails to theorize the nature of the idea itself. It treats scale as if it were an external 'fact' just waiting to be discovered and used, and in itself essentially neutral and simply a matter of operational choice, as noted above. However, even a cursory thought about how scale may actually shape or frame how we see the world must lead us to reject this position. For example, and to state the most obvious example, nation states are not just a fact. They have not always been there. In Europe they are still being created and even the largest and economically most powerful of them are relatively recent creations; for example, Germany, unified as late as 1870 and whose borders were still being modified in the last decade of the twentieth century. They come in different shapes, sizes and functional organization. Or take 'local': is 'local' the same for boys and girls, men and women, rich and poor? When 'locality studies' were proposed as part of the National Curriculum in England and Wales in 1991, many teachers had serious difficulty agreeing what this meant, including the question of whether Wales was a locality, a region or a country. The point here is that scales are constructed, not only by individual geographers needing a framework through which to teach a course or conduct some research, but socially by the people who use them.

Marston discusses this in her article 'The social construction of scale', taking a lead from Howitt (1998):

> His central aim is to argue that scale should be understood ' . . . as a factor in the construction and dynamics of geographical totalities – rather than simply as a product of geographical relations' (1998: 56). Scale, like environment, space or place, is one of the elements from which geographical totalities are built. Rather than accept scale as a naturalized category, Howitt insists that we see scale not as size (census tract, province, continent) and level (local, regional, national) but as a relational element in a complex mix that also includes space, place and environment – all of which interactively make the geographies we live in and study.
>
> (Marston 2000: 220–1)

Such a view, showing that scale is created and is part of the material world that geographers actively study (as opposed to being merely the predetermined lens through which the material world is observed and ordered) is a radically different view from Kantian idealism. Thus, scales such as the 'global' do not simply exist, but are brought into being, and are in a constant, evolving relationship with other scales: 'Global' has a pre-existing meaning in the sense that it denotes the given limits of the planet Earth, but in fact 'global' implies much more than simply that. It is this additional meaning that is brought into being. Different scales may become more important at different times in order to communicate a particular meaning or view of the world and how it 'works'. For example, think what is meant by:

- 'Making globalization work for the world's poor' (a New Labour Department for International Development (DfID) slogan from the early twenty-first century) or
- 'The world's local bank' (an advertising slogan from one of the world's largest banks).

In both cases an idea is being created. They illustrate the politics of scale. The messages contrast with each other, but they have the same root, in neoliberal economics. In the first case, the UK government sets out to persuade the public that late-stage, global capitalism is benign and a force for good (we need to accept it – and embrace a 'globalized' view), *and* can be 'put to work' by a national government. In the second case, a bank with a turnover in excess of many, if not most, nation states, tries to show that it is friendly to you and me by showing it is responsive to local interests, but at the same time is 'reassuringly' global. Thus, both the local and global are scales in a constant state of becoming. They do not have fixed meanings, but nonetheless are created and recreated often to contribute rhetorically to a discourse that can powerfully shape how we understand the world. Think for example about the famous phrase 'Think Globally, Act Locally': this denotes a lot of meaning, emphasizing a sense of impotence we may feel as individuals in relation to global processes in comparison to localized real lives we are supposed to lead (and as we have seen, at least one multinational bank has tried to capture this feeling for its own purposes).

Progress has been made in clarifying this more complicated appreciation of scale, ever since the 'politics of scale' was presented in the 1980s (as we shall see more fully in the following section). The point is that the discipline of geography has evolved a perspective on scale that invests it with critical significance. More than merely offering a cartographic, geographic or operational 'lens' through which to make sense of the world, geography now takes account of the very fact that scale itself is in part a human creation and often a political act. Each of the four given categories we habitually use – the global, the national, the regional and the local – may carry ideological significance. Some geographers such as David Harvey and Noel Castree insist on using the phrase 'global capitalism' rather than 'globalization' for this very reason, and the 2008 global 'credit crunch' provides the justification: increasingly into 2009 political and economic commentators have discussed responses to the crisis in global capitalism in terms of the possible actions of nation states (e.g. Skidelski 2009).

Talk of 'the global' in the late twentieth and early twenty-first centuries was not just of facts therefore: it was also of messages designed for a purpose. Geography in education is well placed to help us question the potentially profoundly disabling messages wrapped up in the 'global' challenges of climate and capitalism (which of course are linked). It can do this by studying real people in real (local) places who not only face differential impacts but also may have uniquely different responses to make. It is interesting in this context to ask why politicians often seem to seek refuge in the notion that some problems are 'global'. By the same token, it is also interesting to think about why contemporary politics also seeks to focus on the neighbourhood and 'communities'.

What we learn from the politics of scale

One of the most influential books in geography from the last quarter of the twentieth century has been Peter Taylor's *Political Geography: World-economy, Nation-state and Locality*, first published in 1985 and subsequently in its fifth edition in 2007. This book reworked Wallerstein's (1975) 'world systems' theory of political economy that divided the world space into three realms: the global, the national and the local, refining the very useful geographical concepts of core and periphery. It influenced another important book of this era, Smith's *Uneven Development* (1984), and the principle reason for this was Taylor's main task to refocus economic geography away from the state, the study of countries' economic patterns, to the scale that (according to him) really matters – the global (see also Peter Dicken's (1998) *Global Shift*). It is on the global scale that capital accumulation occurs. Taylor's task was to use scale as the vehicle with which to modernize geography to become a discipline capable of studying turn of the century capitalism.

In summary, Taylor's framework (see Figure 7.1) provides a language for considering:

- the scale of 'reality' – the global;
- the scale of 'ideology' – the nation state;
- the scale of 'experience' – the local or urban.

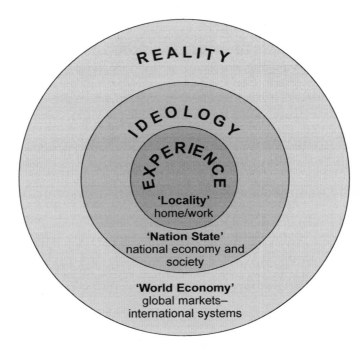

Figure 7.1 A three-tiered structure of separation and control by scale, adapted from Taylor (1993), p. 44.

The scale of *experience* takes in people's lived lives: where people live, where they work, obtain provisions and engage in leisure pursuits. It is the fine grain of geography and is often, rightly, concerned with the unique circumstances of a given place. The scale of *reality* is, as we have seen, the scale that 'really matters'. For example, where are decisions made regarding Chelsea FC, Manchester United or Manchester City? Or Corus steel in Sheffield or Toyota motor cars in Derby? All these concerns are not owned locally. The reality is that English Premier League football clubs are potentially global brands with enormous earnings potential through television and merchandising, and this has knock-on effects on the whole of the football industry. Thus, through the international ownership of several leading football clubs, both production and consumption of football is affected by the reality of global economics. However, the match day experience of the supporter is still to a large degree localized: the chants, the food, the rituals end even where supporters live are best studied through their local geographies.

Coming between the global and the local is Taylor's scale of ideology. The English Premier League has been allowed, even encouraged, to seek foreign ownership. The *Bundesliga* in Germany on the other hand has regulations that prevent this. Thus, the *national* scale, the scale of ideology, is, in Marston's (2000:222) words 'the result of a fragmented capitalist world market predicated on the ideological constructions of statism and nationalism'. This tells us that national governments can choose to respond to global economic processes in different ways. In a way, governments can 'filter' the global scale of reality – through building infrastructure, regional development programmes, incentives or regulations. The Thatcher governments of the 1980s chose a *laissez-faire* approach towards global competition and presided over the destruction of a great deal of manufacturing industry – interestingly, under the famous slogan 'there is no alternative' – appealing to voters to accept the 'scale of reality' and disregarding other policy choices that may have existed. Another interesting and contemporary case in point is to compare, say, the energy policies of the UK and France. The latter produces around 70 per cent of its electricity from nuclear in comparison to closer to 15 per cent in the case of the UK – not for resource reasons alone (though we acknowledge that the UK has benefited from North Sea oil and gas) but for ideological reasons too. There are now signs that the UK government is shifting its position on nuclear power, which is now seen as 'green'.

These scales interplay with each other. They also conflict from time to time, for they are underpinned by real material interests and power, as the destruction of UK manufacturing capacity and the will to establish London as the hub of global finance demonstrates. But what happened to the region, a concept that has been a keystone, especially in the earlier years of geography's development as a discipline? In *Uneven Development*, Neil Smith shows that the regional scale is very elastic – as it always has been in geography. Thus, although we can talk about regions as 'in between' local and national (as we did in the previous section), and this has a common-sense feel to it, it is not the only connotation of the term. Certainly, the government's nine standard regions of England fit the in-between model: North, North-west, Yorkshire and Humberside, West Midlands, East Midlands, East Anglia, South-west, South-east and London. Each is a hybrid region, partly resulting from physical matters (landscape and geology), human patterns, functionality and convenience. But at the same time geographers have talked about the great 'natural regions' of the globe where regions stretch across continents. What Smith showed was that the supranational region was not an idea confined to physical geography. This, according the Smith, resulted from the way capitalism operates over space, whether within national space or global space. Think for example about how school geography tends to divide the world in 'less developed' and 'more developed', or the North and the South (or as it was known in former times, the 'Third World'). In Smith's words:

> ... the crystallization of distinct geographical regions at the national scale has the same function as the global division between the developed and the underdeveloped world. Both provide geographically fixed (relatively) sources of wage labor, one at the international scale and the other under the more direct control of the national capital.
>
> (Smith 1984: 145)

This analysis indicates the creation of global regions based on the international divisions of labour: for instance, separating the manufacturing, research and development, or the making and the knowledge industries. It also accounts for the creation of supranational regions, notably such as the European Union (EU) that quite purposely has tried to reduce the friction of 'traditional' national boundaries on the movement of good, finance and ideas in order to maximize opportunities for capital creation in an intensified global economy. This has created tensions, for as we have seen the European nation states are not only economic units, but have social and cultural meaning established over centuries. The national boundaries were created at a different time, and in some ways expressly to create strong ideologies and identities. No matter what the future of 'the European project', one thing is pretty clear: most Europeans live quite consciously on a number of different scales, with local and regional identity, national allegiance, and an increasingly pan-European economic and cultural lifestyle. And on top of that they exist in a globalized world, a notion that itself is often used ideologically, as we have seen.

The question of 'universal scale' and 'virtual worlds'

So far in this discussion of scale (which is impossible to conduct without reference to the concepts of place and space), we have shown how geographers have developed the idea to help us see and understand the world and how its works. Scale is useful because it relates to social practice, though we must be careful not to reify scale-as-given, giving prominence to pattern over process. There are, however, other perspectives that so far we have virtually ignored, which may be especially pertinent to geography in *schools* that claims to contribute to young people's understanding of the world. Young people of course inhabit the world, or parts of it, and therefore have everyday experience to draw from. Geographers have in recent years been interested in the geographies of young people (see www.youngpeoplesgeographies.co.uk/) and, partly related to this, interested in additional scales to those in Taylor's model. Rather than elevate the global, these geographies have expanded and deepened the scales of experience to include the body, the home and 'community', focusing on easily overlooked matters such as food consumption or fashion (see for example Bell and Valentine 1997; Holloway and Valentine 2000).

The body, being the main physical site of personal identity and the boundary of 'self', is a social construction: you certainly construct your own 'personal space' and do this partly in relation to social space around you. The scale of the body appropriates meaning in terms of gender and sexual relations, 'race' and ethnicity, age, class and ability. The home, manifest as a physical structure in a particular location, is the site of routine social reproduction: eating, sleeping, forming relationships, child-rearing. Again, the home carries meaning, with gendered roles very often evident in 'home-making' for example. The geographies of domestic interiors, functions and activity are worth investigating at one level, while at another level, the scaled meanings of 'home' may be fruitful to explore with young people.

Both the body and the home provide one way into the geographic study of community; in Smith's words, 'the least specifically defined of spatial scales ... (T)he consequent vague yet generally affirmative nurturing meaning attached to "community" makes it one of the most ideologically appropriated metaphors in contemporary public discourse' (Smith 1993: 105). Where and what is the spatial extent of your 'community'?

The way we respond to this question may partly depend on our engagement with the so-called digital revolution. Young people encounter the world increasingly through various media employed in popular culture (see Chapter 11). From the youngest age many children are subject to instant images and communication from around the world. They form friendships with distant people who they have never met and may never meet. Referencing Castells (1997), Kirby observes that:

> ... the veritable explosion of information transfer within the Internet has caused commentators to identify a virtual realm that both transcends and see-mingly undermines the more formal social and political constructions that have determined our previous concepts of scale.
>
> (Kirby 2001: 3)

Enlarging the point still further with extensive references to popular culture through film (e.g. *Independence Day*, *Men in Black*, *X-files*, etc.) and computer games, Kirby goes on to consider the case for a 'universal' scale that transcends world space. He continues:

> ... the scale of public discourse seems to be at odds with our own intellectual constructs. Indeed, global, national and local are not even self-evident contexts for most people, however much it appears that they just 'seem to present themselves' to many academics (Taylor and Flint, 2000, p.43). The truly important thing about identifying a 'universal scale', so to speak, is that it changes the apparent importance of the global scale.
>
> (Kirby 2002: 171)

The trouble with 'global' according to Kirby's position is that it has assumed an all-embracing power. This is beguiling because at the same time, paradoxically, the concept is relatively impotent. The orthodox truth is that climate change is in fact 'global climate change' and yet the results of global climate processes are very diverse. There are many climate changes taking place: warming, cooling, increases in precipitation, drought ... He concludes, ' ... the tyranny of the global scale drives out the possibility of under-standing reality at other scales' (Kirby 2002: 174).

Kirby's call to distinguish the universal scale is literally to put the global in its place which, apart from taking us into extraterrestrial imaginings, may help us connect the virtual worlds of the Internet and, ultimately, the 'armchair' cited by Tuan (page 96). Why is this useful? Because it enables us to diminish the global, which although cur-rently heretical is almost certainly necessary if climate change, or extreme poverty are to be addressed. What we seem to have in the early twenty-first century is the creation of globalism; but at the same time, we can from our favourite armchairs, zoom in and zoom out, land here and put down there. Google Earth symbolizes the universal scale we now inhabit and our ability to fragment it. We will give Kirby the final word in this discussion:

> By taking globalism as something new, as something compelling, something threatening, we stand ready to make social and political choices that will define the twenty first century. On the one hand, we see the elevation in importance of global organizations created in order to deal with global crises, although they are lacking in accountability. On the other hand, and to restate this from the other

direction, we are in danger of marginalizing the state-centered perspectives that defined the twentieth century. This manifests itself in turn in two ways: first, the needs of specific, usually weaker states are marginalized – we see this in the current environmental debate – while second, the power of economically powerful states to dictate strategy and policy is overlooked, with obvious implications for political practice at the local scale and at the national scale. It is not coincidental that an emphasis upon global discourse has coincided with the shrinkage of voter turnout in national elections over the last thirty years.

(Kirby 2001: 20)

Conclusion

This chapter has opened up and has offered a framework for thinking about the key idea of scale. Hopefully, it illustrates how the idea, in the ways it has been developed by geographers, is powerful. It is a taxonomic device, but it is also a socially constructed product, and as such needs to be kept 'on the boil'. Views about scale in geography continue to evolve, and this matters, because the way we conceptualize the local and the global influences how we understand social, economic, political and physical processes, and the impact they have on the worlds we inhabit. Andrew Herod (2003: 243), in his introductory chapter, offers a summary of how the local and the global have been placed in relation to each other in geography. Within the 'universal' setting that Kirby (2002) has outlined above in his critique of globalism, we think this is a useful way to conclude our discussion of scale. As you read this list reflect back on the narrative in this chapter:

1   The global and local are not 'things' but ways of framing situations.
2   The global and the local are defining partly from what they are not.
3   The global and the local offer different perspectives on social networks.
4   The global is local: transnational firms are more multi-local than global.
5   The local is global: the local is where global processes 'touch down' on Earth.
6   All spaces are hybrids of the global and the local: giving us the ugly new word glocal.

What we have also done in this chapter is not only add national and regional layers to this fundamental division between local and global, but acknowledge the body, the home and 'community'.

8   Interdependence and development

Geography in schools has a long history. The first textbooks for primary schools were published in the early nineteenth century and by the beginning of the twentieth century geography was one of the listed subjects recommended for the secondary school curriculum. Throughout this history geography in school has had a significant role in shaping what we might now call the geographical imagination of young people in schools. Interdependence has been an enduring theme – at earlier times this was skewed to an imperialistic or colonial narrative, while more recently notions of global citizenship are more to the fore. Similarly, geography has not had an innocent or neutral role in shaping our ideas of development, whether encouraging ideas of 'darkest Africa' or dividing the globe into 'north' and 'south'. This chapter is not an historical overview of geography's 'sins' however! In the chapter we discuss the nature of the challenge that lies before geography teachers concerning how to represent the world, a challenge that has become increasingly urgent, and is set to become ever more so. We show that geographical perspectives are potentially extremely valuable in this regard.

Introduction

> Achieving a good life for more than 6 billion people, without further threatening the ecological systems on which we all depend, is the greatest challenge of our age.
>
> (Smith and Simms 2008: 242)

In this chapter we are going to survey an idea that seems to have 'come of age' in the last years of the twentieth century and early years of the twenty-first century. *Interdependence* is in this sense a relatively new concept. For some it has become one of the defining ideas of geography. Like so many of the concepts that are valued in geography, the discipline would be narrow-minded indeed to suggest that it had sole proprietor rights to the idea. For example, where would ecology be without the notion of interdependence, or history or physics, or hairdressing for that matter? What we wish to discuss therefore is not how interdependence 'defines' geography, but how geography has used and developed the idea in certain powerful ways. Interdependence, for example, is key to the kinds of relational understanding that underpin what Jackson (2006) has called 'thinking geographically'. Furthermore, the idea has begun to enter a wider public domain, partly through the efforts of those like Joe Smith working in the geography discipline at the Open University.

Thus, Joe Smith and his co-author Andrew Simms of the New Economics Foundation (nef) have promoted the idea of 'Interdependence Day' (www.open.ac.uk/socialsciences/interdependenceday), strongly invoking and establishing a very different meaning from 'Independence Day' introduced over two centuries ago to mark the birth of a nation

(USA). Subtitled *Making new maps for an island planet*, the interdependence day (ID) project has the ambition to 'refresh jaded debates about sustainable development' (which we tackle ourselves in Chapter 10 in the context of 'environment' as a key concept), by reframing debates about environment, globalization and development. For the purposes of this chapter, we take the ID approach as a way in to explore interdependence, with a particular focus on development and the global dimension – themes that have been prominent in school geography for at least three decades, but which are given new purchase with the concept of interdependence.

There is a final introductory point to make. Writing this book in early 2009 provides an inescapably poignant context. The USA has just inaugurated President Obama who seems intent on offering a new global presence and an international leadership role. He does so at a time of possibly unprecedented levels of uncertainty concerning environmental and economic futures. With regard to the latter, and the related developmental issues such as poverty and its eradication, there are journalists, politicians and others asking questions about what precisely the collapse of the global banking system and trade signifies. Is it the 'end' of globalization (as some have said) or the beginning of the next phase of globalization? We can watch, perhaps slightly anxiously, as President Obama takes the reins of the world's most powerful nation on which so much *depends*.

The authors of this book are not in a position to predict the nature of the *interdependencies* playing out over the next decade. But we are clear that a geographical lens helps us to think about these matters and helps us to form judgements in the continuing debates. It does so through (among other things) extending and 'disciplining' our ideas of interdependence and development. Thus, for example, while recognizing in the opening quotation that our times are challenging, Smith and Simms are determined to see the challenges as opportunities and deepen the message of global environmental risk: 'Facing up to current global challenges could, in fact, propel us towards much better ways of living. The message is that good lives don't have to cost the Earth' (Simms and Smith 2008: 1).

This is an optimistic message, and arguably one that can only be grasped in terms of how we imagine people and the planet are interrelated, and what we imagine 'development' to mean. Interdependence is an idea that broadens traditional and sometimes tired notions of 'development' in the geography curriculum.

Interdependence and the 'global dimension'

Let us start by frankly admitting a slight difficulty with 'interdependence' – ie the fact that observing and appreciating global interdependence is little more than stating the self-evident. It is the relatively weak thought that lies behind 'one-worldism' that certainly does not stand up to much scrutiny. However, it is also an idea that can be profoundly unsettling if or common-sense understanding of a world consists of discrete places and bounded spaces such as interdependence nation states. In this section we want to explore how the idea of independent has been deepened and extended in geography.

In the educational literature, we can readily find statements such as 'We live in a world today where everything is literally connected to everything else' (Garlake 2007:

114). This is in many ways a statement of the obvious, a bit like in the children's song that tells us that 'your leg bone is connected to your knee bone'. It tells us everything and arguably very little at the same time. She continues: 'The clothes that young people choose to buy or the food that they eat will affect a producer in another country. The impact of a choice that is as simple as whether to walk to school or not, will be felt across the globe' (p. 114).

We can certainly plan lessons that evidence this kind of thinking, as Box 8.1 illustrates.

Box 8.1

JEAN JOURNEY ACTIVITY SHEET

A pair of jeans
This pair of jeans is normally sold for £29.95 in a High Street store in the UK
Brass rivets and buttons made from Namibian copper and Australian zinc
Jeans sewn by women workers in Tunisia (58 pence an hour)
Cotton grown in Benin
Jeans stone-washed using pumice from Turkey
Jeans cut and dyed in Italy
Synthetic indigo dye made in Germany
Zip teeth made in Japan
Polyester tape for zips made in France
Thread for the seams made in Northern Ireland
Thread for seams dyed in Spain

A simple class exercise can have pupils identifying each country mentioned on a world map. A discussion can follow this, exploring the reasons for the distribution of activities and the environmental and economic effects of a global production process.

Source: adapted from Garlake (2007: 125).

Thus, young people come to 'possess' the fact that the production and consumption of jeans is reliant on interdependent activities across the globe. A problem however, as we discussed in some depth in Chapter 4, is what we expect pupils to do with this information. How does it help them understand the world? In Chapter 4, we quoted a teacher who argued that 'It doesn't matter what I say. It matters what sense the students make of what I say ... ' (Doerr et al. 2007: 296). We went on to write:

> It is exactly at this point that the subject discipline is useful, for the sense (the understanding) that students make is deepened through the use of those structures and ideas that lie outside of themselves and beyond their immediate, direct experience. Thus, understanding is not just a personal view or opinion (see page 58–59 for the full context).

The lesson idea in the box suggests 'discussion' of the implications of global interdependence, clearly designed to take students beyond the simple possession of facts.

However, what is the underlying purpose of Garlake's lesson (which could so easily be a *geography* lesson)? Is it really to share a collective, Western capitalist sense of guilt with young people about who wins and who loses from global interdependence – and to heap on them a sense of responsibility for the state of the world? If so, the accusation that Standish (2009) makes about school geography being corrupted by the moralistic impetus of global citizenship is hard to refute. But unlike Standish, who seems to suggest we stop with the possession of facts, we would suggest that we can go further than Garlake by drawing directly from the discipline, for it offers a framework – or a language – to help young people think geographically about the 'simple fact' of interdependence. And it is very important that we do, for unless we are prepared to go deeper than the possession of fact, we deny opportunities to students, as we argued in Chapter 4, to extend their capabilities through becoming geographic knowledge producers about how to understand an interdependent world, using ideas such as profit, power, production and consumption as, for example, John Huckle attempted in his innovative materials *What we Consume* (Huckle 1988–1993).

To explore this in a little more detail, we can begin with Allen and Massey introducing their perspectives on what they term 'geographical worlds':

> Geography has not slipped unnoticed into our lives. Nowadays you do not have to go far to experience the rest of the world. The world, in fact, comes to us in a variety of ways and means . . . We live local versions of the world and in so doing we have to locate ourselves within wider global context. We only understand the changes taking place in our own backyard when we begin to understand how changes taking place elsewhere affect our world.
>
> (Allan and Massey 1996: 1)

The book shows how geographical thinking enables us to grasp the connection between the local and global world (see also Chapter 7). It begins with the idea that the way in which we see the world is a matter of interpretation: it depends on who you are – a majority world farmer for example or a resident of Los Angeles. It shows how different places are constructed through the economic, political, and social connections that shape and reshape them. This 'global sense of place' (see also Chapter 5) is underpinned by the fact of interdependence, as we have seen, but also requires us to build a relational, or perspectival, view of how 'global interdependence' works.

This is an age of 'time–space compression' and the jeans example is just one example of this. We travel more widely and more frequently; information travels the globe almost instantly; tropical foods are taken for granted, the year round. But we need to take care with these generalizations. As Massey points out, '. . . time–space compression needs differentiating socially. This is not just a moral or political point about inequality, although that would be sufficient reason to mention it; it is also a conceptual point' (Massey 2008: 258). She is making a point about what she calls the 'power geometry' of it all, whereby different social groups and individuals are positioned very differently in relation to the flows and interconnections of global. They also have different measures of control over the initiation and reception of such flows and movements. Some are virtual prisoners, such as the non-car-driving poor or elderly who face 'food deserts' in some towns where the local shops have collapsed in the face of 'competition' from a nearby global supermarket (with free parking). Massey provides a vivid alternative example, 'to illustrate a different kind of complexity':

> (T)here are people who live in the *favelas* of Rio, who know global football like the back of their hand, and have produced some of its players; who have contributed massively to global music, who gave us the samba and produced the lambada . . . ; and who never, or hardly ever, been to downtown Rio. At one level they have been tremendous contributors to what we have called 'time–space compression' and at another level they are imprisoned in it.
>
> (Massey 2008: 260)

There are doubtless millions of people in all manner of social and economic settings around the world who are to some degree 'imprisoned' in their day-to-day lives. There are clearly great differences in people's capacities to break free from their circumstances, but even those with economic means often prefer to stay put. This allegiance to 'home' may hark back to an inward-looking, reactionary sense of place based on belonging and fixed identities, although in truth the world has never really been as static as this view implies. So what Massey is advocating is a more extrovert and progressive concept illustrated through the metaphor of places as *meeting points*. This asks us to think of the world made up not of bounded places where things happen essentially locally but as networks of social relations where the things happening can only be understood fully by looking elsewhere – looking outwards as well as inwards. With such a concept, it is very difficult to describe the essence of any place 'neutrally' or objectively, for places are full of contradictions and complexities and are constantly changing. This is the deceptively simple insight we gain from the idea of interdependence.

This discussion is extended further and in different ways in the chapters on Place (Chapter 5), Space (Chapter 6) and Scale (Chapter 7) in this book. These themes are interlinked and taken together we hope provide a coherent overview of what contemporary geography is about – and specifically how these ideas are 'agentive', in the sense that they are not neutral.

Global citizenship

One of the impacts of interdependence, globalization and the increasing prominence of the global dimension in the school curriculum (DEA 2008; QCA 2009), is the inevitable linking of geography with the citizenship curriculum. Because geographical perspectives can help us understand identities and origins and literally our place in the world, they are vital ingredients in the understanding of citizenship.[1] This is especially the case in global citizenship education even though this is an altogether more controversial idea, for if citizenship is essentially concerned with the relations between individuals and the *state*, we cannot by definition have global 'citizens' in a legal sense (Lambert and Machon 2001). On the other hand, the term has taken hold in acknowledgement of 'the fact' of global interdependence and time–space compression: we live our lives in a global context and this has, in Massey's (2008) words, a 'power geometry'.

The Geographical Association's 'citizenship working group' is a group consisting of teachers, researchers and academics and it has been looking at the relationship between geography the discipline and concepts of citizenship (Cook et al. 2008). Thus, they assert that:

> Geographers study the making of citizens across multiple locales, political units and scales of governance. Geography therefore enables critical insight into ongoing processes of social, political and economic restructuring and their impacts on the relationships between individuals, states and societies. ... It empowers us to reflect critically on the conditions in which 'we' are made citizens. It enables us to rethink that which we take for granted, to unpack concepts and geographical 'facts', and to question the way in which the world operates.
>
> (Cook et al. 2008: 35)

In the light of the preceding discussion on interdependence and the global dimension, it is interesting to read how the group justifies these claims. How does geography enable 'critical insight' and 'empowerment' to 'rethink' (grand claims all)? Again, we can quote their words. First, the group is critical about how the National Curriculum for schools has been framed:

> (T)here is a problem with the prevailing 'geographical imagination' which underpins a national curriculum still embedded in the era *before* de-industrialisation, international migration and globalisation. Here, geographies move 'out' from the local to 'the full range of scales', which implies that places and environments are territorial and the unproblematic object of 'geographical enquiry and skills' ... The notion of the 'bounded territory' is central to all levels of the national curriculum – up to what is referred to as 'exceptional performance' beyond level 8. ... An appreciation of twenty-first century denationalized citizenship geographies requires teachers to adopt and work with an alternative 'geographical imagination'
>
> (Cook et al. 2008: 38)

It then goes on to specify how geography contributes to twenty-first-century citizenship alluding to the development of a geographical imagination that transcends traditional bounded space, echoing the 'progressive' and 'extrovert' idea of place advocated by Massey.

> Places are stabilised through a variety of devices (e.g. the nation-state) wielded by the powerful and modified through struggles of various kinds by the less than powerful. But if space is understood merely as territory, it is hardly surprising that political identities are assumed to spring naturally from such places – especially when they are bedecked in all sorts of symbols of presumed significance – a currency, for example, a flag, a monarch, a football team, a nation, a people, a 'cricket test'. ... In a world of ever-increasing network intensity, neither is it surprising that all sorts of disastrous consequences follow from such a static and limited sense of political identity. And yet, the alternative geographical imagination outlined above can enable students to realise that their

'place in the world' is *de-centred* along a multitude of networks rather than (at least partially and temporarily) *centred* in a set of territories. This alternative geographical imagination elucidates a notion of citizenship as relationally and globally formed. It recognises the open-ended nature of relations in geographical space. But this is quite different from the narrow absolutist notion of citizenship based on national-state territories practised in political relations and in the national curriculum for geography and for citizenship.

Geography as a discipline, then, cannot make citizens, but it can create the language and intellectual space for explorations of the meaning, spatiality and contextualisation of what citizenship is, where it plays a role and what future citizenship rights might or might not entail.

(Cook et al. 2008: 38–9)

This does not deny the relationships people often form with place, usually with great attachment. Massey (2008) does not wish to underplay this and takes it into account. But she simply asks whether a strong identification with place need be exclusive, reactionary and introverted. In this section we have provided an account of how a geographical perspective helps us see the limits of nation-centred geographical imaginations. Nations are of course important to learn about and doubtless their importance in society will from time to time be reasserted by some interest groups. Geography helps shine a light on some of the reasons why this may happen, which in some cases may be in reaction to the real processes of the global shift and the decentred geographical imagination this implies.

Development and developmentalism

The discussion so far has been suggesting that within the context of the global dimension a geographical view of interdependence asks us to consider, and perhaps reconsider, how individuals see themselves in the world – apart from it or a part of it. In this section we carry the discussion forward more specifically, to revisit a widely taught topic in school geography at all levels, development. The topic has grown in parallel with the increasing public and political concern over massive wealth disparities across the world – fuelled by the impressive lobbying from the likes of Oxfam and Save the Children in the latter half of the twentieth century. Development studies in schools has been colonized by geography, perhaps understandably, but it is worth noting that there is a full A-level (the examination taken by 18-year-olds in England) in development studies. Development is an important and popular topic. But as we have been arguing throughout this book, we do not feel it is viable to teach with a complex idea such as development without some kind of consideration of what the concept refers to; what it means and how it has been shaped over the years in the light of research and experience. Geography teachers, developing the concept of interdependence, may once and for all be able to avoid the 'error of developmentalism' that arguably still exerts an influence on the school curriculum. This section opens up this discussion by attempting to relate a narrative of teaching development in school with how the idea of development has evolved in the wider discipline.

Teaching 'radical development geography'

Many teachers' formative experiences of teaching about development in geography are framed by humanitarian events such as the droughts and famines that scourge much of the African continent. Famine was catapulted into the public consciousness by the BBC reporter Michael Buerk in 1984 and the public interest was reflected in the release of the Band Aid record 'Do they know its Christmas?' This was followed by the spectacular Live Aid events in London and Philadelphia. These events are still remarkably fresh, even in the minds of the students who were not even born then – the association of celebrity and fund raising for the poor and dispossessed is now an established cultural phenomenon, now taken up by Comic Relief. Of course, teachers often try to use these events to enable students to understand the 'deeper' causes of the crisis. For example thinking and planning at the time of Band Aid was supported by Lloyd Timberlake's *Africa in Crisis* which provided a fresh and powerful analysis of the problems and suggested the need to move beyond the immediate causes to longer-term underlying problems. Timberlake's book put environmental issues at the heart of Africa's 'crisis'. For example, the way in which prime agricultural land was used to grow cash crops in order to earn foreign currency, with the result that farmers were forced to cultivate marginal land (on hillsides) that was vulnerable to soil erosion. The 'fact', we heard at that time, that UK shoppers could buy strawberries grown in Ethiopia at the same time Michael Buerk was filing his 'biblical famine' report brings a stark new meaning to the 'fact' of global interdependence – and geography is able to reveal and explain some of the behind the scenes issues such as this.

As schoolteachers looking back on this period, it is interesting to reflect on the way development was tackled in our classrooms, and analyse what was shaping this. It was clear how easily students' genuine concern for the 'victims' of famine were shaped by the media, particularly television, and how this tended to be seen as simply the result of the failures of the rains (the immediate cause). Armed with the publications of various campaigning non-governmental organizations (NGOs) (such as Action Aid, Oxfam, Third World First), a fledging understanding of the academic literature on development, and the models of 'anti-racist' teaching practice about which there was considerable interest at the time (e.g. see Dawn Gill's, work co-editing the radical but short-lived journal, *Contemporary Issues in Geography and Education* and David Wright's (1985) publications of the period), lessons were designed that provided students with the historical, political and social contexts of Ethiopia (and the movements for independence in Eritrea and Tigray). Students were encouraged to 'deconstruct' stories in the press and the images and adverts that were produced by aid agencies. Line by line we examined the words of 'Do they know its Christmas?' ('where nothing ever grows, no rain nor rivers flow'), examined the contradiction of Ethiopia's record coffee harvests and the effects of deforestation and soil erosion on run-off, and discussed the limits of foreign aid and even the issues surrounding schemes to sponsor a child in the developing world.

The context for this approach to teaching development was, looking back, a reaction to two strands or ideologies in the development of geographical thought. The first of these was *environmental determinism* suggesting that differences in the wealth and well-being of people around the world could be explained in terms of the physical conditions of places. This has been a deeply influential and pervasive idea and although we may acknowledge (as in Chapter 10) that the *bottom* bottom line may well be the environment, the idea is totally inadequate to the task of explaining levels of development and well-being in the world.

The second contextualizing strand of geographical thought was the more recent *modernization theory*. Again, this became a textbook orthodoxy and deeply influenced geography teaching through the models of Walt Rostow and Gunnar Myrdal. Throughout the 1960s and 1970s geographers had taken up the idea that 'modernization' was transmitted across space through a matrix of cities and transport links. Diffusion theory became *de rigeur*. Poverty was understood to be a lack of development. Inhabitants of the 'Third World' ('less developed countries') lacked modern values and lifestyles and the goal of development was Western style, urban, industrial, market-economic progress. The 'radical' approach to teaching about development was a reaction to these ways of thinking about development geography. Thus, modernization theory was challenged by 'dependency' theory, which argued that the act of development in fact was about 'the development of underdevelopment'. This view was deeply suspicious of capitalism and its increasingly global operations and was also conscious of the negative backwash effects of colonial histories. Dependency theory held that 'Third World' nations should resist calls for greater integration into the global system of trade, and instead seek to follow their own pathways to self-determination.

Post-development geographies

There is, with the benefit of hindsight, a large problem with the above. Apart from the obvious pedagogic issues, for example, of it sounding like the teaching was directed to finding guilt and someone to blame for the victims of poverty (and by implication the students themselves were being asked to share some of this), the late twentieth century was a period in the development a new world-view or ideology – that of neoliberal economics. This was to become hegemonic by the end of the century. The notion that development might involve countries delinking from the global economy is no longer possible. This has led to a crisis in development theory.

There has therefore been a rise in what could be called post-development geographies. These emerged in the mid-1990s and have become increasingly influential within geography as an academic discipline. It is important to note that they developed from work within the radical tradition in geography, but looked to go beyond some of the categories or structural straitjacket, often associated with this tradition. We can explore some of these ideas through a discussion of some influential texts that make use of this approach.

The first is *Power of Development*, which was published in 1995, and was edited by Jonathan Crush. The focus of the book is on the 'texts and words' of development – on the ways that development is written, narrated and spoken. This means that the focus is on the discourse of development. In his introduction, Crush argues that 'the forms in which it [development] makes its arguments and establishes its authority, the manner in which it constructs the world, are usually seen as self-evident and unworthy of attention' (p. 3). This desire to try and make the self-evidence of development problematic was the result of three developments in critical theory:

1   The first was the so-called textual turn that has focused on the idea that our *representations* of the world are constructions or texts that do not simply mimic the 'real world'. Thus, development reports, theories and texts should be read critically, as texts – as one version of events.
2   The second was the rise of postmodern, post-colonial and feminist thought that have challenged the truth claims of 'modernism'. From this perspective development is a modernist project, and as such has a particular purpose and set of objectives
3   Finally, deeply influenced by Edward Said and his concept of Orientalism, has been the struggle within post-colonial thought to challenge the authority of Western accounts of the world and foreground alternative knowledges.

Power of Development (Crush 1995) was published around the same time as Derek Gregory's influential book *Geographical Imaginations* (1993). The idea of the 'geographical imagination' shows that particular ways of imagining or viewing the world become so natural as to appear to be 'common sense'. Geographical imaginations are constructed through the media and popular culture, travel guides and school textbooks. From this perspective, discourses of development have the power to suggest how the world should be imagined. To give some examples, it has become commonplace to see the world as divided into three worlds, or to be divided into the 'North' and 'South' as suggested in the 1970s by the Brandt Commission (1980). These become highly abbreviated but powerful ways of imagining global space, and global development organizations such as the United Nations (UN) or World Bank put forward dominant spatial imaginations of other people and places to provide 'truths' about successful growth, and 'miracle' economies.

The idea that development relies on 'geographical imaginations' informs Marcus Power's *Rethinking Development Geographies* (2003). The approach Power takes is influenced by the philosophers Foucault and Derrida. From Foucault he takes the notion of *discourse* and applies it to development. 'Development' serves to construct people and places in particular ways. It creates them as subjects and urges them to act and think in ways that will lead to their development. Thus, nation states are urged to open up their economies to adopt particular policies in order to catch up with the West. Individuals in this discourse become units of human capital to be utilized in the project of development. From Derrida, Power takes the insight that there is always another way to 'read' the world, always something other at the centre of development discourses that interrupts or challenges the dominant view. Development is a contradictory term that can be challenged and interpreted in unexpected ways.

These may seem difficult ideas to grasp at first. One of the chapters in *Power of Development* is written by Arturo Escobar. His argument is that development is an idea that links 'knowledge about the Third World' with Western power and intervention, and that it has resulted in the production of Third World societies. In this way, individuals, governments and communities are seen as 'underdeveloped' and are treated as such. For example, the World Development Report presents a definition of 'poor people' as the 2.8 billion people who live on less than $2 per day. Though the report goes on to point out differences in poverty by gender and geographic region, the emphasis is on this definition as the characteristic that justifies targeting 'poor people' with developmentalist interventions. The target becomes to move these people from $2 to $5. However, this construction of 'poor people' obscures the complexity of their relationships and identities. There is no doubt that this process of defining people in simple and one-dimensional terms is very often prevalent in geography lessons. In studying tables of statistics that point out the 'facts' that some are rich and others are poor (or studying maps that show the average gross national product (GNP) per capita) students come to 'know' that Bangladeshis or Africans live in 'underdeveloped' countries. They learn that they 'rank' higher. This leads to a particular way of making sense of the world with young people that is not entirely 'innocent'.

So what does a geography that seeks to go beyond these categories – a post-development geography – look like? Perhaps the most important feature is that it seeks to resist the idea that places are homogenous and people share similar characteristics. Instead, as we have seen in the previous sections of this chapter, and in Chapter 6, geographers understand places relationally, which means that they see them as constituted by multiple social relations that are stretched across time and space. The effect of this is to suggest how we are all implicated in the lives of others. For example, Freidburg's (2004) *French Beans and Food Scares* investigates the green bean commodity chain that links Zambia and the UK, as well as Burkina Faso and France. She shows how these connections have their roots in past colonial histories as well as contemporary cultures of 'good' food and locally specific food scares.

Another example of the spirit of post-development geographies is found in Rigg's (2006) book *An Everyday Geography of the Global South*. The term 'global south' itself suggests that the idea of 'north' and 'south' is no longer (if it was ever) meaningful when global social relations affect the lives of us all. Rigg's approach is informed by his concern that it is hard to think about or imagine the non-Western world without conjuring up images of poverty, underdevelopment and inequality. He explains, 'I wanted to extract the Global South from the tyranny of the development discourse and to examine the myriad geographies of the majority world unshackled from such associations'. His book seeks to start with the 'personal geographies' of people making a living, working, looking after one another, albeit in challenging situations.

Finally, there is an increasing concern to 'deconstruct' the categories that serve to suggest that the world is uniform and that economic and social change follows one trajectory. A good example of this is Williams's (2005) *A Commodified world? Mapping the Limits of Capitalism*. In this book Williams examines the evidence for accepting the idea that the economic relations are becoming increasingly linked to the exchange of money. This is the 'commodification thesis', which argues that more and more people are being forced to give up ways of life based on subsistence and sell their labour in a money economy. Williams finds contradictory evidence for this, and this suggests that there may be other trajectories for economic change, other ways for 'development' to take place. In simple terms, 'another world is possible'.

Developing development geographies

Some 20 years after the publication of Timberlake's (1988) *Africa in Crisis*, a new book was published as an update to this 'classic' work. It was called *A New Map of Africa* and noted that the crisis in Africa is the same crisis:

Chronic hunger and disease, war, abuse of power and poor governance still affect large parts of the continent. World market prices for many of Africa's raw materials are at an all time low, and most countries remain highly dependent on foreign aid. However, many of the underlying causes and processes that might lead to more sustainable development are much better understood at the beginning of the 21st century.

(Wisner et al. 2005: 1)

The editors argue that there is still a tendency to think of the continent in aggregate terms. Indeed the book's main contribution is to display a greater sensitivity to the range of scales of African development and the diversity of approaches.

What does this mean for geography teachers who want to teach development geography? Self-evidently, it is helpful to have a clear understanding of the genealogies of 'development'. As we have argued, many of the geographical concepts associated with development (such a 'modernization', 'globalization', 'take-off', 'post-development') are not neutral. These terms have histories, and understanding something about these histories, where the ideas come from and what purposes they serve is central to teaching about development effectively.

Not everyone is sympathetic to the arguments associated with 'post-development' geographies. For some, the focus on 'discourses' or the 'languages' and 'texts' of development seems to risk diverting us away from the hard and material facts of real, observable, existing poverty. They worry that it is perhaps no coincidence that 'post-development geographies' came to prominence at the same time as neoliberal ideologies that proclaimed the 'end of history' and the claim that there is no alternative to a global market economy. For instance, in his recent book *Geography of Power* Peet (2007) insists on the need to understand how ideas about 'development', globalization', 'trade', and so on are always linked to the material interests (money and power) of the powerful groups who promote them.

This serves to remind us that the development of development geography is certainly ongoing. Indeed, geography teachers who take up the challenge of teaching about development may find it rewarding to seek out the perspectives that come from other subjects too – how does development look from the perspective of the economics or business teacher? What do historians have to say about development? This is part of the excitement of engaging young people in the important issues of our time.

Conclusion

The fairly obvious fact that 'development' and the closely related concept of 'interdependence' are cross-curricular has in some ways been to spur to a relatively new academic field, that of 'development education' (Bourn 2008). This is a field that self-consciously declares that it is not well understood either in the academy or among the general public: in this regard, there may be parallels with geography itself! The DEA (formerly known as the Development Education Association) declared on its inception in 1993 that development education was about:

- Enabling young people to understand the links between their own lives and those of people throughout the world;
- Increasing understanding of the global economic, social and political environmental forces which shape our lives;
- Developing the skills, attitudes and values which enable people to work together to bring about change and to take control of their own lives;
- Working to achieve a more just and sustainable world in which power and resources are equitably shared.

(DEA 2006, cited in Bourn 2008: 3)

The first two points in this list, highlighting 'understanding', state aims that can be shared with geography. Given the emphasis we have placed on teaching for understanding in Chapter 4, it is worth pausing for thought. Understanding is not a given quality. *What* we understand depends to a substantial degree on what we bring to the task. Geography provides theoretical insights, constructs or frameworks which, as we begin to grasp them, enable us to see things in new ways.[2] For example, this chapter has discussed the nature and value of geographical perspectives broadening understanding of 'the links' mentioned in the first point above (through a geographical take on 'interdependence'). Other chapters have addressed other aspects of this list – such as Chapter 10 that discusses environment and the difficulties with the idea of 'sustainability' in an educational context.

What may, arguably, distinguish geography and development education is the trajectory given to development education in the second two points on the list. As we have noted in this chapter, geography 'cannot make citizens'. The DEA is clearly committed to certain values that underpin what it would regard as global citizens. Although many schoolteachers may share those values personally, they are not 'geographical'. But geography has a role to play that is to help us think critically and creatively about an interdependent world. In this way it is a resource that may be used by teachers to serve the aims of development education. Perhaps the key point is that 'geography' is not just the neutral context for development. A morally defensible geography is one that is ironic and knowing about claims to represent reality. It is concerned with much more than delivering the 'fact' of interdependence.

Notes

1   Citizenship has been a statutory subject in the school curriculum since 2000, introduced by a government concerned to address issues of social, cultural and political fragmentation and disengagement in young people. We prefer to treat citizenship not as a subject but as a political idea or concept – and like the many other concepts discussed in this book useful in the study of geography.
2   This resonates well with the Geographical Association's 2009 'manifesto': *A Different View* (www.geography.org.uk/differentview).

9 Cultural understanding and diversity: promoting community cohesion?

A central argument of this book is that geography education reflects, and responds to, broader developments in society. Nowhere is this clearer than in the inclusion in the National Curriculum of the concept of 'cultural understanding and diversity', which is an explicit attempt to promote aspects of citizenship. In the course of writing this chapter, schools were mandated to promote 'community cohesion'. For some geography teachers, this will be interpreted as an example of attempts to 'politicize' the teaching of geography, and our argument in this chapter is that if geography teachers are to maintain a critical approach to their work, it will be necessary to reflect on how the subject offers frameworks and perspectives that can help students develop their understanding of this complex and controversial issue. In doing so, we suggest that ideas from the field of 'social geography' will be invaluable.

Introduction

> Britain is more and more often portrayed as a broken society. Politicians, religious leaders, media commentators and academics appear increasingly convinced that the social cement that binds local and national systems together is crumbling and the established standards and values essential for maintaining civic order are collapsing around us. The demise of 'community' is presumed, by Left and Right alike, to be the key driver of this breakdown in society.
>
> (Flint and Robinson 2008: 1)

This chapter explores the contribution that geography teachers can make to the theme of cultural understanding and diversity, and specifically the subject's contribution to promoting 'community cohesion'. We start by exploring the genealogy of the concept of cultural understanding and diversity, and discuss its links with the more recent notion of 'community cohesion'. The following section focuses on the challenges of teaching about cultural understanding and diversity through a discussion of the theme of ethnicity. At that point, we argue against a narrow interpretation of this concept through the lens of 'race' and ethnicity and for a broader engagement with ideas from social geography.

Though we think the concept of 'cultural understanding and diversity' represents an opportunity for geography teachers, we argue that there is a need for critical reflection on the meanings that are attached to the concept. In our experience, developing intellectually robust approaches in 'real' classrooms is a significant challenge, and it is perhaps understandable that some geography teachers are reluctant to address issues of diversity.

However, we do not think this is defensible and this chapter seeks to provide some perspectives helpful to geography teachers.

Cultural understanding and diversity in the National Curriculum

For geography, the inclusion in the National Curriculum of the concept of cultural understanding and diversity is a new departure. Although it has been common to argue that the subject should play its role in helping students to understand the nature of life in a multicultural society, it is only quite recently that the National Curriculum states that geography teachers should now teach about and for cultural diversity. Indeed, the original National Curriculum established in 1990 was seen by many commentators as promoting a distinctly mono-cultural approach to the subject. This is a far cry from the revised National Curriculum with its 'identity and cultural diversity dimension', which explains that the concept involves:

> Considering how people and places are represented in different ways involves questions such as: Who am I? Where do I come from? Who is my family? Who are the people around me? Where do they come from? What is our story? This contributes to pupils' understanding of diversity and social cohesion.
>
> (National Curriculum for Geography 2009)

The term 'social cohesion' in this definition is significant, since from September 2008 all schools have a duty to promote 'community cohesion', which is defined as a 'society in which there is a sense of belonging across all communities, where diversity is appreciated and valued, and where there are similar life opportunities for all'. Given that community cohesion was not present in the lexicon of either urban theory or public policy (including education) before 2001, it is important for teachers to enquire into the origins of this concept and its relationship to cultural understanding and diversity.

Towards community cohesion

In 1997 a New Labour government was elected to power. After a long period of Conservative rule, there was, among many sections of society, widespread optimism that 'things could only get better'. Labour's first term of office was marked by initiatives to develop social inclusion, increased levels of public spending and a sense, for many, of increasing economic prosperity. The Labour government was re-elected in May 2001, and within weeks, a series of events occurred that threatened the rosy glow of New Labour's Britain. On a scale not seen since the early 1980s, a series of urban disturbances erupted in towns and cities in the north of England. These were towns with high concentrations of ethnic minority populations, and there was a serious collapse of law and order for several nights. Earlier, in 1999, the MacPherson report into the murder of the black teenager, Stephen Lawrence, had concluded that the London Metropolitan Police Force suffered from 'institutional racism' that led it to fail to properly investigate the killing. As a result of these events, the issue of 'race' was back at the heart of the political agenda.

The geography of these events is important. As Kundnani (2007) explains, the northern 'mill' towns of Bradford, Oldham and Burnley were the sites of post-war immigration from the New Commonwealth and Pakistan (NCWP) from the 1950s. This post-war migration was encouraged by the UK government in order to solve the problem of labour shortages in key industries. The pattern of settlement was closely related to these economic opportunities, and, as a consequence, subsequent processes of de-industrialization were closely linked to the emergence of ethnic and social segregation. Kundnani describes how, in the 1960s, Pakistanis had been recruited to work night shifts, which were unpopular with the existing white workforce. However, improvements in technology meant that the demand for labour was reduced, and production was shifted to the developing world. As the mills declined, entire towns were left on the scrap heap. The only future for the Asian community lay in the local service economy. This took the form of family-run restaurants, shops or takeaways, or, more riskily, mini-cabbing. Industrial collapse led each community to turn in on itself. The depressed inner-city areas were abandoned by those whites who could afford to move out to the suburbs. Others were allocated to new housing estates cut off from Asian areas. Those Asians who did find themselves on white estates were subject to racial harassment. The simple option was to stay in your own community. This was exacerbated by the mechanism of parental choice enshrined in the 1988 Education Act, which led to the development of a segregated school system.

Seen in a longer historical perspective, the 2001 riots can be seen as marking the point when the limits of an earlier model of citizenship and welfare were exposed and officially recognized. This can be seen in the report of Ted Cantle into the context of these events. The Community Cohesion Review Team published its findings in 2001 and, in an important passage, drew attention to the idea of communities living 'parallel lives':

> Whilst the physical segregation of housing estates and inner city areas came as no surprise, the team was particularly struck by the depth of polarisation of our towns and cities. The extent to which these physical divisions were compounded by so many other aspects of our daily lives, was very evident. Separate educational arrangements, community and voluntary bodies, employment, places of worship, language, social and cultural networks, means that many communities operate on the basis of a series of parallel lives. These lives often do not seem to touch at any point, let alone overlap and promote any meaningful interchanges.
> (Community Cohesion Independent Review Team 2001: 9)

In this statement we have a strong narrative of the events that led to the 2001 disturbances. That narrative is one of different communities living 'parallel lives', with the result that the notion of social citizenship central to the idea of the welfare state has failed to cohere in the towns and cities of contemporary multi-racial Britain. Consequently, since 2001, community cohesion has been an important part of urban and social policy. This focus on community cohesion is also found in contemporary education policy. For example, The Diversity and Citizenship Review published by the Department for Education and Skills in 2007 states that: 'We passionately believe that it is the duty of all schools to address issues of "how we live together" and "dealing with difference" however controversial and difficult they might sometimes seem'.

Similarly, the Department for Children, Schools and Families (2007b) guidance on the recently introduced duty for schools to promote community cohesion stresses that: 'Through their ethos and curriculum schools can promote discussion of a common sense of identity and support diversity, showing pupils how different communities can be united by shared values and common experiences' (p. 1).

These statements are indicative of the official story line that underpins the community cohesion agenda. Residential segregation leads to social isolation and limited cross-cultural contact, which allows misunderstanding and suspicion to flourish. The answer is to challenge the 'them and us' attitude and develop common goals and a shared vision, although the document also recognizes that educational attainment is related in complex ways to wider social factors:

> Whilst acknowledging the role of schools at the heart of their local communities, it should be acknowledged that schools face tensions and problems stemming from societal factors outside of their control and which they may not be able to solve.
>
> (Department for Children, Schools and Families 2007b: 6)

So far we have discussed how the idea of community cohesion can be traced to concerns about the relations between communities based on ethnicity. However, recent moves to strengthen the relationship between schools and communities is also linked to the challenge of promoting social inclusion, especially in those communities where educational attainment is low and young people risk becoming part of the 'NEET generation' (not in employment, education, or training) Schools are seen as central to improving links with their communities. As West-Burnham et al. argue in *Schools and Communities: Working Together to Transform Children's Lives*:

> Schools, like other institutions, find themselves operating as silos: out of touch and no longer an integral part of the community. Given this reality, schools cannot only be about the business of improving themselves; they also need to address this isolation and alienation. Schools must transform their relationship with the community. This involves changing attitudes, relationships and the deployment of resources.
>
> (West-Burnham et al. 2007: 13)

West-Burnham et al. argue that official models of school improvement cannot address the long-standing and enduring patterns of educational inequality that exist in Britain. Instead, they argue that schools must be at the centre of attempts to reinvigorate communities. This is to be achieved through the process of 'building social capital' (West-Burnham et al. 2007: 73). This represents an important shift in educational thinking, one which realizes the necessity of 'bringing together a diverse set of stakeholders to discover common ground through a democratic process, thereby developing social capital and reconnecting schools and communities'. For West-Burnham et al., there are four factors influencing educational success or failure. These are: the quality of family life, the level of wealth or poverty, the level of social capital in the community and the social class of the family. Social capital is defined with reference to the work of the US political scientist,

Robert Putnam (2000), whose *Bowling Alone* provides evidence for an apparent decline in the density of quality networks within communities. This definition emphasizes the importance of shared social norms and values, sophisticated social networks, high levels of trust and civic engagement (people vote, stand for elections etc), a strong shared sense of identity, interdependence and reciprocity (caring and sharing), and high levels of volunteering and community action.

While many of these features are desirable, it can be argued that they tend to valorize particular forms of social interaction and set up an idealized notion of 'community'. There is little doubt that community is meant to be interpreted as the 'locality', and that schools are to play a central role in compensating for any deficits. Increasingly within policy circles, it is stressed that education is central to meeting the needs of communities and the populations they serve. This requires that schools have a sophisticated understanding of the 'needs' of their communities, the challenges and problems these communities face, and are able to utilize and develop the resources and networks that exist in those communities.

In this section, we have explored the background to the drive to develop 'community cohesion' in schools. At this point it will be useful to acknowledge that there are many unresolved issues concerning this drive to develop community cohesion through schools.

First, critics argue that the community cohesion agenda 'represents the contemporary manifestation of a civilizing offensive through which governments seek to inculcate particular values and to reshape the morals and behaviour of the population' (Flint and Robertson 2008: 259). Given this, it is quite legitimate for teachers to critically examine the 'community cohesion' agenda and ask what purposes it is made to serve.

Second, the agenda has focused on cultural explanations based on assumptions about the motivations and allegiances of particular groups within society; for instance, the idea that people live 'parallel lives', that they blame society's problems on immigrants. In doing so, it neglects the wider structural processes that constrain the choices of individuals.

Third, there is a lack of empirical evidence how the dynamics of diversity are playing out in different localities. Indeed, research by Phillips et al. (2008: 84) conclude that the 'justification for a policy approach that focuses on "breaking down" segregation is, we would argue, rather shaky'. This is because (1) statistical indices show that the residential segregation of ethnic groups is not increasing; (2) it cannot be assumed that ethnic residential segregation is necessarily a 'bad' thing; (3) what is meant by 'integration' is highly contingent on political discourses and can be defined in different ways.

Fourth, there is a moral geography of 'good' and 'bad' places. The use of normative notions of social capital enables the construction of particular locales as 'problem' places. Communities, groups and individuals are poor and disadvantaged because they have not networked enough and have insufficient social capital. As Johnston and Mooney (2007: 134) suggest, what we have here is a 'rather sheltered middle-class outlook, a world of neighbourliness, painting classes, neighbourhood watch schemes, a world in which the community is responsible and self-policing'.

Fifth, the model is behavioural not political – the focus is on changing aspects of individual or group behaviour – urging people to change their attitudes and actions, rather than encourage political mobilization.

Sixth, there is little sense of history – no recognition that schools have always been linked with their communities and have been involved in work that seeks to create cohesive and functional links with the world around them.

In view of these criticisms, it seems clear that geography teachers cannot uncritically accept calls to promote 'community cohesion'. An alternative approach is to help students to examine the notion of community and explore the factors that serve to bring people together or drive them apart. An obvious place to start is to explore students' social networks within and beyond school. Inevitably, the notion of a single, homogenous 'community' is replaced by recognition of diversity and difference. From this starting point, geographical inquiry might focus on the processes (social, historical, geographical) that serve to construct communities and which can undermine them. Local studies can be usefully supplemented with examples from other times and places.

From no problem here to we're all white, thanks

The concept of 'cultural understanding and diversity' is most commonly interpreted as a call for geography teachers to acknowledge and recognize the fact of a 'multicultural society'. As the title of this section suggests, there is still a tendency to suggest that there is 'no problem here' and the geography taught in schools generally assumes that, in lessons on Britain's geography, the landscape is populated by a 'white' population, other than in the 'inner cities' (see Morgan and Lambert (2003) for an elaboration of this argument).

Geography as a school subject was relatively slow to rise to the challenge of teaching in a multicultural society. As explained in Chapter 1, from the 1960s geography was strongly influenced by 'scientific' approaches that stressed the role of objective regional description or, later, the production of law-like generalizations. As a result, it was not until the 1980s that the academic subject began to take seriously the geographies of 'race'. This was part of a more general shift in understanding. By the 1970s race relations policies had shifted from seeking to promote the 'assimilation' of migrants to the values and ways of life of the 'indigenous' population to a focus on 'integration' that recognized the existence of distinct cultural differences. One result of this was the realization that the development of a multiracial or multicultural society had important implications for education.

In her review of policies surrounding race and education since 1945, Tomlinson notes that:

> The urban schools most migrant and minority children attended during the 1970s were housed in deteriorating buildings, with high teacher turnovers, little access to playing fields or open spaces, and with a low-level curriculum, followed by low-level youth training courses with no guarantee of permanent work.
>
> (Tomlinson 2008: 53)

As a result of this 'problem', from the early 1970s there was sustained pressure on central government to produce national policies and funding to deal with the incorporation and successful education of minority children. The 1977 Green Paper *Education in Schools* accepted the need for curriculum change in a society that was now routinely referred to as multiracial and multicultural. It noted that the comprehensive school reflects the need to educate for a different sort of society: 'the education appropriate to our Imperial past cannot meet the requirements of modern Britain'. (Department of Education and Science 1977: 2)

Despite these developments, it is important to note that no national policies existed as to what a curriculum for a democratic multicultural society would look like, and official publications continued to stress the 'problems' of children from other cultures. The result of this lack of curriculum direction was that it was possible for many schools (and geography departments within them) to revert to the argument that there is 'no problem here', especially in schools where the intake was overwhelmingly white. However, some geography teachers who were working in the context of towns and cities characterized by processes of change and racial conflict and tension came to adopt a more 'politicized' approach that linked the fact of Britain's former empire with that of migration from the New Commonwealth and Pakistan. As a result, from the late 1970s and early 1980s a minority of geography teachers were actively involved in the discussions and activities associated with multicultural and anti-racist education. The most notable result of this engagement was a public discussion (which reached the pages of the national press) of racism in school geography.

The so-called 'GYSL affair'[1] was precipitated by Dawn Gill (1983), a geography teacher at a school in Inner London, who had studied how questions about race were treated in the major syllabuses taught in London schools. She was commissioned by the Schools' Council to produce a report about the problems of assessment in a multicultural society. She pronounced on the way that school geography served to promote racist ideas:

> It tends to use explanatory frameworks which fail to mention the trade relationships between First and Third World as a reason for the relative poverty of the latter; it presents the notion that third world peoples are responsible for their own poverty and thus implicitly supports the view that they are ignorant or stupid; population growth, if mentioned in the texts at all, is rarely linked explicitly with levels of economic development – more often with hints that the uneducated are failing to use contraceptives; developing countries are presented as places which are important only because they provide us with certain commodities; urbanisation is considered a major problem – its cause, immigration into cities; immigration is presented as an important cause of inner city decline.
>
> (Gill 1983: 13)

Gill concluded that the problems lie in the nature of geography as a discipline. She suggested that geography tends to be descriptive, but the explanations offered for the trends identified require interdisciplinary understandings. She urged teachers to ask whether geography should be studied in isolation from history, politics, sociology and economics. The reluctance of the Schools' Council, which had commissioned the study, to publish Gill's research sparked a vocal debate among geography educators.

In response, the Geographical Association set up a Working Party on Multicultural Education (Walford 1985). The report is set within a liberal perspective on multiculturalism. We can see this in a number of ways; for instance, the recommendation that 'teachers should be prepared to examine thoroughly their own practices and viewpoints and ensure that there is representation of different cultural viewpoints'. The Working Party's report effectively side-stepped any question of power in the discussion of racism. The report seems to imply that racism is something that can be overcome by making more information available to pupils and multiplying perspectives in the classroom. Prejudice is seen as an irrational barrier that will be overcome by better resources and knowledge and that is amenable to a treatment of liberal 'fair-mindedness'.

As we have argued elsewhere, the 'GYSL affair' can be seen as part of a broader controversy in education in the 1980s that focused around whether schools and teachers should adopt 'multicultural' or 'anti-racist' approaches in classrooms. These debates developed in the 1990s and beyond (again see Morgan and Lambert (2003) for an account of more recent discussions); however, they have not influenced the mainstream of discussion in geography education, as evidenced by the fact that Rawling's (2001) study of the changing fortunes of the subject between 1980 and 2000 makes no reference to the debate about multicultural and anti-racist geography teaching.

More recent approaches to the question of race and ethnicity within geography as a discipline have been concerned with the ways in which 'whiteness' has been constructed as an ethnic identity. Critical studies of Whiteness appeared in the late 1980s in the fields of literary criticism and cultural studies (Dyer 1997; Gabriel 1998). These were less concerned with simply mapping difference and more concerned with producing nuanced studies of the processes of *racialization* by which difference is produced. There was a tradition of interest in issues of racism and segregation in geography, but until recently few geographers had taken up Jackson's (1987) challenge for geographers to study the white institutions that generate racial inequality. Bonnett (2001) argued that the subject of geographical enquiry was still resolutely 'other' (i.e. geography tended to study exotic or other cultures). Instead, Bonnett urged geographers to examine the production of white identities.

Interestingly, Bonnett's early research in this area was on the different approaches to teaching about cultural diversity in schools. Anti-racist educators were concerned to develop approaches in areas where it was assumed that because there were few or no black people, there was 'no problem here'. Bonnett argues that anti-racists have often placed a 'myth of whiteness' at the centre of their discourse. Being white is a condition with some clear moral attributes. These include: being racist; not experiencing racism; being an oppressor; not experiencing oppression; silencing; and not being silenced: 'Thus anti-racism has been developed in white areas as a way of encouraging white people to rethink their attitudes to non-white people. It has not sought to enable whites to understand themselves as racialised subjects' (Bennett 2001: 127).

The result of this, Bonnett argued, is that it becomes difficult for white people to see how they might see anti-racism as a project in which they may have a stake. In this way, white ethnicity was made absent from critical analysis. Other educators have reached similar conclusions. For example, Mac an Ghaill (1999: 140) argues that, 'there is an urgent need to deconstruct whiteness in terms of identity formation and racialisation'. Mac an Ghaill makes this point in his discussion of his research in a school in the West Midlands. He notes that when he first arrived in the school he was told by some white pupils that the school is 'racist'. At first he saw this as a sign that the school's policies on multiculturalism and anti-racism were working. However, he later discovered that the white pupils felt the school discriminated against white pupils. He found that the school curriculum and buildings had many positive representations of African-Caribbean and Asian people, but little evidence of awareness of the existence of other ethnic groups, notably the large number of Irish students. Most notable was the absence of concern for the needs of white, English, working-class students. When Mac an Ghaill asked the teachers about this, they queried whether white, English working-class students have any culture.

In response to these arguments, some geographers have become interested in deconstructing the historical geographies of whiteness. For instance, as hinted above, lumping together whole categories of people as 'white' tends to ignore the complex heterogeneity of this group (e.g. the experience of the Irish or regional cultures). Nayak (2003) has attempted to expose the diverse geographies and histories of white students. The activities drew on family life histories as students traced their ethnic and social class lineage. The approach allowed some of the complexity of the terms 'Whiteness', 'Britishness' and 'race' to be unpacked and reflected on. Again, this is in line with the approach adopted in this chapter, which is to suggest that cultural diversity should not simply be accepted at face value, but that the ways in which these categories are constructed be examined in geography lessons. As Gillborn argues:

> If anti-racist approaches are to be fully effective across a school it is necessary for all subject areas to acknowledge their responsibilities and take advantage of available opportunities ... All subjects can make a contribution; if subject specialists decide not to reflect anti-racism in their classroom work this can send a powerful message to students: the school's wider commitment to antiracism may be undermined where students perceive some subjects to be 'neutral' or exempt from the need to challenge racism.
>
> (Gillborn 1995: 132)

Geographies of difference

> Once we accept that people have a place in human geography, then we also have to accept that they do not fall out of packets like so many green jelly-babies. They are sorted ('structured') by culture and class, age and sex; and yet how much of human geography continues to represent the world of the white, middle-class, middle-aged man as its 'ideal type'?
>
> (Gregory 1985: 63)

There is a danger that the concept of 'cultural understanding and diversity' will simply become associated with the issue of race and ethnicity. Against this, we argue that the inclusion of this concept within the national curriculum for geography presents geography teachers with the opportunity to draw on and develop important insights from the field of social and cultural geography. This is not simply a case of importing ideas and perspectives from academic geography, but is essential if we are to take seriously calls to develop an 'inclusive education'.

A serious engagement with 'cultural understanding and diversity' requires an examination of the 'models' of human activity that inform geographical teaching. One of the features of geography in the past two decades is how it has been influenced by and contributed to debates about how to conceptualize and understand the categories that make up the 'social'. Perhaps the key to this shift was the impact of feminism on the social sciences. Once the existence of a gendered geography was recognized, it was a short step to acknowledge other 'axes of difference', with the result that, as Jacobs and Fincher argue:

> Recent developments in contemporary social theory have intensified interest in issues of identity and difference ... Along with this enlivened attention to difference has come a new sensitivity to the processes by which identities are constituted and negotiated.
>
> (Jacobs and Fincher 1998: 1)

The post-war settlement that emerged after 1945 was based around a model of universal citizenship. The state undertook to ensure that health, social security and education would be available to all. This was the promise of the Beveridge Report of 1942. Following the removal of austerity measures in the early 1950s, Britain experienced a period of full employment, expanded welfare provision and a programme of large-scale house building. However, in the face of social and cultural change through the 1960s and 1970s, this tradition of 'welfarism' was criticized on the grounds that its 'ideal' citizen was in fact an able-bodied, white, male worker, and that those who deviated from this norm were unable to access the full range of welfare goods. Another way of putting this is to say that it was increasingly recognized that the welfare settlement was predicated on assumptions about what was the 'normal' or 'natural' way to live, and that critiques of this model stressed that there was nothing natural about the nuclear family, about a set of gender relations that assumed that men would work and women stay at home, or that black or disabled people would assume the role of 'second-class citizens'. Throughout the 1970s and 1980s, and through the actions of what sociologists call the 'new social movements', there were attempts to 'denaturalize' these social categories and show that they reflected aspects of cultural politics. An earlier, exclusive focus on social class was joined by the dimensions of ethnicity, gender, sexuality and disability.

This is the important context for understanding how and why human geographers became more and more interested in questions of social and cultural diversity. In the 1970s, in the face of economic slowdown and the so-called 'rediscovery of poverty', many geographers became interested in the classic problem of welfare geography – who gets what, where and why. While early approaches to this problem were largely conducted through the process of mapping the spatial distribution of phenomena, the highly politicized context of the 1980s meant that many geographers in universities became influenced by the critical perspectives in the social sciences. These arguments saw the problem of welfare as one that required an understanding of how the state operated to oppress and marginalize minority groups. Aspects of identity such as race, gender, sexuality and disability were seen as political and social constructions. As a result of this, social geography has become increasingly concerned to understand how society and space are mutually constituted.

The result of these developments is that social and cultural geographers have become increasingly focused on questions of difference and diversity. In particular, they question the idea that social categories (such as 'male', 'female', 'old', 'young' and so on) are natural and can be simply classified and mapped, and focus instead on the processes by which these categories are constructed in and through space. It is not common to find this type of approach in geography teaching, where it is rare to examine the different ways in which space is socially constructed.

In concluding this chapter, we want to discuss the implications of using the concept of cultural understanding and diversity in the construction of geography education. It seems to us that our answers to these questions will depend on the meaning we attach to the word *understanding*. The trap that most teaching of social geography in schools falls into is that of spatial fetishism, by which we mean the tendency to explain complex social processes in terms of spatial concepts. The result is a focus on low-level mapping and/or simplistic and one-dimensional explanations for spatial patterns. There is no 'set' curriculum or body of knowledge that can inform planning for teaching about cultural understanding and diversity. There are intellectual frameworks, which are more or less useful in making sense of the diverse patterns on the map. Social geography provides resources for understanding these issues, as the following example illustrates.

Who dies of what, where *and why?*

The Grim Reaper's Road Map: An Atlas of Mortality in Britain provides a useful way to think about the issues involved in teaching about cultural understanding and diversity. This publication asks the question, *who dies of what, where?*

> This is an atlas of death. On these pages we show how death came to people on one small island over the course of some 24 years ... Each of our individual deaths cannot be predicted with great accuracy. However, collectively, mortality rates and variation by cause are known to be strongly patterned, according to our age, sex, when and where we were born, where we have moved to, the jobs we have done or not done, rewards we did or did not receive, and all the myriad environmental, social and economic 'insults' and benefits that our minds and bodies have suffered or rejoiced in.
>
> (Shaw et al. 2008: ix)

There are 99 'official' causes of death, and the atlas provides maps for them all, showing where people in a particular place are more likely to die from that cause. They reveal some interesting patterns:

- The *murder* map reveals a concentration of higher murder rates in Scotland, especially on the west coast, one part of Liverpool and one neighbourhood in South London. There is a strong age–sex bias, with higher rates among males, and those aged 15–65.
- The *transport* deaths map shows that there are lower than average death rates in London, the Welsh valleys, many south coast towns, the west midlands, and cities of the north west, Sheffield and Newcastle. Higher rates are found in the far

north of Scotland and the outer Home Counties ring. Again, there is a strong male bias, and death from this cause is more likely between the ages of 15–29.

- Higher rates of *suicide* are found in the central areas of cities such as London, Brighton, Manchester and Glasgow, as well as remote northern parts of Scotland. Lower rates are found in affluent parts of southern England. Once more, this cause is more prevalent among males aged 15–60.

- Deaths rates from *infections* are twice the national average in most of Inner London, inner Glasgow, parts of Edinburgh, Manchester, Middlesbrough and Birmingham. There is a strong rural–urban gradient in rates of deaths from this cause to the extent that rates are four times lower in remote rural areas.

- *Cancer* accounts for about 25 per cent of all deaths, of which one-quarter of cases are lung cancer. There is no significant difference between males and females. However, there is a strong, north–south divide, with clusters of above-average rates in northern cities, especially Glasgow.

- *Cardiovascular disease* accounts for 44.5 per cent of all deaths, of which more than half are from heart attacks or coronary heart disease. The risks of dying from this cause increase as you move north and into large cities, and peak in the very centre of Glasgow. The lowest rates are found in parts of Oxford and Reading, Surrey, west London by the banks of the Thames and in the 'commuter belts' between Bristol and Southampton.

This is a 'cartography of distress' if we have ever seen one. However, its role as a piece of social geography is crucial, and of course, it illustrates the challenge of teaching for 'cultural understanding and diversity'. As the authors note, this is not an atlas for undertakers who need to know where the greatest numbers of people die. It is about the health of us all. Simply looking at these patterns and beginning to think about the underlying reasons for them takes us into some complex social processes.

For example, how can we begin to explain gender differences, and the fact that young men are more likely to die violent, premature deaths, as well as their disproportionate involvement in traffic accidents? What is the relationship between poverty and premature deaths (and, vice versa, wealth and longevity)? This is particularly significant in a society where 'absolute' poverty no longer exists, and which offers the message that individuals are responsible for their own health. Some of these patterns appear to be linked to the type of places in which we live: is the countryside healthier than towns and cities? Is this true for all groups?

Conclusion

The maps found in *The Grim Reaper's Road Atlas* prompt many questions that could form the basis for exploring the concept of 'cultural understanding and diversity'. In line with the argument in this chapter, an understanding of aspects of diversity in relation to health requires an understanding of social processes that are influenced by and shape places and spaces. Mapping the causes of health problems is the starting point for enquiry, but understanding and attempting to explain the patterns mapped invariably requires knowledge of aspects of economic, social, cultural and political processes. This example also prompts the question of the *utility* of this knowledge. As Harvey (1973) once argued, perhaps we do not need any more studies that 'map man's inhumanity to man'. Instead, the point is to improve the quality of our geographies, as Del Casino (2009: 281) suggests, geographers: 'can further implode the notion that the individual is somehow distinct from society and that those far away are somehow less significant than those close by.'

Notes

1   GYSL is an acronym for Geography for the Young School Leaver.

10 Environment, sustainability and futures

To many geography teachers the conceptual contents of this chapter go to the real, substantial core of the subject in schools. If sustainable development rests on the three pillars of economic security, social justice and environmental quality, then pretty well the same case can be made for geography. Geography, particularly in education, often claims its strength is in 'unifying' the physical and the human worlds, or 'synthesizing' the environmental and social realms. In one sense this chapter provides substance to those claims by carefully unpacking the ideas such as nature and environment and showing the origins of 'social nature'. The chapter refuses to accept too easily the part that 'sustainable development' (an idea identified as 'key' to school geography in the state National Curriculum) can play to guide or even rejuvenate geography with a renewed sense of purpose. Instead, we argue that the idea is very difficult to use in the classroom, and we contend that what geographical study may bring is some critical distance to it. Interestingly, the QCA's 2009 guidance on Sustainable Development, a companion booklet to the 2007 QCA guidance on the Global Dimension, has surprisingly little geography in it. This does not mean, of course, that brilliant work is not possible in geography classrooms, as this chapter goes on the argue – using the language of environment critically with young people and encouraging futures thinking with them.

Introduction: ethical and political perspectives

> The key point is this: the skills, aptitudes and attitudes that were necessary to industrialise the Earth are not the same as those that are needed now to heal the Earth, or to build durable economies and good communities.
>
> (Orr 1999a: 232)

In this chapter we are going to explore the small constellation of concepts that often become conflated to become the complex idea of *sustainable development*, as has happened in the list of 'key concepts' in the 2008 National Curriculum revised geography programme (QCA 2008). Thus, we see in the QCA's guidance publication:

> Identified as one of the key concepts in the geography national curriculum, *'environmental interaction and sustainable development'*, geography teachers can be expected to take on and develop their teaching schemes accordingly. For example, through their geography lessons pupils will:
> - develop their understanding of climate, and use this knowledge to analyse the evidence of current climate change and projections for the future;
> - study how a growing economy in the UK and, for example, the rapid

economic growth of India and China place pressure on sustainable use of resources;

- analyse global patterns of population growth and resource use and within the context of globalization consider the challenge of sustainable development at the national and international scales;
- investigate first hand their neighbourhood's environmental quality and consider the social and economic factors that effect its quality and the actions necessary to improve it.

(QCA 2009)

The widespread 'endorsement' of sustainable development – in the National Curriculum itself, by the government's curriculum agency and by the leaders of the UK's leading organizations for geography – is essentially a political act. Thus, taking each in turn:

- *The government* of the day want to harness the publicly funded education system to help service the political goal of providing information and hopefully influencing public opinion (the Secretary of State at the time of the launch of the new curriculum was quite explicit about this, that young people would be in a position to influence their parents' thinking and behaviour in relation to their carbon footprints).
- *The QCA* on the other hand, see sustainable development (and related ideas such a global dimension) as unifying big ideas or grand themes to provide some 'coherence' and applied relevance to the school curriculum.
- *The GA*, representing school geography as a subject discipline, have a felt need to express the contribution that geography is able to make to the understanding of the idea (e.g. Grimwade et al. 2000) – including, as we shall see more extensively in this chapter, a critical awareness of its limits and potentials.

None of these political motives need be seen cynically, although each in its way demonstrates attempts at strategic thinking and intervention. If you agree with the prominent environmentalist, David Orr, in the opening quotation, then you might welcome the adoption of sustainable development as a key idea, because you may see the potential for unsettling and perhaps breaking up the hold that 'traditional' (and Western) subject knowledge has on the school curriculum – and on which Orr heaps blame:

Towards the natural world, this education system, like that which produced the butchers of the Holocaust, emphasises theories, not values; abstraction rather than consciousness; neat answers instead of questions; and technical efficiency over conscience.

(Orr 1999b: 166)

On the other hand, you may have a different view. Standish (2009) for example is deeply suspicious of the position adopted by Orr and others who embrace the 'ethical turn' in education whereby 'values' usurp 'knowledge and understanding'. The ethical curriculum, he argues, is 'designed entirely' (p. 41) to engage young people in a focus on their own personal response to – and responsibility for resolving – environmental crises or following Al Gore's lead, the 'planetary emergency' (Gore 2006). Standish is highly critical therefore of the geography curriculum being utilized for political purposes. Drawing on Marsden's analyses in the 1990s, which showed how rigorous disciplined enquiry can be lost when education processes and/or social purposes dominate (Marsden 1997), and bolstered by the Civitas critique that talked about the 'corruption of the curriculum' (Whelan 2007), Standish explains that:

> ... beneath the rhetoric of empowerment, social justice, citizenship education and personal transformation lies a strong moral imperative with authoritarian consequences. The new ethical geography may superficially present itself as more enlightened and considerate of non-Western cultures than previous curricula with their Western-centrism, yet behind this veil of tolerance lies a new intolerance. The new ethical geography curriculum does not allow young people to develop their own moral compass; instead the issues and questions presented to students are designed to reinforce some strong contemporary moral messages. These are based around the ideas of environmentalism (etc).
>
> (Standish 2009: 40)

The purpose of this chapter is not to adjudicate between these positions. We acknowledge from the start that these are fundamental issues that have their resolution in what we think education itself is for – a discussion that lies beyond the scope of this book. However, neither can we ignore these debates. As with 'diversity' and 'cultural cohesion' (Chapter 9), when it comes to 'sustainable development' school geography has an inescapable contribution to make. Indeed, geography as a school subject has for at least 30 years more or less adopted the study of 'economic development' (see Chapter 8) and 'environment' into its mainstream. The question that interests us here is how 'carefully' the subject has managed to integrate these ideas (see Morgan and Lambert 2005: 157-8, 62–5 for a discussion of 'moral carelessness' in geography teaching), including sustainable development. To do this, we need to examine the ideas themselves, especially how they continue to evolve and change as academics shed new light and produce new ways to see.

Not least, and notwithstanding Standish's observations, we emphasize that the 'ethical turn' in geography is of enormous significance. While sympathetic to some of the warnings sounded by Standish and aware of the dangers of 'careless' teaching, one of the main arguments we make is that teachers of geography in schools today need to take into account the role of values, ethics and morality: it is an historical shift. One of the major developments in geography in recent years is the realization that knowledge production is neither neutral nor value-free (e.g. Castree 2005; Kobayashi and Proctor 2003; Proctor and Smith 1999). When we teach geography in schools, therefore, we are to a greater or lesser degree inducting young people into ways of knowledge-making, not a given or predetermined window on the world. Teaching geography well is careful *not* to provide a moral code or right and wrong 'that encourages them to consume less, have fewer children, take public transport rather than drive cars, be less money grabbing, support charities and so forth' (Standish 2009: 41), for that is not a moral education (it is more like indoctrination). Moral education 'is concerned with the ways in which individuals and groups make judgements about right and wrong. This is not (about) teaching *what* is right or wrong but *how to make* worthwhile distinctions' (Morgan and Lambert 2005: 154, our emphasis). Geography is a discipline and a body of knowledge, therefore, that teachers can use and engage with as a resource to contribute to this goal. Clarifying the conceptual landscape, which this book attempts to do, makes a crucial contribution to this task.

Sustainable development: a short reprise

Elliot (1999) asserts that 'understanding the characteristics of successful sustainable development projects will be essential for meeting the ongoing and evolving challenges worldwide of balancing present needs against those of the future' (p. 1). She goes on to say that when she was writing there were at least 70 definitions of sustainable development in circulation. It has a genealogy that we will attempt to trace, partly by going back to its roots through the ideas of *development* (see Chapter 8) and *environment*, both of which are indisputably core elements of geographical thought and enquiry. As Figure 10.1 shows, the third pillar of sustainable development (after economic security and environmental quality) is social justice, an idea we deal with to some extent in Chapter 9. Because most definitions of sustainable development take in the idea of inter-generational responsibility, we are also in the chapter going to examine the place of *futures* study in the geography curriculum. This will draw heavily from the writings of David Hicks who has stated that geography is a good subject context in which to ask young people to think about futures, and that geography was the first curriculum subject to begin to take futures thinking seriously (Hicks 2007).

But before embarking on this account, we should spend a little time on sustainable development in order to capture some of the profound disputes concerning this almost ubiquitous 'twenty-first century idea'.

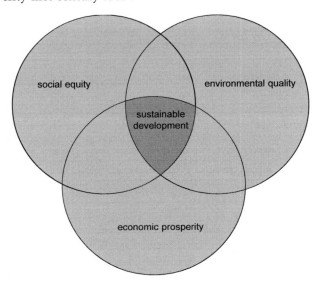

Figure 10.1   A simple model of sustainable development

Perhaps the most enduring definition is that used by the World Commission on Environment and Development (WCED) in 1984, produced the Bruntland Report (WCED 1987). According to Bruntland, sustainable development is 'Development that meets the needs of the present without compromising the ability of future generations to meet their own needs' (p. 43). This definition has been adopted widely in the school curriculum. In one school textbook, for example, aimed at primary and younger secondary-age pupils, we can read that the idea of sustainable development suggests that:

> ... the environment will be damaged if economic development continues without giving thought to how it might affect the future. It emphasizes the need to balance social development with the way in which the environment and economies develop, so that what happens now will not jeopardize the future. Sustainable development is now recognized as critical for the future of the planet.
>
> (Brownlie Bojang 2008: 13)

The profound challenges in this idea are becoming well recognized, though barely even acknowledged in a school text such as this. In the long term we may accept that social and economic progress depends on the '*bottom* bottom line', that is the environment, as is strongly implied in this passage. But the difficulty is that restoring environmental resources, or protecting the environment, is difficult to accept with no expense being incurred to social and economic advantage.

Elliott addresses this dilemma with reference to how the idea of sustainable development has been interpreted in the literature. Redclift (1997), for example, has commented that 'Like motherhood, and God, it is difficult not approve of it. At the same time, the idea of sustainable development is fraught with contradictions' (p. 438), while O'Riordan (1995) has written that 'its very ambiguity enables it to transcend the tensions inherent in its meaning' (p. 21). But in the 10 years or so since these comments were made, has any further clarity been achieved? Possibly not, given the title of a more recent volume drawing from research on both sides of the Atlantic Ocean: *The Sustainable Development Paradox* (Krueger and Gibbs 2007).

Citing Campbell (1996: 312), this book begins with the affirmation that 'in the battle of big public ideas, sustainability has won: the task of the coming years is simply to work out the details, and to narrow the gap between its theory and practice' (Krueger and Gibbs 2007: 1). As they also show, it is not so straightforward. Swyngedouw sets the scene for the revision of any sense of security by destabilising the idea – indeed showing its 'impossibility' – in the context of contemporary politics. He writes:

> I have not been able to find a single source that is against 'sustainability'. Greenpeace is in favour, George Bush Jr. and Sr. are, the World Bank and its chairman (a prime warmonger on Iraq) are, the Pope is, my son Arno is, the rubber tappers in the Brazilian Amazon forest are, Bill Gates is, the labor unions are. All are presumably concerned about the long-term socioenvironmental survival of (parts of) humanity; most just keep doing business as usual.
>
> (Swyngedouw 2007: 20)

This echoes Redclift's (1997) point about 'motherhood and God', but it also takes us further. For what Swyngedouw is showing us is the impossibility of sustainability *as an idea* in the post-political conditions that exist today. At the risk of misrepresenting his complicated arguments, we identify three interconnected main points that are important to take into account when planning to engage young people in sustainable development debates: all these put flesh onto the 'post-political' and what this means.

First, is the claim that we live in an age of consensual politics, in which it seems everything is 'politicized' including the environment, but in a way that denies genuine conflict and which eliminates spaces of disagreement. What disagreements that are aired publicly tend to be false, or at least distractions, such as in the case of the dwindling number of climate change sceptics. And yet, Swyngedouw argues, questions of sustainability 'are fundamentally political questions revolving around attempts to tease out who (or what) gains from and pays for, who benefits from and who suffers (and in what ways), from particular processes of (the workings of capitalism)' (Swyngedouw 2007: 37). Questions of sustainability need then to be fully contextualized and properly located (and not talked about on a general level and in the abstract): what does it *mean* for these people living in this place and in these circumstances? Put another way (and linking with Chapter 7 on Scale), there is no such thing as a global climate change in the sense that you can be for or against it politically, but instead a million local climate changes of variable speeds and effects.

The second, connected, point concerns the concept Nature, or more precisely how natures are conceptualized (see also Castree 2005). We shall return to the idea of multiple natures later in the chapter in the context of 'environment'. Swyngedouw's (2007) main point however is to signal the debilitating effect of the tendency to reify Nature as a singular entity with particular properties: it is, for example, assumed to be harmonious and 'in balance'. This requires us to think that we must protect Nature, or at least manage it 'properly'. This view of Nature also allows us to imagine environmental apocalypse by climate, disease or 'natural' hazard, which is a true sign of the post-political condition: we are disabled by this imaginary.

This brings us to the third point which, again, is closely connected. Realizing a genuinely viable concept of sustainable development means, first and foremost, rediscovering the economic domain in geography. We do not mean classic models of industrial location that tend to be static and evoke the politics and economics of the past, but building on the long-established question of 'who gets what, where, and why?' This requires attention in school geography because it is the 'economic' that structures the processes that govern the geographical outcomes. Realistic decision-making exercises possibly form the key to developing and applying these understandings, whether in the context of a local planning issue or the question of a third runway at Heathrow. But in Swyngedouw's (2007) words, the key is 'traversing the fantasy that the "economic" is the determining instance of the political' (p. 38). Put another way, 'who gets what, where and why?' are political questions for which there are always disputes and contests and alternatives in determining the economics.

Sustainable development is an idea that should be addressed in school geography. The opportunity that greets us is to do so in a way that helps young people understand the political contexts that operate in particular settings: *who decides* on who gets what, where and why? Where does the power to decide reside? This is what we meant by 'realistic' decision-making exercises in the previous paragraph, designed not only to engage young people in active process-based learning, but to introduce them to instances of how the world is made through economic, social and cultural *argument* (see next section). Such an approach may reveal the values basis for decision-making, including people's attitudes to 'nature' itself.

As Proctor (1999) writes in his chapter 'A moral earth': 'The earth – at least the critical, thin life-supporting biosphere enveloping the earth – is now in many ways a product of humankind' (p. 149). John Huckle, who was commissioned by the Training and Development Agency (TDA) to produce a briefing document for trainee teachers on education for sustainable development (Huckle 2005), adds further weight to the values dimension. Huckle argues not only for the consideration of values as a variable to take into account in order to understand people's actions and society's decisions, but as an aspect of a teacher's identity:

> The meanings of nature, the environment, development and sustainability are central to the human sense of identity or being in the world. All are the bearers of multiple meanings and much academic and everyday knowledge. While the search for a single body of professional knowledge that will equip teachers to deliver ESD is unrealistic, the paper argues that all trainees should be exposed to sustainability as a frame of mind underpinned by values that support the development of both human and non-human nature.
>
> (Huckle 2005: 1)

This, for some, may be a step too far as we have already seen. On the one hand, like motherhood and apple pie, how can we *not* support sustainable development? On the other hand, if Huckle wants teachers to promote particular ways of seeing the world we are in danger of teaching for a 'good cause' and indoctrination rather than education. In fact, Huckle's advocacy of a sustainability 'frame of mind' is not to promote certain 'answers' but to enable effective democratic participation, an ideal entirely congruent with the notion of argument developed later in this chapter and education for 'capability' discussed in Chapter 4.

Environment, environmentalism and the culture of argument

'Environment' is a much used term today and a part of public discourse. It is a modern term in the sense that it was little used until the second half of the twentieth century. It is often 'claimed' by geographers, but mistakenly, for it is an idea that now transcends usual disciplinary boundaries: it belongs to practically every discipline and to none. In this section we are going to (albeit briefly) examine the place of environment in topical discourse and the role of geography in schools to help prepare young people to take an intelligent part.

For many 'environment' is synonymous with nature, or the natural surroundings. Others see it as having a human dimension, as in the 'built environment' of cities, for example, or in ecological studies emphasizing people–environmental 'interrelationships'. Some academics, particularly since the cultural turn in geography, are prepared to accept that the traditional dualism of 'man and nature' is actually hard to justify. There are partly philosophical reasons for this, for as Castree (2005) discusses at length, nature is a concept that can apply equally well to the human and non-human domains. In geographical enquiry, there are physical geographers, human geographers and a smaller group of environmental geographers with different disciplinary traditions and practices, but all of whom are in the business of producing knowledge as 'representations of nature' (p. 33). He goes on to write, perhaps rather provocatively for some tastes, that

> ... knowledges of nature are not the same as nature itself, even though they are always *about* those things classified as 'natural' phenomena. Geographers produce *understandings of nature*: knowledge, not the reality itself. It is an open question whether those understandings are true or false, good or bad, accurate or partial.
>
> (Castree 2005: 34, original italics)

Thus nature, like culture, is a large, ill-defined and wide-ranging concept that in effect can take on a life of its own. The physical geography part of the discipline tends to take an empirical science approach to nature, observing it and accounting for it, often as a system. Human geographers, on the other hand, tend to look through a human lens and are thus more perspectival, showing how nature can be interpreted in different ways often drawing from human cultural expression; for example, through literature, art or food, rather than claiming to represent the world 'as it is'. Perhaps the power of geography as a school subject is to show that different 'understandings of nature' are possible – and literally to keep an open mind so that understandings can be deepened, broadened and extended.

Environmental geography tends to see human activity as a component of, and as a mechanism in, the making of the environment. Human beings are therefore seen as part of what are called 'environmental issues' at all scales from local to global, typically to do with: the deterioration in atmospheric and water quality, soil degradation, biodiversity loss, population pressure, waste management and disposal, resource use and conservation and the big one that is climate change (e.g. Kemp 2004). At the end of his comprehensive textbook Kemp is abundantly clear about the nature (*sic*) of environmental issues and on human culpability:

> People are an integral part of the environment and, being responsible for the environmental deterioration that has occurred, they must also participate in the search for solutions, working proactively and decisively. Sustainable development offers the greatest promise, but it is also the approach that demands the greatest change in current socio-economic and cultural patterns and the greatest individual sacrifice. Success or failure in slowing and then reversing environmental deterioration will depend on society's willingness to face these challenges and accept the sacrifices or ignore them and suffer the consequences.
>
> (Kemp 2004: 406)

This appears to be a very loaded statement: we are apparently all *responsible* for environmental deterioration; we need to make *sacrifices*, or *suffer the consequences*. There may be truth in this, but it may not be helpful to load the study of environment with such burdensome ideological purpose. It may be useful therefore for teachers to draw a distinction between environment and environmentalism, which to be fair to Kemp, he does (see Figure 10.2).

In order to avoid geography lessons in school falling into an environmentalist trap, becoming, either overtly or tacitly, exercises inculcating environmentalism as ideology, we can gain much from the critical reading of environment, nature and sustainability by Castree, Swyngedouw and others referred to earlier in this chapter. We can also learn from an interesting and significant 'cross-disciplinary' discussion by George Myerson (and English academic specializing in rhetoric) and Yvonne Rydin (a geographer specializing in environmental evaluation and planning) in *The Language of Environment* (Myerson and Rydin 1996). The central idea is that language matters, which sounds on the face of it unremarkable. But they show that 'language is more than words' and that key environment words (e.g. global warming; unsustainable; overpopulation, etc.) should be studied in order to understand 'the arguments that are made through them' (p. vi). You might try reading Kemp's words again, quoted in the passage above, with this observation in mind.

One of the recurring claims in this book is the significance of argument. It can be considered a 'capability' outcome (Chapter 4), and one of the reasons that geography can claim to contribute significantly to the educational goal to raise pupils' capabilities is that it deals with the fast-changing, uncertain and in some ways 'super-complex' (Lambert 1999) world. We have maintained throughout this chapter the need to keep meanings open and developing, implying the need for geography education to resemble a conversation, dialogue – or argument – rather than the delivery of closed or predetermined gobbets of knowledge. Myerson and Rydin add powerful authority to this position, not least by juxtaposing what they call the 'answer culture', which dominates today (especially in schools) with its antithesis the 'culture of argument' that they see as a prerequisite of the new democratic culture they advocate to make sense of the rhetoric of environment.

There clearly is not the space here to deal with this in full. But even though written over 12 years ago, the analysis remains profound and is indeed timely. While recognizing that the answer culture is deep within us – and in some ways 'is admirable, necessary and encouraging' (Myerson and Rydin 1996: 208), they point to the reasons that it needs to develop and be dragged into a culture of argument. First, they show the fallacy of the 'information principle' – not only that it is impossible to reduce the world to information but the belief that when we have better or more information we can make better decisions (in 2008, the world's politicians, bankers and captains of industry had never had more information, and yet it seems not one predicted the full extent of the late summer credit crunch until in happened). The second and third fallacies are the 'therapeutic paradigm' (that knowledge in itself makes us better people) and the 'managerial paradigm' (that the world is manageable). Finally, they also question the 'professional rule' that competence in the modern world is locked up in specialized skills and expertise. They go on to say:

> Contemporary culture demands new ways of thinking, and particularly new
> ways of thinking about 'unsolved' problems. We need to outgrow the old

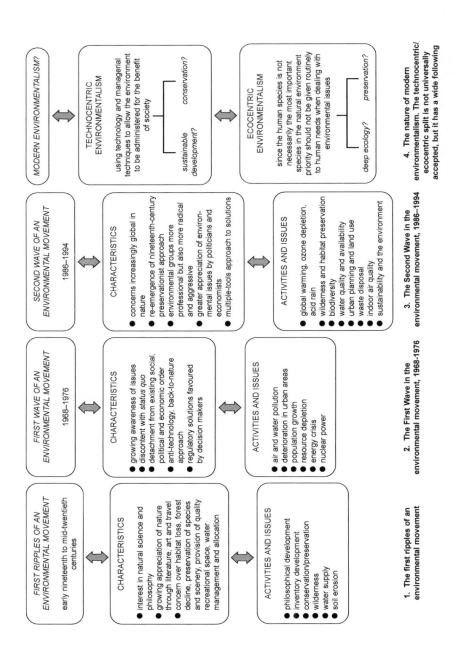

Figure 10.2 Three waves expressing the growth and evolution of the environmental movement and environmentalism in the late twentieth century. Bringing this to the present, it is probably correct to say that environmentalism is now more 'theorized'. Broadly split into the two camps of 'technocentrism' (an optimistic belief in the possibility of sustainable development) and 'ecocentrism' (aligned to deep ecology which, like the Gaia hypothesis (Lovelock 1995), does not necessarily see human survival as of paramount importance). Adapted from Kemp (2004: 16–21).

models, the models where truth comes to the rescue, where the viewpoints are gradually eliminated until only the right answer remains. ... (Argument) helps to rethink 'problems', to see them as arguable worlds we live in, rather than puzzles we design and dissolve.

(Myerson and Rydin 1996: 216–17)

This sentiment echoes the famous phrase of Peters (1965) who wanted us to see that to be educated is not to arrive at a destination, but rather 'to travel with a different view' (a phrase picked up by the Geographical Association in its 2009 'manifesto' for geography in education (www.geography.org.uk/differentview). In the contemporary study of environment, the classic Enlightenment metaphor of *discovery* is amended (in a culture of argument) to become *reconsideration*. This has implications for learning, but also for teaching, both of which will need to become more reflexive. Myerson and Rydin themselves are aware of some of the profound challenges, such as the not so small matter that people usually expect arguments to finish or be resolved in some way: 'If the argument is perpetual, it is disturbing, it seems "pointless"' (p. 217), perhaps even leading to environment fatigue and the fading of interest. The skills of the teacher, plus their conceptual grasp of the understandings they are trying to achieve with their students, has never been more important. Generic argumentation skills *per se* are indeed 'pointless'.

Futures

The twenty-first century is now well under way. It is now quite amusing to look back at the hyperbole that accompanied 'the Millenium' celebrations, the level of anticipation and excitement that greeted the dawn of a new century – and the inevitable anticlimax. The *New Statesman* carried an interesting editorial that commented on the 'veritable orgy of prediction' that took place (New Statesman 1999: 7), observing that 'the one certainty is that the future will take us by surprise'. It is worth quoting from the piece at length:

If it is futile to predict the future, it must be equally futile to predict that new forms of technology will have such-and-such an effect on society. Some writers suggest that the Internet is the quintessential democratic technology ... This is an absurdly over-optimistic view. The Gutenberg printing press – which made possible the rise of Protestant individualism – may have seemed to hold similar promise. Yet the succeeding centuries saw examples of despotism as stern as any known before ...

In short, the world in the 21st century, like the world in any previous century, will be what we want it to be. Ideas, political convictions, cogent arguments, faith, hope and charity (or their opposites): these will shape the future, not some scientist's box of tricks. Ignore those bastard children of Marx who argue that the free market or the mighty multinational or death of the welfare state or the genetically modified tomato is inevitable and irresistible. If we don't want these things, we needn't have them.

(New Statesman 1999: 7)

No one at that time – or as recently as mid-way through 2008 – predicted that the banking industry in the UK and the USA would effectively be nationalized in that year, or even that such a step would be possible to contemplate. The passage emphasizes the futility of even trying to make particular predictions. But it also, perhaps paradoxically at first glance, urges us to embrace the idea of choice and the possibility of making decisions that can shape possible outcomes.

It is for this reason that David Hicks and other educationists working in the field prefer to discuss futures rather than 'the future' (see Hicks 2001; 2002; 2007; Hicks and Holden 1995; Slaughter 1996), denoting the notion of alternatives rather than tacit acceptance of inevitable or taken-for-granted futures. The key is to develop ways to help young people (and indeed, ourselves) to think more critically and creatively about futures in order that they can understand their own lives in the context of their place in the present (see both Chapters 6 and 7 – on 'Place' and 'Scale') and their links with the past *and* future. This requires, as we have argued throughout this book, an *understanding* of social, economic, cultural and political influences that shape people's perceptions of themselves in nature, and in space and through time.

A culture of argument as described in the previous section is entirely conducive to the kinds of practical techniques developed by Hicks and others to bring about a futures dimension. In terms of realistic decision-making exercises advocated in this chapter, while we might be quite comfortable and familiar in using such techniques to help students examine 'where are we now?' and 'how did it come to be like this?'. What a futures dimension asks is 'where do we wish to get to?' and 'what ways can we imagine getting there?'

Conclusion

This chapter has tackled what for many is the obvious, core idea in geography, particularly if we define geography as the study of the Earth as the home of humankind (Johnson 1985). This is the environment. From the beginning to the end, however, we have not shirked the immense complexity involved in opening up this idea. It is impossible today to examine the environment as if it was separate from the social and economic worlds. Development is therefore a related concept and we have therefore examined the nature of sustainable development – a twenty-first century idea if ever there was one, and one that geography teachers in particular need to grasp.

This is not to imply 'delivering' sustainability education through geography lessons as if it were a stable, or even known, body of knowledge and skills. What this chapter makes clear, we hope, is that education for sustainable development is impossible within the confines of the answer culture that tends to dominate so much of school curriculum. We need to build and develop this concept of education, which is bolstered by the metaphorical expression of 'delivery', into something more resembling a culture of argument. The appropriate metaphor here is 'conversation' in which ideas about possible and preferred futures can be put forward, challenged, reconsidered and modified in a way that prepares young people to embrace positively choices and challenges that they will face as citizens.

PART 3
CURRICULUM CHALLENGES

11 Geography, media and education

This chapter explores the role of the media in shaping people's geographical imaginations. We suggest that knowledge of the world is increasingly mediatized, and that this has important implications for geography teachers, who routinely use the products of media culture to teach about the world. We suggest that perspectives found in media education are useful here, and outline some of the important debates about how media texts construct meaning. The second part of the chapter summarizes some of the recent claims made about how learning is being transformed in the face of the development of 'new media', and we conclude by offering some alternative scenarios for the relationship between geography teaching and media.

A world in crisis?

In the past two decades, school geography teaching has become increasingly focused on the scale of the 'global' and aware of the interdependence of people and places. This process whereby the scale of analysis has shifted from the national to the global is, in part, a response to the emergence of a series of 'global shifts' and 'global crises', and mirrors broader concerns about global processes talked about by scientists, politicians and the media. The result is that, for many of us, the parameters of existence and imagined horizons now extend beyond neighbourhoods and nations, cities and countries, encouraging a sense of the world as a singular, shared, space.

This consciousness of the world as a whole is constructed through various means but largely through the media. In teaching and learning about 'global issues' geography teachers and students are increasingly likely to make use of the products of media culture. For instance, news coverage of events such as the floods in the UK in 2007, the aftermath of the South Asian tsunami or Hurricane Katrina provides ready-made source material, and these are supplemented by material available through search engines on the Internet. There is no doubt that these materials serve to produce the impression that geography is a subject that provides students with an important 'window on the world'. Though there may sometimes be cause to examine whether resources are telling the truth or are 'biased', the idea that media products provide an account of reality is widespread. This chapter sets out to examine that assumption, and argues the case for geography teachers to develop a theoretical understanding of the role of the media in constructing geographical knowledge.

From this perspective, accounts of global crises need to be seen more as a reflection of the processes of media selection and dissemination than a reflection of 'reality'. Indeed, it is increasingly argued that global crises are not simply mediated (i.e. experience through the media) but *mediatized* in the sense that they are actively constructed and framed in particular ways by the media. An explanation of what this entails is provided by Cottle's (2009) discussion of the coverage of what he calls '(un)natural disasters'. Cottle demonstrates the existence of a 'terrible calculus of risk' in media coverage of disasters. He provides evidence to show that it is not the scale of the disaster that determines the amount of coverage, but whether or not the home country's citizens are involved. In addition, in most events there is a rapid peak of coverage followed by a decline as other stories are favoured. The focus tends to be on human interest and the coverage of local people. Cottle suggests that this reflects the geopolitical interests involved, as the media provides coverage from the perspective of its own nation.

But the quantity of coverage is only one aspect of how 'disasters' are reported. Cottle argues that there is a particular 'ritualization of catastrophe', which involves ways of representing the events. In the case of the South Asian tsunami, a familiar pattern of reporting unfolded. It started by focusing on the scale of the event, then the grief of local people, followed by highly publicized shows of community and solidarity on the part of powerful nations and ordinary people. Once more, this is all framed in line with dominant geopolitical interests (as in the case of national governments showing their humanitarian side to help those in need).

Cottle provides an interesting way of thinking about this process. He suggests that newspapers provided a moral infusion into the wasted human landscape – this allowed for a' recolonization' of space and place momentarily lost to the amoral forces of nature. It allowed for the construction of a global community and shows of solidarity. In other words, media coverage of this event was less about the disaster than the need to promote a sense that we are all part of 'one world'.

Not all disaster coverage follows this pattern though, and Cottle discusses the example of media coverage of Hurricane Katrina in New Orleans in 2004. He suggests that newspapers quickly shifted from the disaster itself to the social control issues that were raised in its wake. Thus, the victims of the disaster were forgotten and media portrayed the city as at the mercy of gangs of lawless black men who were looting homes and businesses. This was then seen as clearing the ground for strong law and order policies. The general framing was in terms similar to riot reporting. It stressed the stereotypical views of young blacks and ignored the many acts of solidarity and kindness that ensued in the aftermath of the disaster.

This example illustrates an important point about the ways in which our geographical imaginations are shaped by media culture. One response to these arguments is to suggest that geography teachers are in a position to see through the partial framings of these accounts and arrive at a version of what *actually* happened. The problem with this, of course, is that unless we were actually present, all we can go on are representations of the geographical phenomena we are studying, and these representations are constructed and framed in particular ways. This suggests the need for the development of forms of media literacy that allow teachers and students to understand the role that the media plays in shaping geographical knowledge and understanding. Accordingly, this chapter seeks to provide an overview of some important debates in media education and their implications for geography teaching.

The importance of television

It is difficult to overestimate the importance of television in shaping our understanding of the world, though of course this is a relatively recent development. Handbooks written for geography teachers in the 1950s make only passing reference to television, while Gospill (1956) noted 'It is not possible to give any considered opinion on the potential merit of television broadcasting in geography teaching'. (p 238). Murdock and Phelps (1973) explored the attitudes of teachers to television and found that many were fearful of its effect on young people. However, the widespread acceptance of television as a central part of people's experience had significant implications for all teachers, including geography teachers, because it blurred the boundaries between schools and the wider culture. In the 1960s a number of factors brought about a conceptual shift. First, the emergence of a visible youth culture, initially concentrated on music and radio. Second, as, we have seen, the emergence of television at the centre of domestic space. At first this was source of anxiety for teachers. However, as it settled into domestic culture, it 'became a source of remarkable richness for all teachers' (Goodwyn 2003: 5); notably, geography teachers who were well served by the variety of formats available, from holiday programmes that depicted distant locations, to crime series shot in inner urban locations.

We can speculate that many geography teachers were (and still are) doubtful about the educational value of television. However, from the mid-1960s there were important shifts taking place in education. These included the development of comprehensive schooling and the raising of the school leaving age, and the acceptance that schools needed to work with the experiences of pupils. This was reflected in the influential Bullock Report (1975), *A Language for Life*, which led to the movement for 'Language across the Curriculum'. It emphasized the value of pupils' talk: and invariably, much of that talk was about television. This focus on pupils' language also allowed for a greater variety of resources as objects of classroom study, such as newspapers and magazines. The authors of the geography book in the series 'Language, Teaching and Learning' recognized that:

> Geography teachers are generally aware of the importance of children's leisure-time reading and television viewing in their geographical learning ... pupils are just as likely to quote from what they have recently seen in programmes on television. Westerns, urban crime programmes, children's television programmes yield as many examples of geographically interesting phenomena as do documentaries. The geography teacher can use these experiences by encouraging the pupils to draw on them in their classroom discussions.
>
> (Williams et al. 1981: 27)

We would suggest that this statement remains the dominant position in relation to the value of the media in geography teaching. It is seen as a resource for making links with pupils' experience, stimulating classroom discussion and allowing for the elaboration of geographical concepts. In this approach, the media is seen as effectively a transparent 'window' on reality, and the value of the media is to make the subject come to life. This way of thinking about the media has continued to gain ground in geography education, and is reflected in the recent work of Durbin (2006), Roberts (2003) and Taylor (2004). Though these texts are likely to highlight that media representations are selective and may offer 'biased' views of reality, their usefulness as educational texts is undermined by their lack of any link to theoretical ideas from media education. The following two sections introduce perspectives from media education that can inform curriculum development in geography.

Teaching the media

In this section, we discuss one version of media education that became influential in the 1980s and focus on its implications for geography teaching in schools. In *Teaching the Media* Len Masterman (1985) argued that rather than being confined to the media studies classroom, media education should be seen as part of a general education that develops students' capacities for critical autonomy. Masterman noted the paradoxical situation in which: 'As communication systems and information flows become increasingly central components of social, economic and political activity at all levels, media education remains marginal within educational systems everywhere' (p. 1).

Masterman offered seven reasons why media education should be an 'urgent priority':

1. The high rate of media consumption and the saturation of contemporary societies by the media
2. The ideological importance of the media, and their influence as consciousness industries
3. The growth in the management and manufacture of information, and its dissemination by the media
4. The increasing penetration of media into our central democratic processes
5. The increasing importance of visual communication and information in all areas
6. The importance of educating students to meet the demands of the future
7. The fast-growing national and international pressures to privatise information
   (Masterman 1985: 20)

Some of the language used in this list provides clues to the position Masterman (1985) adopts towards the media. It is concerned with 'ideology', consciousness shaping, saturation and the 'manufacturing of consent'. His book outlined a method for developing media education, which follows from the first principle that: 'the media are symbolic (or sign) systems which need to be actively read, and not unproblematic, self-explanatory reflections of external reality' (p. 20).

In other words, the media should be seen as actively *constructing* people's views of the world rather than reflecting some pre-existing reality, and from this four general areas for investigation emerge. These are: (1) the sources, origins and determinants of media constructions; (2) the dominant techniques and codes employed by the media to convince us of the truth of their representations; (3) the nature of the reality constructed by the media, the values implicit in media representations; and (4) the ways in which media constructions are read or received by their audiences.

For Masterman, the role of the teacher is to 'demystify' the myths that the media presents as common sense. In an influential edited collection based on the idea of 'myth' associated with the French theorist Roland Barthes, Masterman states:

> We need to demonstrate precisely how and why television's representations are produced – by whom, in whose interests, using what kinds of rhetorical techniques, and producing what kind of consciousness – rather than simply accepting them as 'reflections', part of the way things are.
>
> (Masterman 1984: 5)

This is no easy task, since it involves developing 'in pupils enough self-confidence and critical maturity to be able to apply critical judgement to media texts that they will encounter in the future' (Masterman 1984: 5).

Masterman argues that this approach to media education should not be confined to media studies, but should be developed *across* the curriculum. The final chapter of *Teaching the Media* discusses the implications of these arguments for geography teaching, and remains one of the most interesting and thoughtful accounts of the role of the media in geography teaching. Masterman states that to argue for the importance of media literacy in the study of geography may seem, in one sense, perverse, since geography is a subject in which visual images have a particularly prominent place. He suggests that geography teachers should ask questions about the sources of information or images, selection, captioning and agenda-setting. Visual images are used to provide a short-cut way of making the world available to students. Too often, however, these images are treated as a transparent window on the world.

Many geography teachers would accept these arguments, but Masterman argues that there is a need to go beyond simply questioning the sources of geographical material. This is because the very substance of geography as a subject cannot be viewed innocently or transparently. Landscapes can be interpreted in a variety of ways, and we always interpret them through particular frames. These frames are not innocent, but often reflect the views and interests of those who promote them. For Masterman (1985) these images 'crystallise enormously powerful ideological values' (p. 250), and one of the cornerstones of media literacy is the ability to relate content to the interests of the sources who produce it:

> Functional media literacy could be invaluable in raising questions about the taken-for-granted visual illustrations which are used in all classrooms, and in encouraging teachers and students to treat school books and images not as transparent carriers of knowledge, but as culturally loaded texts which need to be actively deconstructed and critically read.
>
> (Masterman 1985: 250)

It is worth stressing the main features of this version of media education. To start with, Masterman adopts an *oppositional* stance to the products of media culture. He recognizes the media as a central element of young people's lives, but also as the primary means whereby the dominant ideology is imposed on them. He emphasizes the need for the 'objective analysis' of media texts and images. Such detached, critical analysis would enable teachers and pupils to identify how media texts are constructed and selected, and thus reveal their suppressed ideological function. Teaching the media is thus a process of 'demystification'.

This focus on the importance of media education was mirrored in the work of some geographers influenced by the 'cultural turn' in the mid-1980s. As noted in Chapter 6, an important contribution in this respect was Burgess and Gold's (1985) *Geography, the Media and Popular Culture*. The editors' introduction serves as a useful account of ideas about the media. Burgess and Gold point out that much early work on media was rooted in behavioural geography, with a simplistic and individualized model of communication. The important limitation of this work was that it tended to avoid the social and cultural contexts in which communication takes place. In particular, it relied on a false division between 'direct' and 'indirect' experience (this is mirrored in ideas in geography education about the value of direct rather than indirect experience). It denies the fact that in the contemporary world most images of places and environment are indirect. There was also a concern with comparing the images of places with the reality, without exploring the role that meaning could play. Humanistic geography ought, in theory, to have allowed for a more interpretivist approach to the media, but geographers were more likely to explore images produced in art and literature rather than the full range of popular culture.

The essays in *Geography, the Media and Popular Culture* are varied in approach. They include chapters that draw on a behavioural and communications studies approach, an article on musical lyrics that allows for the personal preferences of the author, studies of documentary tradition of films and landscape documentaries on television, as well as an article that explores the myths surrounding inner cities in the wake of the race riots of the early 1980s and a study of the effects of newspaper coverage of race relations. This was a landmark text that reflected the beginnings of the cultural turn in geographical studies. It was followed by Jackson's (1989) *Maps of Meaning*, which contained a number of references to popular culture and made use of media analysis. Since then, cultural geographers have contributed a wide range of studies of the products of media and popular culture.

Children making meaning

The idea that media education should be primarily concerned with 'demystifying' media products was challenged in the 1990s. One of the most influential figures in these debates is David Buckingham, Professor in media education at the Institute of Education. His (1987) book, *Public Secrets: EastEnders and its Audience*, was an analysis of the ways in which children made sense of the BBC television soap opera, *EastEnders*. Through interviews with viewers, Buckingham argued that there is no fixed or final meaning to the *EastEnders* texts. Instead, children read and made sense of the texts in terms of their own experiences and social relationships. In more formal terms, the *EastEnders* text did not contain a set of ideological meanings but instead offered a set of discourses that audiences made sense of through their active reading of the text. There are important educational implications of this, and these were set out in Buckingham's (1986) critical review of Masterman's (1985) *Teaching the Media*.

In 'Against demystification', Buckingham (1986) argued against an approach that sees ideology as something that is inherent in the text, and that 'real' meanings can be uncovered by the removal of apparent or surface meanings. Meaning does not reside in the text, but is produced by readers, who may interpret them in different ways. This has implications for teaching since it suggests that we should not see readers as potential 'victims' of media ideology. Buckingham provides the most succinct educational version of the wider argument found in cultural studies that see the question of 'audience' as key to understanding how texts are consumed.

Buckingham's work has spawned a wide range of classroom studies that focus on the ways in which students interpret and use media texts. A recent statement of Buckingham's (2003) position is found in *Media Education* that argues for a 'new paradigm' in media education. In the new paradigm, the notion of media as bearers of a singular set of ideologies and beliefs is no longer so easy to sustain. Though it is important to recognize that there are still limits on the diversity of views and cultural forms represented in the media, in general the development of modern communications has led to a more heterogeneous media environment. In addition, the idea that the media are an all-powerful consciousness industry has come into question. Children are a much more autonomous and critical audience than they are conventionally assumed to be.

The critical stance towards media is increasingly outdated. Technological changes are making it more difficult to prevent children gaining access to material and there is a move towards providing advice about media use rather than restriction. This is linked to a generational shift within the teaching profession, since younger teachers who have grown up with electronic media are more relaxed in their attitudes towards media culture and are less likely to see themselves as 'missionaries' denouncing the influence of the media and more enthusiastic about young people using the media as forms of expression.

For Buckingham, the new paradigm adopts a more student-centred perspective beginning from young people's existing experience and knowledge of media. Rather than seek to protect children from the media or lead them on to better things, it looks to enable them to make decisions for themselves:

> it aims to develop a more reflexive style of teaching and learning, in which students can reflect on their own activity as both 'readers' and 'writers' of media texts, and understand the broader social and economic factors that are in play. Critical analysis is seen here as process of dialogue, rather than a matter of arriving at an agreed or predetermined position.
>
> (Buckingham 2003: 14)

Buckingham argues that media education should be based around a series of concepts – production, language, representation and audience. In geography, we would argue that the selection of content is likely to come from substantive themes in the curriculum, and that the starting point will be that of representation.

The debate between Buckingham and Masterman was acrimonious, and revisiting the arguments in the writing of this book, we would suggest that they are unnecessarily polarized, and can be seen as part of a wider argument with media and cultural studies about whether texts were the carriers of 'ideological' meaning or whether viewers or readers were free to 'construct' their own meanings. The common-sense answer is that media texts *do* carry preferred meanings, and seek to 'sell' particular values and products, but that there is no guarantee that readers will accept the preferred reading. As

Buckingham argues, 'Readers make meanings, but not in conditions of their own choosing'. Masterman's position, that ideology is present at every stage of the production and consumption of media, still holds good. Some of the best work in the 'new cultural geography' has examined the ways in which films, television programmes and adverts use place and space to create an imagined geography. Much of this work focuses on the texts themselves, rather than their reception by diverse audiences. Geography teachers who make use of media representations will explore for themselves the appropriate balance between the ideology of the text and the active response of the reader in determining meaning.

Box 11.1

REEL CITIES

One of the most obvious ways in which geography teachers introduce media into their teaching is through the inclusion of clips from popular cinema. This is a way of connecting with the experience of students and also offering highly condensed visual illustrations of geographical ideas. In this chapter we are arguing for an approach which explicitly recognizes these images as productions, and which therefore reflect particular values and ideologies.

Gibson (2007) raises an interesting set of questions in relation to the representation of US cities on television. He starts from the observation that the cast photo from the series *Grey's Anatomy* is taken against the Seattle skyline, suggesting that the location for this drama is important. He suggests that 'establishing shots of glittering city skylines and vibrant urban street scenes proliferate on contemporary television – to the point where one might conclude six decades of rapid suburbanization have been abruptly reversed'. Gibson suggests that in recent years there has been a shift in how US cities are represented on television, with reference to a book by Steve Macek (2006) called *Urban Nightmares*. The premise of Macek's book is that during the 1980s and 1990s representations of US cities focused on the negative, dystopic aspects of city life, and that these were fuelled by and served to reinforce the idea of central cities as sites of crime, drug-dealing, violence and prostitution. According to Macek, these representations amplified conservative political discourses about the causes of the 'urban crisis'. Though such representations continue to exist, Gibson (2007) suggests that: 'American television now offers a new vision of the city as a bourgeois playground – a bright lights stage upon which popular fantasies of wealth, power and distinction can be indulged'.

So far, Gibson's argument is set within a resolutely standard framework of media analysis – one that draws on long-standing distinctions between city as heaven and city as hell (Short 1991). However, he then seeks to locate these cultural representations in the concrete political economy of US cities. He does this by linking these images to policies of urban 'boosterism' by which urban leaders seek to envision the city as 'a playground of upscale consumption and leisure', which is reflected in policies of gentrification and displacement. The focus is on nurturing 'loft living', subsidizing museums and performance spaces: 'Turn key neighbourhoods into real-life versions of *Sex and the City*, complete with art galleries, funky clubs, and sidewalk cafes' (Gibson 2007).

Gibson draws on the work of the geographer Neil Smith and his notion of the 'revanchist city' in which gentrification is an act of class warfare as the middle classes seek to reclaim valuable urban space from working-class residents. It is these moves that are central to exploring the cultural politics of media representations. In this way, Gibson prompts us to consider the question of what is the relationship between these images of cities and actual shifts in the political economy of cities.

Similar arguments can be made in the case of British films. Dave (2006) suggests that what marks the representations of class in the 1990s is the split between a fairy-tale world of privilege and an underclass world of working-class origins. This is reflected in a number of films that represent London as a global city. Thus, in the highly successful film *Notting Hill*, the central character is William Thacker who describes Notting Hill as a 'small village in the middle of London'. He adds, 'what's great is that lots of friends have ended up in this area'. In *Sliding Doors* the central character Helen tries to jump through the sliding doors of an underground train on her way home from being fired from her job in the City. There are two cuts of this – in the first she catches the train, in the second she misses it. From this point the film pursues parallel stories. One where Helen is consigned to the world of temporary and low-wage service employment and the other where she finds the strength to realize her creative talent and sets up her own business.

Again, it is possible to speculate about the relationship of these representations to the underlying material processes shaping cities. In the case of *Notting Hill*, much was made of the romantic representation of what is a mixed area of west London. The area has a long history of social deprivation and unrest. The Ladbroke Estate, with its communal garden, which is an important part of the film as the central characters aspire to living there as a couple, was designed to minimize contact with the poorer areas. In 1958 the area was the scene of Britain's first 'race riots', and the Notting Hill Carnival is an important symbol in multicultural London. This meant that 'even the most conservative of British film reviewers commented that there was something funny about a Notting Hill with no black people'. Brunsdon (2007: 115) suggests that the film works to 'add a formerly "edgy" area to the repertoire of city attractions', and Murphy (2001) argues that it belongs to a growing band of films that celebrate the pleasures of middle-class life in London. These films were produced at the height of the city's house-property price boom, which turned even ostensibly 'low achievers' such as William's friends into 'paper millionaires'. Indeed, Thacker's comments about how it is strange that all his friends have ended up living there might be better explained by geography teachers as an outcome of the process of gentrification. Brunsdon also reads the film as a mediation on the tensions involved in becoming a 'global city' as the central characters represent an 'olde world' Englishness and a brash US movie star. This is reflected in the way the film moves between Notting Hill and the West End. Films such as *Sliding Doors* and *Notting Hill* can be read as representations of wider economic, social and cultural processes. In this respect, Dave argues that they serve to resolve the contradictions of late capitalist society by papering over the divisions between social groups.

There is no final, authoritative reading of these films. However, we would suggest that their value lies not in simply offering visual illustrations of what actual cities are like (though that may be appropriate). Instead, the approach we are suggesting here is to enquire as to how such representations serve to offer particular narratives and interpretations of places and spaces. The films are best read in the context of social and geographical processes.

The rise of 'new media'

So far, this chapter has focused on film, television and newspaper coverage of geo-graphical phenomena. However, many people have argued that the development of new digital media has far-reaching implications for children and young people. The technical possibility of 'digitizing' a diverse range of different forms of communication is part of a broader convergence of media, in which the boundaries of between print, television and computer-generated media are beginning to break down. These are complex develop-ments. Hesmondlagh (2007) explains how they have been driven by the need to restore economic profitability since the 1970s and the deregulation of media and copyright regulations so as to allow innovation in the information industries. In this sense, new media must be seen as part of a move to a more market-led media system. This has implications in terms of who gets access to these new media, since they are not available to all (the so-called 'digital divide'). More optimistically, it is suggested that these tech-nologies enable the blurring of the distinction between producers and consumers, since anyone can potentially produce and publish material using technologies that were pre-viously the preserve of a small elite.

These arguments have important implications for teaching and learning, since it is asserted that there exists a new generation of children who were 'born digital'. That is, they have grown up around new forms of digital media and this affects their relationships to school and learning. The following quote is typical of the argument that the very nature of learning has changed in the 'digital age':

> Born and raised in a digital, networked age, these students ... are as much shaped by the dominant cultural logic of the early twenty-first century as they reproduce it through their creative practices and social interactions: they are members of the *born digital generation*. Their beliefs and assumptions about the way 'learning' occurs have been shaped by their early encounters with pervasive digital worlds and network technologies, and the ubiquity of 'smart' and responsive environments. They present themselves as just-in-time learners, confident that when they need to know something, they'll know where to find it.
>
> (Anderson and Balsamo 2008: 244)

This quote is reminiscent of Green and Bigum's (1993) argument that children are 'aliens in the classroom' and is reproduced in journalistic terms such as 'generation Y', 'the i-Pod generation', the 'Nintendo generation', 'the Playstation generation' and notions of 'cyberkids'. The idea of a generation gap is nothing new, but this time, it is suggested, the generation gap is based on a digital gap. Technology offers a new form of empowerment for young people and is producing a generation gap as the habits and preferences of the older generation are coming to be superseded. As Buckingham (2007) points out, from an academic vantage point, these claims lack scholarly caution and qualification, and the evidence on which they are based is unrepresentative and often anecdotal. Osgerby (2004) notes that all too often the experiences associated with new technology use – namely, new forms of social participation and interaction, informational access and knowledge creation – are overgeneralized with little or no account taken of the variety of other factors that influence young people's actions.

Despite these criticisms, these types of idea are increasingly taken seriously by policy-makers. One of the most thoughtful accounts to date is Lankshear and Knobel's (2006) *New Literacies: Everyday Practices and Classroom Learning*. Lankshear and Knobel suggest that we are presently at a point in the historical-cultural development of literacy where educators are struggling to deal with the 'new literacies' associated with Web 2.0:

> What seems to be happening is that the day-to-day business of school is still dominated by conventional literacies, and engagement with the 'new' literacies is largely confined to learners' lives in spaces outside of schools and other formal educational settings.
>
> (Lankshear and Knobel 2006: 30)

This is not to claim that new technologies are absent from schools, but rather that schools and teachers tend to use them in ways that operate within an old 'mindset'. For instance, the web page or PowerPoint slide show stands in for paper, pencil and crayon as a medium for presenting stories or work. The way in which schools and teachers seek to fit new technologies into existing practices is an example of the tendency for schooling to revert to the 'deep grammar' of schooling, which assumes that the teacher is the ultimate authority on matters of knowledge and learning. Whatever is addressed in the classroom needs to fall within the teacher's 'competence parameters' because he or she has to direct or control learning.

Lankshear and Knobel conclude that teachers (and the dominant models of teacher training) are wedded to an old mindset, based on the management of the physical space of the classroom, centralized authority and expertise invested in the teacher, an attachment to long-standing conceptions of teaching and learning and their social relations, the perpetuation of the book, and time-honoured forms of language practice like story-telling, recounts and reports.

The final chapter of Lankshear and Knobel's (2006) book considers the implications of these arguments for formal education which, as they suggest, has historically been based on the idea that 'the role of education has been to make available to learners the opportunity to master a range of systematic ways of understanding and engaging with the world that they cannot be presumed to encounter elsewhere' (p. 252). While they recognize that this is still important, they note that contemporary schools are failing in this endeavour for the majority of students. Indeed, with its focus on the 'basics' of literacy and numeracy 'skills', 'current education policy seems to be pushing elementary education away from anything approximating the kind of systemic/holistic mastery that young people get free in so many out-of-school discourses' (p.252).

Buckingham summarizes what he calls the 'new digital divide':

> ... we are witnessing a widening gap between the culture of the school and the culture of chidren's lives outside school. In their leisure time, children are encouraged to see themselves as active participants, navigating their way inde-pendently through complex multimodal media environments. Yet in school, they are expected to submit to a pedagogic regime that is fundamentally

premised on the testing of decontextualized skills and knowledge. By and large, the use of information and communication technology in school signally fails to engage with the ways in which young people are now relating to information, and with the ways they choose to communicate.

(Buckingham 2007: 178)

These arguments have important implications for geography education, not least because in recent years many teachers have started to accept the argument that these technologies suggest a radically new way of learning and the need to change curriculum and pedagogy. This might entail: abandoning the persistent non-negotiability of a fragmented, discipline-based curriculum; placing greater responsibility for the content and direction of learning in the hands of students; reconceptualizing the teacher's role away from transmitter of skills and knowledge to co-constructor of knowledge; and emphasizing learning as a opposed to knowledge acquisition.

Box 11.2

CASE STUDY: GOOGLE EARTH

Google Earth is a database technology that uses satellite images to present a dynamic, streaming photographic 3D map of the world. Users can explore by inputting location, global coordinates or areas. There is also the ability to simply scroll around using a compass and a zoom function.

The consequences of the information found on Google Earth are clear. A seemingly 'real-time' image of the world gives access to the world as well as imaginatively disciplining space. For the initiated, there is potential to manipulate and create unique maps. Google Earth publishes application programming interfaces (api) that allows the user to embed maps in their web pages. The software allows the user to add images overlays, literally to impose their own images on the map. Crampton and Krygier (2006) suggest that 'map-hacking' and open source technologies allow the bypassing of standard practice in map-making. This means that cartography is no longer in the hands of cartographers and Geographic Information Science (GIS) scientists.

This is potentially liberating: if users can escape the gatekeepers of cartographic knowledge and begin to construct and use their own maps (particularly of contested sites or places), they can create their own geographies. Technology here allows for the disruption of hierarchies, given the user the power to create and control their own sense of space. This fits in very neatly with the notion that there are multiple ways of experiencing and making sense of the world, and with the broader understanding of 'mapping' as something that is personal and subjective.

However, there are problems with this view of Google Earth. Over the past two decades there have been moves to develop a more critical cartography that understands how maps and mapping have been used to control space in the interests of power. This sees maps as technologies of power that are used to divide space in the interests of capital and the state, and the strategy has been one of 'deconstructing the map' in order to show how it is a human construction rather than a neutral and technical representation of 'reality'. This suggests that we should ask the same type of questions as we would of any media product.

Buckingham provides a useful framework for this type of 'digital media literacy', based around themes of representation, language, production, and audiences.

Representation: Like all media, Google Earth represents the world, rather than simply reflecting it. Informed users need to be able to evaluate the material they encounter. This may mean assessing the motivations of those who created it and by comparing it with other sources. In the case of information texts, this means addressing questions about authority, reliability and bias, and also broader questions about whose voices are heard and whose viewpoints are represented, and whose are not. As Bonnett has commented:

> Google Earth is a political event. The further one ranges from the USA and other Western countries the more likely one is to find that one is dropping into unresolved mud. Type in 'Birmingham' or 'St Petersburg' and you will be led to cities in the United States.
>
> (Bonnett 2008: 94)

Languages: digital literacy involves an understanding of the grammar of communication, but also the broader codes and conventions of particular genres. This would involve awareness of the functions of verbal language, still and moving images in the design of Google Earth (e.g. the rotation of the globe as Google Earth zooms in on your chosen location); how the hypertextual structure encourages users to navigate in particular ways; how users are addressed in terms of formality and informality; the kinds of interactivity on offer, such as the space for authorship, uploading images and feedback.

Production: literacy involves knowing who is communicating to whom, and why? Although Google Earth appears to offer the promise of accessing anywhere in the world, that information is highly structured, and commercial influences are increasingly important. Advertising, promotion and sponsorship influence the nature of the information that is available in the first place. Awareness should also extend to non-commercial groups that look to use Google Earth to persuade and raise awareness of contentious issues. Students also require an understanding of the nature of ownership. For instance, does it matter that when faced with a need for information we first look to 'google it'? What happens to other forms of geographical information such as atlases and guidebooks in an interactive age? What are the significance of commercial influences and the role of advertisers, promoters and sponsorship in shaping Google Earth?

Audiences: finally, literacy also involves an awareness of one's own position as an audience. This involves asking questions about who is the audience for Google Earth? Is that audience segregated by age, class, gender, ethnicity? What do audiences do with Google Earth? What do they search for, and find? How do they use the information? How do users interpret the information they find on Google Earth?

Conclusion

This chapter has covered a lot of ground. It started with a discussion of how our geographical imaginations are always mediatized, in the sense that there is no obvious place to stand outside of the frameworks and representations offered by media culture. Geography, as a subject that makes great use of visual representations, is thus one where the *question of who produced that image, for whom, and why* should be posed with urgency. The chapter explored two different models of media education, and argued that both can be useful in developing approaches that allow students to investigate the meaning of media representations. The second part of the chapter summarized some recent arguments about how the nature of learning might be changing in response to the development of 'new media culture', and in many ways that is a good place to leave this discussion, since this is perhaps the area where the question of what type of geography education for what type of society will be debated most intensely. At the present time, we would suggest that there are three likely scenarios for geography teaching and new media:

1. *Geography 1.0 (Keep it basic)*: in this version there will be an acceptance of the role of technology in all aspects of geography teaching, but it will be harnessed to existing models of teaching and learning. Thus, technology will be seen as a way of delivering the geography curriculum more effectively. In this scenario, interactive whiteboards replace blackboards, lessons are turned into PowerPoint presentations, students submit work by email and resources are put onto VLEs, but the 'basic grammar' of teaching and learning are unchanged. The teacher decides the important questions about what to teach, how learning should take place and how it should be assessed.

2. *Geography 2.0 (Neat geography or 'CyberGeography')*: in this version there is an acceptance of the ideal that there exists a credibility gap between the cultures of young people and the formal regimes of schooling. Geography teachers attempt to close this gap by adopting a 'tech-savvy' approach to teaching that capitalizes on the use of the interactivity of Web 2.0. In this scenario, PowerPoint presentations are turned into YouTube presentations and shared freely using shareware technologies. There is experimentation with forms of web-based writing, so that students produce blogs rather than essays, and teachers and students contribute to wikis. The appeal of this approach is its potentiality to engage students in sharing the content and pedagogy of geography classrooms. However, it continues to reflect existing models of teaching and learning. In addition, we might be concerned that the very nature of information required of these new media forms (informal, rapid, soundbites) might be directly opposed to the more disciplined thought and reflection required in education.

3. *Geography 3.0 (Critical media)*: this is the version that we argue for in this chapter and which underpins the book as a whole. It sees all geographical knowledge as socially constructed and therefore requires that students and teachers are able to examine the nature of that knowledge. In order for this to happen, teachers need to find ways to both engage with the geographical imaginations and experiences of the students they teach, and draw on concepts and ideas within the subject to develop a systematic understanding of geographical issues.

12 A mind for the future

This chapter is shorter than the others in this book. It is best read as a 'coda' to the book as a whole. Not a conclusion, but a brief reflection on what we have tried to achieve in the previous chapters. Hopefully, this will encourage your own reflections on this book. Possibly you may even be persuaded to reread parts of it.

Back to the front

> If we want a passive population, leave well alone.
> Bernard Crick,
>
> (cited in Ward and Fyson 1973: 14)

In the Preface we set ourselves a task, which was to explore some of the conceptual terrain of contemporary geography as a subject discipline. We did this under the heading 'The promise of geography in education'. Using a photograph of an ordinary chalk landscape in south-east England, we tried to show the nature of this promise. We can apply geographical perspectives in order to interpret what we see. We can 'read' the landscape. But we suggested that the promise of geography in education lay deeper than this. Using some of the big, complex ideas developed in geography – such as space and scale, interdependence and environment, and culture and diversity – we can bring much deeper understanding to the picture. We can develop a 'politics of place'. We can explore ideas such as 'power geometries'. Our overall point was that while geography is concerned to make sense of the real world (such as that piece of it in the photograph), it does so through its ideas. The ideas we bring to the task contain the promise. What we realize from this is that modern geographic thought has acquired a kind of ironic self-awareness of the kind that we believe is exceedingly helpful for young people to be exposed to in their task of making sense of the world that bombards them daily through the various media. What this means first and foremost is that we realize that we can no sooner describe and explain this 'ordinary English landscape' *objectively*, than we can say what it means to be a 'Londoner' or 'English'.

We know that some readers may be uncomfortable with this. What we would say is, please do not misread what we mean. A mushy, anything-goes form of relativism, which implies that there are no limits or frameworks, no standards or discipline to judge the quality of a description or explanation, is out of the question. There is so much we can say about this ordinary English landscape through a geographical lens (reread the Preface if you need to); there is no need to resort to 'anything-goes'. However, we need ideas with which to focus the lens. For example, a 'progressive sense of place' helps us realize that another's gaze, from a different perspective, may have things to say that we hadn't realized or had failed to see.

Facing the future

The purpose of this book then is to deepen and extend our understanding of the potential of geography as a school subject. Each chapter, in effect, is an essay that stands in its own right: we have tried to be clear about the scope and limits of each essay and what are the main threads of its argument. We have also attempted to show links between them, and there are many. Here, we shall try to show what this amounts to; whether there is a coherence and overall concept of 'geography' that is fit for the secondary school curriculum.

This may appear as a strange and somewhat limited aim – after all geography has been an established part of the school curriculum for well over a century. But we have self-consciously not made any prior assumptions in this book. We simply do not make self-evident claims for geography in school without going to an immense amount of effort to justify them. We have gone back to the subject discipline and how this has developed in recent years and asked: is school geography a subject for today and tomorrow? Or, is it stuck in the past (which in some ways was far from innocent) and in a shadow from times gone by? If there is any truth in the latter, then how may that limit the potential of geography's contribution to education? The world in which young people live, learn and develop is different from the one in which many of us developed and learned our geography: the contemporary study of geography tells us this – and furthermore, contemporary geography is less certain about how it claims to represent and explain the world. To what extent can we learn from geography and judiciously apply this to our curriculum-making in schools? What are the implications for school geography if we do not?

The opening quotation has as much resonance now as when it first appeared nearly 40 years ago. Bernard Crick was later to lead the introduction of citizenship education in schools, and as this statement implies, was in favour of schools encouraging in young people an informed, active participation in making the world. What this statement reminds us is that a static unchanging curriculum was the recipe for quite the reverse. This is how we see the geography curriculum: if we leave 'well alone', it will become marginal to the needs of young citizens prepared for tomorrow. We agree with the Geographical Association,[1] that teachers are the curriculum-makers, and to be effective we need to engage with the subject and its promise. This is not always easy work. But it is vital.

Making geography work for the future

The title of this chapter is a deliberate echo on Gardner's (2006) book *'Five Minds for the Future'* in which he makes a persuasive case for modifying what we might call the 'educational imagination' in the context of the urgency of our times. He points out that in general educational thought is often quite conservative in practice, which he says is 'no bad thing'. Nonetheless, there are two legitimate reasons for undertaking new educational practices in his view:

The first reason is that current practices are not actually working. We might think, for example, that we are educating young persons who are literate, or immersed in the arts, or capable of scientific theorising, or tolerant of immigrants, or skilled in conflict resolution. But if evidence accrues that we are not successful in these pursuits, then we should consider altering our practices ... or our goals.

The second reason is that conditions in the world are changing significantly.

(Gardner 2006: 10)

We have already noted and stated our agreement with Gardner's second reason. In this book we develop a compelling argument about the changing world and changing geographies (in particular in Chapters 2 and 11). But what of his first reason? Is geography 'actually working' in schools? It all depends of course on what we think 'what works' really means, and as Gardner says himself, this depends what we expect from it – 'our goals'. Whether school geography is working is a question for you – we have addressed the issue (especially in Chapters 3 and 4), but it is for you in your school in relation to the young people you teach to decide. How you tackle the question may take in some or all of the following:

- Is the subject 'popular' at options time?
- Do students do well in geography?
    - In examinations (are they 'successful learners'?)
    - In their engagement with the material (are they 'confident individuals'?)
    - In their making sense of the world (are they informed and 'responsible citizens'?)
- Is geography valued, not only by the students but by parents and other teachers?

No matter how the question is tackled, somewhere in the mix is how we express geography. What is it and what is it for? What contribution does geography make to the education of young people?

Our position argued throughout this book, is that dynamic relationships, based on a disposition to 'resee' classrooms and young people, is crucial. We argue that this critical engagement is considerably strengthened and nourished through the teacher's dynamic relationship with the subject.

What kind of geographer are you?

The world of geography can appear very fragmented. In higher education students are taught by specialists, many of whom may even have difficulty with their geographic identity, preferring to attend conferences and publish their research in their specialist field, rather than in 'geography'. This state of affairs has resulted in the commonplace question: what *kind of* geographer are you? The reply typically starts with 'human' or 'physical' and develops from that point. In extreme circumstances the conversation is fairly short, for there may be very little apparent common ground.

In this sense geography is an *elusive* subject. Unlike physics or mathematics, geography has difficulty presenting itself with a look of disciplinary unity or coherence, being instead a subject that has relied on the import of methods and approaches from many disciplines. There is no need to envy physics or mathematics in this regard, although it is worth noting that the rush to models and quantification in the post-Second World War period of the twentieth century (and which deeply influenced school geography in the 1970s – see Walford 2001) was almost certainly tied up with geography's felt need for academic and intellectual respectability: quantification, models and a search for 'laws' provided the rigour that the subject was presumed to need.

Whatever the predilection of a schoolteacher of geography, their *geographic* identity is almost certainly very significant to them. But as Clare Brooks has found in her research with geography teachers, probably no more so than their overarching identity as a teacher (Brooks 2007). This requires a professional balancing act between pedagogy and subject, and a mix of sociological and psychological perspectives on young people themselves. Thus, to the question 'what kind of geographer are you?' in a school setting, the only answer that makes sense is 'geographer in *education*'.

Such a position has implications. Primarily, to be a geography educationist implies that the geography needs to be understood within the context of education and not in terms of its sub-specialisms. Teachers, we assume, possess a philosophy of education: they have beliefs and knowledge of education that shape their understanding of its goals, purposes and processes. It is this that contributes to their identity, and motivates them professionally. Furthermore, as *geography* teachers, it is just as important to have a philosophy of geography: they have an understanding of geography that serves, or at least complements, their educational philosophy. This notion of 'philosophy' (if that is not overstating the point) is exceedingly important and needs some explanation. It is important because it provides the basis for autonomous professional activity such as is required in localized and successful 'curriculum making', which is underpinned by some clarity over what is being taught and why this particular selection of what to teach has been made (see also Lambert 2009b).

We certainly need to avoid becoming too encumbered with deep epistemological or ontological debates. At this point, we merely want to signal the need to be aware, as a geography teacher, of what it is you think geography 'brings to the table'. Note that this kind of question can be addressed to all schoolteachers. For example, are teachers of *science* introducing young people to:

- a selection of 'essential' scientific *knowledge*, or
- how to be a *scientist*, or
- the scientific *method*, or
- *questions* of how scientific knowledge is made and evaluated, or
- the idea of *scientific literacy*?

The answer may be a carefully judged combination of these things, even in the realization that perhaps some of these priorities may not sit comfortably with each other. But without teachers being part of a debate about what science education is for, personally and within a wider specialist community of practice, the science curriculum may simply become a version of the 'curriculum of the dead' (or at least of persons unknown). We think the curriculum needs ownership by teachers, and in some way by the young people for whom it is made.

Conclusion

To bring this discussion to a 'conclusion' is impossible – or at least undesirable. In many ways this book has the expressed purpose of opening up a process of thinking and development of geography in the school curriculum: we do not wish now to close this down.

A different view

This approach is supported by the Geographical Association's 'manifesto', *A Different View*, which claims to be a stimulus for a national conversation about geography in schools (GA 2009). Drawing from a very broad array of individuals, including academics, educationists, novelists and broadcasters, it sets out an ambitious series of challenges for teachers. For example, it asks them:

- to use geography as a 'curriculum resource';
- to clarify what it means to 'think geographically';
- to examine the potential of school geography to:
  - engage with young people's geographical experiences;
  - help young people to envision themselves in the world now and in the future;
  - encourage curiosity and investigation of the world (including first hand in the 'real world');
- to see themselves as the curriculum-makers.

We hope this book provides a framework and a resource to support teachers responding to these challenges.

Notes

1   See the GA's (2009) 'manifesto' for school geography: www.geography.org.uk/adifferent view. This website also contains a downloadable version of the photograph used in The Promise of Geography.

References

Abrams, M. (1959) *The Teenage Consumer*. London: Policy Press Exchange.

Allen, J. and Massey, D. (eds) (1996) *Geographical Worlds*. Oxford: Oxford University Press.

Ambrose, P. (1969) *Analytical Human Geography*. London: Longmans.

Amin, A. (2005) Local community on trial, *Economy and Society*, 34(4): 612–33.

Anderson, S. and Balsamo, A. (2008) A pedagogy for original sinners, in T. McPherson (ed.) *Digital Youth, Innovation and the Unexpected*, pp. 241–59. Cambridge, MA: Massachusetts Institute of Technology.

Armitage, S. (2006) *Tyrannosaurus Rex Versus the Corduroy Kid*. London: Faber. (Poem last accessed on 22nd October 2009 at http://www.simonarmitage.com)

ATL (2006) *Subject to change: new thinking on the curriculum*, Association of Teachers and Lecturers Position Statement.

Audit Commission (2006) *More than the Sum*. London: Audit Commission.

Ball, S. (2008) *The Education Debate*. Bristol: Policy Press.

Bauman, Z. (2000) *Liquid Modernity*. Cambridge: Polity Press.

Bell, D. and Valentine, G. (1997) *Consuming Geographies: We Are Where We Eat*. London: Routledge.

Bereiter, C. (2002a) *Education and the Mind in the Knowledge Age*: Mahwah, NJ: Erlbaum.

Bereiter, C. (2002b) Artifacts, canons, and the progress of pedagogy: a response, in B. Smith (ed.) *Liberal Education in a Knowledge Society*. Chicago, IL: Open Court.

Bereiter, C. and Scardamalia, M. (1998) *Beyond Bloom's Taxonomy: Rethinking Knowledge for the Knowledge Age. Developing Higher Level Approaches to Knowledge*. Toronto: Ontario Institute for Studies in Education at the University of Toronto. Available online at: www.ikit.org/fulltext/1998BeyondBlooms.pdf (accessed 2 April 2001).

Berman, M. (1983) *All that is Solid Melts into Air: The Experience of Modernity*. London: Verso.

Blair, T. (2001) *Social Exclusion Unit (SEU): A New Commitment to Neighbourhood Renewal*. London: Social Exclusion Unit.

Bloom, B.S. (ed.) (1956) *Taxonomy of Educational Objectives, Handbook 1: Cognitive Domain*. New York: Addison Wesley.

Bondi, L. (1993) Locating identity politics, in M. Keith and S. Pile (eds) *Place and the Politics of Identity*. London: Routledge.

Bonnett, A. (2001) *White Identities: Historical and International Perspectives*. London: Prentice Hall.

Bonnett, A. (2008) *What is Geography?* London: Sage Publications.

Bourn, D. (2008) *Development Education: Debates and Dialogue*. London: Institute of Education, University of London.

Brandt Commission (1980) *North–South: A Program for Survival*. London: Pan Books.

Briggs, K. (1977) *Introducing Urban Structure*. London: Hodder & Stoughton.

Brown, C. (2001) *The Death of Christian Britain: Understanding Secularisation 1800–2000*. London: Routledge.

Brown, P. and Lauder, H. (2001) *Capitalism and Social Progress*. London: Palgrave Macmillan.

Brownlie Bojang, A. (2008) *Aid and Development*. London: Evans Brothers.

Brooks, C. (2007) *Towards understanding the influence of subject knowledge in the practice of 'expert' geography teachers*, unpublished Ph.D. thesis, Institute of Education, University of London.

Bryman, A. (2004) *The Disneyization of Society*, 2nd edn. London: Sage Publications.

Buckingham, D. (1986) Against de-mystification: a response to 'Teaching the Media', *Screen*, 27: 80–85.

Buckingham, D. (1987) *Public Secrets: EastEnders and its Audience*. London: British Film Institute.

Buckingham, D. (2003) *Media Education: Literacy, Learning and Contemporary Culture*. Cambridge: Polity Press.

Buckingham, D. (2007) *Beyond Technology: Children's Learning in the Age of Digital Culture*. Cambridge: Polity Press.

Bullock Report (1975) *A Language for Life*. London: Her Majesty's Stationery Office.

Bunge, W. (1966) *Theoretical Geography*, 2nd edn. Lund Studies in Geography. Series C: General and Mathematical Geography, No. 1. Lund, Sweden: Gleerup.

Burgess, J. and Gold, J. (eds) (1985) *Geography, the Media and Popular Culture*. Beckenham: Croom Helm.

Burt, T. (2003) Scale: upscaling and downscaling in physical geography, in S. Holloway, S. Rice and G. Valentine (eds) *Key Concepts in Geography*. London: Sage Publications.

Brunsdon, C. (2007) *London in Cinema: The Cinematic City since 1945. London: British Film Institute.*

Campbell, S. (1996) Green cities, growing cities, just cities: urban planning and the contradictions of sustainable development, *Journal of the American Planning Association*, 62(3): 296–312.

Cantle, T. (2008) *Community Cohesion: A New Framework for Race and Diversity*. London: Palgrave Macmillan.

Carr, D. (2007) Towards an educationally meaningful curriculum: epistemic holism and knowledge integration revisited, *British Journal of Educational Studies*, 55(1): 3–20.

Carson, R. (1962/2000) *Silent Spring*. London: Penguin.

Castells, M. (1997) *The Information Age*. Oxford: Blackwell.

Castree, N. (2005) *Nature*, Oxford: Routledge.

Castree, N., Coe, N., Ward, K. and Samers, M. (2003) *Spaces of Work: Global Capitalism and Geographies of Labour*. London: Sage Publications.

Clark, N., Massey, D. and Sarre, P. (eds) (2006) *A World in the Making*. Buckingham: Open University Press.

Cloke, P. (ed.) (2003) *Country Visions*. Harlow: Pearson.

Cloke, P. and Little, J. (eds) (1997) *Contested Countryside Cultures: Otherness, Marginalization and Rurality*. London: Routledge.

Clout, H. (1972) *Rural Geography: An Introductory Survey*. Oxford: Pergamon.

Club of Rome (1972) *Limits to Growth*. New York: Universe Books.

Community Cohesion Independent Review team (2001) *Community Cohesion: A Report of the Independent Review Team*. Cantle Report. London: Home Office.

Cook, I., Anderson, J., Askins, K. et al. (2008) What is geography's contribution to making citizens', *Geography*, 93(1): 34–9.

Cook, I.G., Horde, B., McGuhan, H. and Ritson, P. (undated) *Geography in Focus*. London: Hodder.

Copnall, G., Crundwell, M., Horsfall, D. and Miller, G. (1999) *People, Production and*

Environment. London: Hodder Arnold.

Cottle, S. (2009) *Global Crisis Reporting: Journalism in the Global Age*. Maidenhead: Open University Press.

Crampton, J. and Krygier, J. (2006) An introduction to critical cartography, *ACME*, 4(1): 11–33.

Cresswell, T. (1996) *In Place/Out of Place: Geography, Ideology and Transgression*. Minneapolis: University of Minnesota Press.

Cresswell, T. (2004) *Place: A Short Introduction*. Chichester: Wiley-Blackwell.

Cresswell, T. (2006) *On the Move: Mobility in the Modern Western World*. London: Routledge.

Crush, J. (1995) *The Power of Development*. London: Routledge.

Daniels, S. (1985) Humanistic geography, in R. Johnston (ed.) *The Future of Geography*. London: Methuen.

Dave, P. (2006) *Visions of England: Class and Culture in Contemporary Cinema*. London: Berg.

DEA (2008) *Questioning Education*. London: DEA. See also www.dea.org.uk/questionning education.

Del Casino, V. Snr. (2009) *Social Geography* Chicester: Wiley-Blackwell.

Department for Children, Schools and Families (2007) *Diversity and Citizenship Review*, London: DCSF.

Department for Children, Schools and Families (DCSF) (2007b) *Guidance on the Duty to Promote Community Cohesion*. London: DCSF.

Department for Children, Schools and Families (2008) *Guidance on Community Cohesion*. London: DCSF.

Department of Education and Science (DES) (1977) *Education in Schools*. London: HMSO.

Dicken, P. (1998) *Global Shift: Transforming the World Economy*, 3rd edn London: Paul Chapman Publishing.

Dicken, P. and Lloyd, P. (1981) *Modern Western Society: A Geographical Perspective on Work, Home and Well-being*. London: Harper & Row.

Doel, M. (1999) *Poststructuralist Geographies: The Diabolical Art of Spatial Science*. Edinburgh: Edinburgh University Press.

Doerr, A., Ruffus, M., Chambers, E. and Keefer, M. (2007) The changing role of knowledge in education, *Education, Knowledge and Economy*, 1(3): 279–300.

Dove, J. (1999) *Theory into Practice: Immaculate Misconceptions*. Sheffield: Geographical Association.

Drucker, P. (1969) *The Age of Discontinuity*. London: Heinemann.

Durbin, C. (2006) Media literacy and geographical imaginations, in D. Balderstone (ed.) *Secondary Geography Teachers' Handbook*. Sheffield: Geographical Association.

Dyer, R. (1997) *White: Essays on Race and Culture*. London: Routledge.

Ecclestone, K. and Hayes, D. (2008) *The Dangerous Rise of Therapeutic Education*. London: Routledge.

Elliott, J. (1999) *An Introduction to Sustainable Development*, 2nd edn. London: Routledge.

Evans, J., Rich, E., Davies, B. and Allwood, R. (2008) *Education, Disordered Eating and Obesity Discourse: Fat Fabrications*. London: Routledge.

Fairgrieve & Young (1952) *Real Geography*. London: George Philip & Son (first published 1939).

Fien, J. and Gerber, R. (1988) *Teaching Geography for a Better World*. Edinburgh: Oliver & Boyd.

Flint, J. and Robinson, D. (eds) (2008) *Community Cohesion in Crisis? New Dimensions of Diversity and Difference*. Bristol: Policy Press.

Freidberg, S. (2004) *French Beans and Food Scares*. Oxford: Oxford University Press.

Gabriel, J. (1998) *Whitewash: Racialized Politics and the Media*. London: Routledge.

Gardner, H. (1999) *Intelligence Reframed: Multiple Intelligences for the 21st Century*. New York: Basic Books.

Gardner H. (2006) *Five Minds for the Future*, Boston: Harvard Business School Press.

Gardner, H. and Boix-Mansilla, V. (2006) Teaching for understanding within and across the disciplines, in H. Gardner (ed.) *The Development and Education of the Mind*. London: Routledge.

Garlake, T. (2007) 'Interdependence in Hicks D. and Holden C. (eds) *Teaching the Global Dimension: Key principles and effective practice*, London: Routledge.

Garner, R. (2008) Teachers urged to 'take risks' inspires pupils, *Independent*, 22 September.

Gates, B. (2005) *National Education Summit on High Schools* [speech]. Available online at: www.gatesfoundation.org/MediaCenter/Speeches/Co-ChairSpeeches/BillgSpeeches/BGSpeechNGA-050226.htm (accessed 17 March 2007).

Geographical Association (2009) *A Different View: A Manifesto from the Geographical Association*, Sheffield: GA. (Also accessed from www.geography.org.uk/adifferentview.)

Gibson, T. (2007) *Urban Fortunes: Television, Gentrification and the American City. Flow TV: a critical forum on television and media culture*. Available online at www.flowtv.org/?p=826 (accessed 28 April 2009).

Gibson-Graham, J.-K. (1996) *The End of Capitalism (as we knew it)*. Oxford: Blackwell.

Giddens, A. (1991) *Modernity and Self-Identity*. Cambridge: Polity Press.

Gilbert, D., Matless, D. and Short, B. (eds) (2003) *Geographies of British Modernity*. Oxford: Blackwell Publishing.

Gilbert, J. (2005) *Catching the Knowledge Wave? The Knowledge Society and the Future of Education*. New Zealand: NZCER.

Gill, D. (1983) *Geographical Education in a Multi-cultural Society: Research Report Commissoned by the Schools Council*. London: Commission for Racial Equality.

Gill, D., Mayor, B. and Blair, M. (1993) *Racism and Education: Structures and Strategies*. London: Sage/Open University Press.

Gillborn, D. (1995) *Racism and Anti-racism in Real Schools*. Buckingham: Open University Press.

Goodson, I. (1983) *School Subjects and Curriculum Change*. Beckenham: Croom Helm.

Goodwyn, A. (2003) *English Teaching and the Moving Image*. London: Routledge.

Gore, A. (2006) *An Inconvenient Truth: The Planetary Emergency of Global Warming and What We Can Do About It*. London: Bloomsbury.

Gospill, G.H. (1956) *The Teaching of Geography*. London: Macmillian

Goudie, A. (1993) Schools and universities: the great divide, *Geography*, 78(4): 338–9.

Goudie, A. et al. (1994) *The Encyclopaedic Dictionary of Physical Geography*. Oxford: Blackwell.

Gough, J., Eisenschitz, A. and McCulloch, A. (2006) *Spaces of Social Exclusion*. London: Routledge.

Gould, P. and Strohmeyer, U. (2004) Geographical visions: the evolution of human geographic thought in the twentieth century, in G. Benko and U. Strohmeyer (eds) *Human Geography: A History for the 21st Century*. London: Arnold.

Graves, N. (1979) *Curriculum Planning in Geography*. London: Heinemann.

Graves, N. (2001) *School Textbook Research: The Case of Geography 1800–2000*. London: Institute of Education, University of London.

Graves, N., Kent A., Lambert, D. and Slater, F. (1990a) National curriculum: first impressions, *Teaching Geography*, 15(1): 2–5.

Graves, N., Kent A., Lambert, D. and Slater, F. (1990b) Evaluating the final report, *Teaching Geography*, 15(4): 2–5.

Green, B., and Bigum, C. (1993) Aliens in the classroom, *Australian Journal of Education*, 37(2): 119–41.

Gregory, D. (1985) People, places and practices: the future of human geography, in R. King (ed.) *Geographical Futures*. Sheffield: Geographical Association.

Gregory, D. (1993) *Geographical Imaginations*. Oxford: Blackwell.

Gregory, D. (2004) *The Colonial Present: Afghanistan, Palestine, Iraq*. Oxford: Blackwell.

Gregory, D. and Urry, J. (eds) (1985) *Social Relations and Spatial Structures*. London: Macmillan.

Grimwade, K., Reid, A. and Thompson, L. (2000) *Geography and the New Agenda: Citizenship, PSHE and Sustainable Development in the Secondary Curriculum*. Sheffield: Geographical Association.

Grosvenor, I. and Burke, C. (2008) *School*. London: Reaktion Books.

Groundwater-Smith, S. and Sachs, J. (2002) The activist professional and the reinstatement of trust, *Cambridge Journal of Education* 32(3): 341–58.

Haggett, P. (1965) *Locational Analysis in Human Geography*. London: Edward Arnold.

Haggett, P. (1980) *Human Geography: A Modern Synthesis*, 3rd edn. New York: Harper & Row.

Hall, D. (1976) *Geography and the Geography Teacher*. London: Allen & Unwin.

Hargreaves, D. (1994) The new professionalism: the synthesis of professional and institutional development, *Teaching and Teacher Education* 10(4): 423–38.

Harrison, B. (2009) *Seeking a Role: The United Kingdom 1951–1970*. Oxford: Oxford University Press.

Harrison, S., Pile, S. and Thrift, N. (eds) (2004) *Patterned Ground: Entanglements of Nature and Culture*. London: Reaktion Books.

Harvey, D. (1969) *Explanation in Geography*. London: Edward Arnold.

Harvey, D. (1973) *Social Justice and the City*. London: Edward Arnold.

Harvey, D. (1974) What kind of geography for what kind of public policy? *Transactions of the Institute of British Geographers*, 63: 18–24.

Harvey, D. (1996) *Justice, Nature and the Geography of Difference*. Oxford: Blackwell.

Harvey, D. (2000) *Spaces of Hope*. Edinburgh: Edinburgh University Press.

Harvey, D. (2005) *A Brief History of Neoliberalism*. Oxford: Oxford University Press.

Hendrick, H. (2003) *Child Welfare: Historical Dimensions, Contemporary Debate*. Bristol: Policy Press.

Herod, A. (2003) Scale: the local and the global, in S. Holloway, S. Rice and G. Valentine (eds) *Key Concepts in Geography*. London: Sage Publications.

Herod, A. (2009) *Geographies of Globalisation*. Chichester: Wiley-Blackwell.

Hesmondlagh, D. (2007) *The Cultural Industries*, 2nd edn. London: Sage Publications.

Hicks, D. (1981) Teaching about other peoples: how biased are textbooks? *Education 3–13*, 9(2): 14–15.

Hicks, D. (2001) *Citizenship for the Future: A Practical Classroom Guide*. Godalming: World Wide Fund for Nature UK.

Hicks, D. (2002) *Lessons for the Future: The Missing Dimension in Education*. London: RoutledgeFalmer.

Hicks, D. (2007) Lessons for the future: a geographical contribution, *Geography*, 92(3): 179–88.

Hicks, D. and Holden, C. (1995) *Visions of the future: Why We Need to Teach for Tomorrow*. Stoke on Trent: Trentham.

Hicks, D. and Townley, C. (eds) (1982) *Teaching World Studies: An Introduction to Global Perspectives in the Curriculum*. London: Longman.

Hillyard, S. (2007) *A Sociology of Rural Life*. Oxford: Berg.

Hinchliffe, G. (2007a) Special issue on the concept of capability and its application to questions of equity, access and the aims of education, *Prospero*, 13(3).

Hinchliffe, G. (2007b) Beyond key skills: the capability approach to personal development, *Prospero*, 13(3): 5–12.

Hirsch, E.D. (1988) *Cultural Literacy: What Every American Needs to Know*. New York: Houghton Mifflen Co (Vintage Books edition).

Hoggart, R. (1957) *The Uses of Literacy* London: Chatto & Windus.

Holloway, S. and Valentine, G. (eds) (2000) *Children's Geographies: Playing, Living, Learning*. London: Routledge.

Holloway, S., Rice, S. and Valentine, G. (eds) (2003) *Key Concepts in Geography*. London: Sage Publications.

hooks, b. (1994) *Teaching to Transgress*. London: Routledge.

Hoskins, W.G. (2005) *The Making of the English Landscape*. London: Hodder & Stoughton (reissued in 2005 with a new Introduction by Keith Thomas).

Howitt, R. (1998) Scale as relation: musical metaphors of geographical scale, *Area*, 30: 49–58.

Huckle, J. (ed.) (1983) *Geographical Education: Reflection and Action*. Oxford: Oxford University Press.

Huckle, J. (1985) The future of school geography, in R. Johnston (ed.) *The Future of Geography*. London: Methuen.

Huckle, J. (1988–1993) *What We Consume*. A module of the WWF's Global Environmental Programme consisting of a teacher's handbook and 10 curriculum units. London: Richmond. See also http://john.huckle.org.uk.

Huckle, J. (2005) Education for Sustainable Development, briefing document prepared for the TDA, Available online at www.ttrb.ac.uk/viewarticle2.aspx?contentId=12789 (accessed 29 December 2008).

Huckle, J. (2009) Sustainable schools: responding to new challenges and opportunities, *Geography*, 94(1): 13–21.

Hudson, R. (2001) *Producing Places*. New York: Guilford Press.

Huppert, F., Bayliss, N. and Keverne, B. (eds) (2005) *The Science of Well-being*. Oxford: Oxford University Press.

Isard, W. (1956) *Location and the Space Economy*. New York: Wiley.

Jackson, P. (ed.) (1987) *Race and Racism: Essays in Social Geography*. London: Allen & Unwin.

Jackson, P. (1989) *Maps of Meaning: An Introduction to Cultural Geography*. London: Unwin Hyman.

Jackson, P. (2006) Thinking geographically, *Geography*, 91(3): 199–204.

Jackson, P. and Smith, S. (1984) *Exploring Social Geography*. London: Allen & Unwin.

Jackson, P. and Thrift, N. (1995) Geographics of consumption in D. Miller (ed.) *Acknowledging Consumption*. London Routledge.

Jacobs, J. and Fincher, R. (eds) (1998) *Cities of Difference*. New York: Guilford Press.

James, O. (2007) *Affluenza: How to be Successful and Stay Sane*. London: Vermilion.

Johnson, M. (2008) *Ideas of Landscape*. Oxford: Blackwell.

Johnston, C. and Mooney, G. (2007) '"Problem" people, "problem" places? New Labour and council estates', in R. Atkinson and G. Helms (eds) *Securing an Urban Renaissance*. Bristol: Policy Press.

Johnston, R. (1977) On geography and the organisation of education, *Journal of Geography in Higher Education*, 1(1): 5–12.

Johnston, R. (1985) Introduction: exploring the future of geography, in R. Johnston (ed.) *The Future of Geography*. London: Methuen.

Johnston, R. (1986) *On Human Geography*. Oxford: Blackwell.

Johnston, R., Gregory, D., Pratt, G. and Watts, M. (1994) *The Dictionary of Human Geography*, 3rd edn. Oxford: Blackwell.

Johnston, R. and Taylor, P. (eds) (1986) *A World in Crisis? Geographical Perspectives*. Oxford: Blackwell.

Jones, K. (2003) *Education in Britain: 1944 to the Present*. Cambridge: Polity Press.

Kemp, D. (2004) *Exploring Environmental Issues: An Integrated Approach*, London: Routledge.

Kirby, A. (2001) *Reconfiguring scale: The spaces of popular culture* paper presented to the conference *Theorizing Space & Time at the Millennium*, Athens, GA, April 1999.

Kirby, A. (2002) Popular culture, academic discourse and the incongruities of scale, in A. Herod and M. Wright (eds) *Geographies of Power: Placing Scale*. Oxford: Blackwell.

Kirk, G. and Broadhead, P. (2007) *Every Child Matters and Teacher Education: A UCET Position Paper*. London: UCET Occasional Paper No. 17.

Kobayashi, A. and Proctor, J. (2003) Values, ethics and justice, in G. Gaile and C. Wilmott (eds) *Geography in America at the Dawn of the Twenty-first Century*, pp 721–29, New York: Oxford University Press.

Knox, P. and Agnew, J. (1998) *The Geography of the World Economy*, 3rd edn. London: Arnold.

Krueger, R. and Gibbs, D. (eds) (2007) *The Sustainable Development Paradox: Urban Political Economy in the United States and Europe*. London: Guilford Press.

Kundnani, A. (2007) *The End of Tolerance: Racism in 21st Century Britain*. London: Pluto Press.

Lam, N. and Quattrochi, D.A. (1992) On the issues of scale, resolution, and fractal analysis in the mapping sciences, *Professional Geographer*, 44: 88–98.

Lambert, D. (1999) Geography and moral education in a supercomplex world: the significance of values education and some remaining dilemmas, *Ethics, Place and Environment*, 2(1): 5–18.

Lambert, D. (2008) Inconvenient truths, *Geography*, 93(1): 48–50.

Lambert, D. (2009a) Being a professional geography teacher, in C. Brooks (ed.) *Studying PGCE Geography at M Level*. London: Routledge.

Lambert, D. (2009b) Geography in Education: Lost in the post? Inaugural professional lecture, London: Institute of Education (www.ioe.ac.uk/publications)

Lambert, D. and Balderstone, D. (2009) *Learning to Teach Geography in the Secondary School*, 2nd edn. London: Routledge.

Lankshear, C. and Knobel, M. (2006) *New Literacies: Everyday Practices and Classroom Learning*, 2nd edn. Maidenhead: Open University Press.

Lambert, D. and Machon, P. (2001) *Citizenship through Secondary Geography*. London: RoutledgeFalmer.

Lawton, D. (1989) *Education Culture and the National Curriculum*. London: Hodder.

Layard, R. (2005) *Happiness: Lessons from a New Science*. London: Penguin.

Leadbeater, C. (2008a) *We-think: Mass Innovation not Mass Production*. London: Profile.

Leadbeater, C. (2008) *What's Next? 21 Ideas for 21st Century Learning*. London: The Innovation Unit. Available online at www.innovation-unit.co.uk.

Leavis, F.R. and Thompson, D. (1933) *Culture and Environment: The Training of Critical Awareness*. London: Chatto & Windus.

Lee, R. (1977) The ivory tower, the blackboard jungle and the corporate state: a provocation on teaching progress in geography, in R. Lee (ed.) *Change and Tradition: Geography's New Frontiers*. London: Queen Mary's College, University of London.

Lee, R. (1985) Teaching geography: the dialectic of structure and agency, in D. Boardman (ed.) *New Directions in Geographical Education*. Brighton: The Falmer Press.

Lee, R. (1985b) The future of the region: regional geography as education for transformation, in R, King (ed.) *Geographical Futures*. Sheffield: Geographical Association.

Lee, R. and Williams, C. (eds) (2003) *Alternative Economic Spaces*. London: Sage Publications.

Lee, R. and Wills, J. (eds) (1997) *Geographies of Economics*. London: Arnold.

Lewis, J. and Townsend, A. (eds) (1989) *The North–South Divide: Regional Change in Britain in the 1980s*. London: Paul Chapman Publishing.

Lloyd, P. and Dicken, P. (1977) *Location in Space: A Theoretical Approach to Economic Geography*. 2nd edn. New York: Harper & Row.

Lovelock, J. (1995) *Gaia: A New Look at Life on Earth*, 2nd edn. Oxford: Open University Press.

Lovering, J. (1997) Global restructuring and local impact, in M. Pacione (ed.) *Britain's Cities: Geographies of Division in Urban Britain*. London: Routledge.

Lowe, R. (2007) *The Death of Progressive Education: How Teachers Lost Control of the Classroom*. London: Routledge.

Mac an Ghaill, M. (1999) *Contemporary Racisms and Ethnicities: Social and Cultural Transformations*. Maidenhead: Open University Press.

Macek, S. (2006) *Urban Nightmares: The Media, the Right, and the Moral Panic Over the City*. Minneapolis, MN: University of Minnesota Press.

Mackinder, H. (1911) The teaching of geography from an Imperial point of view and the use which could and should be made of visual instruction, *The Geographical Teacher*, 6: 83.

Malecki, E. and Moriset, B. (2006) *The Digital Economy: Business Organization, Production Processes and Regional Developments*. London: Routledge.

Marsden, T., Murdoch, J., Lowe, P., Munton, R. and Flynn, A. (1993) *Constructing the Countryside*. London: UCL Press.

Marsden, B. (1997) On taking the geography out of geographical education, *Geography*, 82(3): 241–252.

Marsden, B. (2002) Citizenship education: permeation or pervasion; some historical pointers, in D. Lambert and P. Machon (eds) *Citizenship Through Secondary Geography*. London: RoutledgeFalmer.

Marsden, W. (1976) *Evaluating the Geography Curriculum*. London: Oliver & Boyd.

Marsden, W. (2001) *The School Textbook: Geography, History and Social Studies*. London: Woburn Press.

Marston S. (2000) The social construction of scale: a review and critique, *Progress in Human Geography*, 24(2): 219–42.

Marzano, R.J. (2001) *Designing a New Taxonomy of Educational Objectives*. Thousand Oaks: Corwin Press, Inc.

Massey, D. (1984) *Spatial Divisions of Labour: Social Structures and the Geography of Production*. London: Macmillan.

Massey, D. (2005) *For Space*. London: Sage Publications.

Massey, D. (2008) A global sense of place, in T. Oakes and P. Price (eds) *The Cultural Geography Reader*. Oxford: Routledge.

Masterman, L. (1984) Introduction, in L. Masterman (ed.) *Television Mythologies: Stars, Shows and Signs*, pp. 1–6. London: Comedia/MK Media Press.

Masterman, L. (1985) *Teaching the Media*. London: Comedia.

Matless, D. (1998) *Landscape and Englishness*. London: Reaktion Books.

Matthews, B. (2006) *Engaging Education: Developing Emotional Literacy, Equity and Co-operation*. Maidenhead: Open University Press.

McDowell, L. (1999) *Gender, Identity and Place: Understanding Feminist Geographies*. Cambridge: Polity Press.

McRobbie, A. (2009) *The Aftermath of Feminism: Gender, Culture and Social Change*. London: Routledge.

McWilliam, E. and Hatcher, C. (2004) Emotional literacy as a pedagogical product, *Continuum: Journal of Media and Cultural Studies*, 18(2): 179–89.

Mohan, J. (1989) *The Political Geography of Contemporary Britain*. London: Sheridan.

Mohan, J. (2001) *A United Kingdom? Economic, Social and Political Geographies*. London: Arnold.

Morgan, J. (2003) Imagined country: national environmental ideologies in school geography textbooks, *Antipode: A Radical Journal of Geography*, 35(3): 444–62.

Morgan, J. and Lambert, D. (2003) *Race, Place and Geography Teaching*. Sheffield: Geographical Association.

Morgan, J. and Lambert, D. (2005) *Geography: Teaching School Subjects 11–19*. London: Routledge.

Muir, R. (2007) *How to read a village*. London: Ebury Press.

Murdoch, J. (2006) *Post-structuralist Geography: A Relational Guide to Space*. London: Sage Publications.

Murdoch, J. and Pratt, A. (1997) From the power of topography to the topography of power: a discourse on strange ruralities, in P. Cloke and J. Little (eds) *Contested Countryside Cultures: Rurality and Socio-cultural Marginalisation*, pp. 51–69. London: Routledge.

Murdock, G. and Phelps, G. (1973) *Mass Media and the Secondary School*. London: Macmillan.

Murphy, R. (2001) Citylife: urban fairy tales in late 90s British cinema, in R. Murphy (ed.) *The British Cinema Book*. London: British Film Institute.

Myerson, G. and Rydin, Y. (1996) *The Language of Environment: A New Rhetoric*, London: UCL Press.

National Curriculum for Geography. Available at www.curriculum.qca.org.uk/key-stages-3-and-4/subjects/geography/index/aspx (accessed 14 July 2009).

Nayak, A. (2003) *Race, Place and Globalization: Youth Cultures in a Changing World*. London: Berg.

Neal, S. and Agyeman, J. (eds) (2006) *The New Countryside? Ethnicity, Nation and Exclusion in Contemporary Rural Britain*. Bristol: Policy Press.

New Economics Foundation (2004) *A Well-being Manifesto for a Flourishing Society*. London: New Economics Foundation (available at www.neweconomics.org/gen/uploads/21xvsyytotixxu322pmyada205102004103948.pdf

New Statesman (1999) 'The future belongs to us all', *New Statesman*, 20 December 1999–3 January 2000, p. 7).

Newsom Report (1963) *Half Our Future*. London: Her Majesty's Stationery Office.

Noddings, N. (2003) *Happiness and Education*. Cambridge: Cambridge University Press.

Nussbaum, M.C. and Sen, A. (eds) (1993) *The Quality of Life*. Oxford: Clarendon Press.

O'Riordan, T. (1995) *Environmental Science for Environmental Management*. London: Longman.

O'Shea, A. (1996) English subjects of modernity, in M. Nava and A. O'Shea (eds) *Modern Times: Reflections on a Century of English Modernity*. London: Routledge.

Office for Standards in Education (Ofsted) (2007) *The Annual Report of Her Majsety's Chief Inspector of Education, Childern's Services and Skills*. London: Ofsted. Available at www.ofsted.gov.uk/Ofsted-home/Publications-and-research/Browse-all-by/Annual-Report/2006-07/The-Annual-Report-of-Her-Majestys-Chief-Inspector-2006-07 (accessed 14 July 2009).

Ogborn, M. (1998) *Spaces of Modernity*. New York: Guilford Press.

Orr, D. (1999a) Rethinking education, *The Ecologist*, 29(2): 232–4.

Orr, D. (1999b) Education for globalisation, *The Ecologist*, 29(2): 166–8.

Osgerby, B. (2004) *Youth Media*. London: Routledge.

Peet, R. (1998) *Modern Geographical Thought*. Oxford: Blackwell.

Peet, R. (2007) *Geography of Power: Making Global Economic Policy*. London: Zed Books.

Pepper, D. (1985) Why teach physical geography? *Contemporary Issues in Geography and Education* 2(2): 62–71.

Peter, B. (2007) *Form Follows Fun: Modernism and Modernity in British Pleasure Architecture 1925–1940*. London: Routledge.

Peters, R.S. (1965) Inaugural lecture, Institute of Education, University of London.

Phillips, D., Simpson, L. and Ahmed, S. (2008) Shifting geographies of minority ethnic settlement: remaking communities in Oldham and Rochdale, in J. Flint and D. Robinson (eds) *Community Cohesion in Crisis? New Dimensions of Diversity and Difference*. Bristol: Policy Press.

Philo, C. (1992) Neglected rural geographies: a review, *Journal of Rural Studies*, 8: 193–207.

Popper, K. (1972) *Objective Knowledge: An Evolutionary Approach*. Oxford: Clarendon Press.

Power, M. (2003) *Rethinking Development Geographies*. London: Routledge.

Preece, D. and Woods, H. (1944) *Modern Geography. Book 2: The British Isles*, 2nd edn. London: University Tutorial Press.

Pred, A. and Watts, M. (1992) *Reworking Modernity: Capitalisms and Symbolic Discontent*. Piscataway, NJ: Rutgers University Press.

Priestley, J.B. (1937) *English Journey*. London: Heinemann.

Proctor, J. (1999) A moral earth, in J. Proctor and D. Smith (eds) *Geography and Ethics: Journeys in a Moral Terrain*. London: Routledge.

Proctor, J. and Smith, D. (eds) (1999) *Geography and Ethics: Journeys in a Moral Terrain*. London: Routledge.

Putnam, R. (2000) *Bowling Alone: The Collapse and Revival of American Community*. New York: Schuster & Schuster.

QCA (2008) *The National Curriculum KS3: Geography*, Qualifications and Curriculum, Authority (accessed from www.curriculum.qca.org.uk/ April 2009). The precise link is as follows: www.curriculum.qca.org.uk/key-stages-3-and-4/subjects/geography/index.aspx?return=/key-stages-3-and-4/subjects/index.aspx.

QCA (2009) *Sustainable Development in Action: A Curriculum Planning Guide for Schools*, London: Qualifications and Curriculum Authority.

Rawling, E. (2001) *Changing the Subject: The Impact of National Policy on School Geography 1980–2000*. Sheffield: Geographical Association.

Rawling, E. (2008) *Planning your Key Stage 3 Curriculum*. Sheffield: Geographical Association.

Redclift, M. (1997) Sustainable development: needs, values, rights, in L. Owen and T. Unwin (eds) *Environmental Management: Readings and Case Studies*. London: Longman.

Relph, E. (1976) *Place and Placelessness*. London: Pion.

Rice, R.E. (1991) The New American Scholar: scholarship and the purpose of the university, *Metropolitan Universities*, 1: 7–18.

Rigg, J. (2006) *An Everyday Story of the Global South*. London: Routledge.

Ritzer, G. (2008) *The McDonaldization of Society*, 5th edn. Thousand Oaks, CA: Pine Forge Press.

Roberts, M. (2003) *Learning through Enquiry*. Sheffield: Geographical Association.

Rose, S. (2003) *Which People's War? National Identity and Citizenship in Wartime Britain 1939–1945*. Oxford: Oxford University Press.

Ross, A. (2000) *Curriculum: Construction and Critique*. London: Taylor & Francis.

Royal Institute of British Architects (RIBA) (1943) *Rebuilding Britain*. London: RIBA.

Rutherford, J. (2005). How we live now, *Soundings: A Journal of Politics and Culture*, 30: 9–11.

Rycroft, S. (1997) in R. Walford (ed.) *Land Use UK*. Sheffield: Geographical Association.

Sachs, J. (2003A) *The Activist Teaching Profession*. Buckingham: Open University Press.

Sachs, J. (2003B) Teacher Activism: mobilizing the profession, plenary address to the British Educational Research Association, September.

Said, E. (1978) *Orientalism*. New York: Vintage.

Sayer, A. (1985) Systematic mystification: the 16–19 Geography Project, *Contemporary Issues in Geography Education*, 2(2): 86–93.

Schumacher, F. (1973) *Small is Beautiful*. London: Abacus.

Sen, A. (1985). *Commodities and Capabilities*. Oxford: Oxford University Press.

Sennett, R. (1999) *The Corrosion of Character: The Personal Consequences of Work in the New Capitalism*. New York: Norton.

Sennett, R. (2008) *The Culture of the New Capitalism*. New Haven, CT: Yale University Press.

Sharp, J. (2009) *Geographies of Postcolonialism*. London: Sage Publications.

Shaw, M., Thomas, B., Davey-Smith, G. and Dorling, D. (2008) *The Grim Reaper's Road Atlas: An Atlas on Mortality in Britain*. Bristol: Policy Press.

Sheller, M. (2003) *Consuming the Caribbean: From Arawaks to Zombies*. London: Routledge.

Shields, R. (1992) *Places on the Margins: Alternative Geographies of Modernity*. London: Routledge.

Short, J.R. (1991) *Imagined Country*. London: Routledge.

Shurmer-Smith, P. (2002) *Doing Cultural Geography*. London: Sage.

Sibley, D. (1995) *Geographies of Exclusion*. London: Routledge.

Simmons, I. (2001) *An Environmental History of Great Britain: From 10,000 Years Ago to the Present*. Edinburgh: Edinburgh University Press.

Simms, A. and Smith, J. (eds) (2008) *Do Good Lives Have to Cost the Earth?* London: Constable & Robinson.

Sinfield, A. (1989) *Literature, Culture and Politics in Postwar Britain*. London: Athlone Press.

Sinfield, A. (1997) *Literature, Politics and Culture in Post-war Britain*, 2nd edn. London: Athlone Press.

Skidelski, R. (2009) Where do we go from here?, *Prospect*, 154: 36–40.

Slater, F. (1992) ... to travel with a different view, in M. Naish (ed.) *Geography and Education*. London: Institute of Education, University of London.

Slaughter, R. (ed.) (1996) *The Knowledge Base of Futures Studies*, 3 volumes, Melbourne: Futures Study Centre.

Smith, D.M. (1974) Who gets what, where, and how: a welfare focus for geography, *Geography: an International Journal*, 59: 289–97.

Smith, J. and Simms, A. (2008) One good life; one good planet: what does change look like? in

A. Simms and J. Smith (eds) *Do Good Lives Have to Cost the Earth?* London: Constable & Robinson.

Smith, N. (1984) Uneven Development: nature, capital and the production of space. Oxford: Blackwell.

Smith, N. (1993) Homeless/global: scaling places, in J. Bird, B. Curtis, T. Putman , G. Robertson and L. Tickner (eds) *Mapping the Futures: Local Cultures, Global Change.* London: Routledge.

Smith, N. (1996) *The New Urban Frontier: Gentrification and the Revanchist City.* London: Routledge.

Soja, E. (1989) *Postmodern Geographies: The Reassertion of Space in Social Theory.* London: Verso.

Stamp, D. (1946) *The Land of Britain and How it is Used.* London: Longman.

Stamp, D. and Beaver, S. (1954) *The British Isles: A Geographic and Economic Survey*, 4th edn. London: Longman.

Standish, A. (2009) *Global Perspectives in the Geography Curriculum: Reviewing the Moral Case for Geography.* London: Routledge.

Swyngedouw, E. (2007) Impossible 'sustainability' and the postpolitical condition, in R. Krueger and D. Gibbs (eds) *The Sustainable Development Paradox: Urban Political Economy in the United States and Europe.* London: Guilford Press.

Taylor, L. (2004) *Re-presenting Geography.* Cambridge: Chris Kington Publishing.

Taylor, P.J. (1985) *Political Geography: World-economy, Nation-state and Locality.* London: Longman.

Taylor, P. (1993) *Political Geography: World Economy, Nation State and Locality*, 3rd edn. Harlow: Longman.

Taylor, P.J. and Flint, C. (2000) *Political Geography: World-economy, Nation-state and Locality.* 5th edn. New York: Prentice Hall.

The Guardian (2008) 'Teach creationism' says top scientist, 12 September.

Thrift, N. (1989) Images of social change, in C. Hamnett, L. McDowell and P. Sarre (eds) *The Changing Social Structure.* London: Sage Publications.

Timberlake, L. (1988) *Africa in Crisis.* London: Earthscan.

Tomlinson, S. (2008) *Race and Education: Policy and Politics in Britain.* Maidenhead: Open University Press.

Trend, R.D. (2008) Fostering progress in children's developing geoscience interests, *Geographie und ihre Didaktik*, 35(4): 168–84.

Tuan, Y. (1999) *Who am I?* Madison: Wisconsin University Press.

Walford, R. (1985) *Geographical Education for a Multi-cultural Society: Report of the Working Party Set Up by the Geographical Association.* Sheffield: Geographical Association.

Walford, R. (2001) *Geography in British Schools 1850–2000: Making a World of Difference.* London: Woburn Press.

Wallerstein, I. (1975) Class formation in the capitalist world-economy, *Politics and Society* 5: 367–5.

Ward, C. and Fyson, A. (1973) *Streetwork: The Exploding School.* London: Rouledge & Kegan Paul.

Warren, S. (1993) 'This heaven gives me migraines': the problems and promises of landscapes and leisure, in J. Duncan and D. Ley (eds) *Place/culture/representation.* London: Routledge.

Weeks, J. (2007) *The World We Have Won: The Remaking of Erotic and Intimate Life.* London: Routledge.

Wenger, E. (1999) *Communities of Practice.* Cambridge: Cambridge University Press.

West-Burnham, J., Farrar, M. and Otero, G. (2007) *Schools and Communities: Working Together to Transform Children's Lives*. London: Network Continuum.

Whelan, R. (ed.) (2007) *The Corruption of the Curriculum*. London: Civitas.

White, J. (ed.) (2004) *Rethinking the Curriculum*. London: Routledge.

White, J. (2006) The aims of school education', paper presented at the IPPR Event: *Curriculum, Assessment and Pedagogy: Beyond the Standards Agenda*, 3rd April. Available from www.ippr.org.uk/research/teams/event.asp?id=2006 (accessed 5 May 2009).

Williams, A. (2008) *The Enemies of Progress: The Dangers of Sustainability*. London: Imprint.

Williams, C. (2005) A *Commodified World? Mapping the Limits of Capitalism*. London: Zed Books.

Williams, M., Coleman, D., Lee, G., Plant, P., Stephenson, B. and Turk, R. (1981) *Language, Teaching and Learning: Geography*. London: Geographical Association/Ward Lock.

Williams, R. (1961) *The Long Revolution*. New York: Columbia University Press.

Williams, R. (1973) *The Country and the City*. London: Chatto & Windus.

Williams, R. (1976) *Keywords: A Vocabulary of Culture and Society*. London: Fontana.

Wisner, B. Toulmin, C. and Chitiga, R. (eds) (2005) *Towards a New Map of Africa*. London: Earthscan.

Woods, M. (2006) *Rural Geography: Processes, Responses and Experiences in Rural Restructuring*. London: Sage Publications.

World Commission on Environment and Development (WCED) (1987) *Our Common Futures*. Oxford: Oxford University Press.

Wright, D. (1979) Visual images in geography textbooks: the case of Africa, *Geography: An International Journal*, 64(3): 205–10.

Wright, D. (1985) In black and white: racist bias in textbooks, *Geographical Education*, 5: 13–17.

Index